COMMUNICATION of INNOVATIONS

To Ann —

Ev always
spoke very
highly of
you.

Cordially,

Communication of Innovations
A JOURNEY WITH EV ROGERS

EDITED BY
Arvind Singhal
James W. Dearing

SAGE Publications
New Delhi / Thousand Oaks / London

First published in 2006 by

Sage Publications India Pvt Ltd
B-42, Panchsheel Enclave
New Delhi 110 017
www.indiasage.com

Sage Publications Inc  **Sage Publications Ltd**
2455 Teller Road   1 Oliver's Yard, 55 City Road
Thousand Oaks, California 91320   London EC1Y 1SP

Published by Tejeshwar Singh for Sage Publications India Pvt Ltd, typeset in 10/12.5 Janson Text by Star Compugraphics, Delhi, and printed at Chaman Enterprises, New Delhi.

Library of Congress Cataloging-in-Publication Data available

ISBN: 10: 0-7619-3477-4 (PB)   10: 81-7829-624-1 (India-PB)
        13: 978-0-7619-3477-6 (PB)   13: 978-81-7829-624-1 (India-PB)

Sage Production Team: Deepa Dharmadhikari, Rrishi Raote, Rajib Chatterjee, and Santosh Rawat

Indexes: Jayme Feldman, Ohio University

Contents

List of Tables and Figures

Tables

Figures

List of Plates

Foreword

RALPH WALDO EMERSON WROTE OF GREAT HISTORICAL FIGURES, LIKE George Washington and Plutarch's heroes, that "the largest part of their power was latent." This, Emerson felt, is what we call Character, "a reserved force which acts directly by presence, and without means." Emerson linked other qualities to Character, such as "undiminishable greatness" and "magnetism." Character excites intellect, Emerson believed, not the reverse.[1]

Ev Rogers exuded Character, in the Emersonian way: not flashy, but charged with latent magnetism and able to accomplish a great deal, as the varied contributors to this volume make clear. Less understood, perhaps, was Ev's flair for getting things done on a shoestring budget, an aspect of Character that Emerson especially admired.

I can vouch for the power of Ev's "presence ... without means." He and I were colleagues at two universities where I served as a department chair (the University of Michigan in the 1970s) or as a dean (the University of Southern California's Annenberg School for Communication in the 1980s). I reviewed and approved research budgets, and Ev's proposals seldom boasted many trailing zeroes. Usually, his grants lay in the five-figure and lower-six-figure range, skimpy by comparison with today's fashion in government and foundation support.

Nonetheless, we envy his productivity. We are grateful for the many ideas he originated and research breakthroughs he directed. This anomaly has a simple, but deep explanation: high on the list of Ev's resources for accomplishing great scholarship were the students he recruited into projects.

And these students were not dished up to Ev on a silver platter by the fine academic programs that had the good sense to hire him. Ev earned every one of his student collaborators by paying close

---

[1] Ralph Waldo Emerson (1803–82), a philosopher and leader of the American Transcendental movement, published his thoughts about Character in *Essays, Second Series*, in 1844.

attention to their intellectual and spiritual needs. He deftly handed over responsibilities to apprentice scholars earlier than their years-in-grade would suggest. Ev confidently shared his projects with young people, because he had taken care to learn about their capacity to develop Character, in Emerson's sense.

And, in the final analysis, this was Ev's great gift, beyond his intellectual legacy. He recognized and fed the talents of others. That is why so many colleagues and friends have assembled since his death, as is the case with this volume, to express their gratitude. We understand the debt we owe to a life keenly observed.

Peter Clarke
University of Southern California

Preface

WE BROACHED THE IDEA FOR THE PRESENT EDITED BOOK OVER LUNCH at our favorite Star of India restaurant in Athens, Ohio, a couple of months before Ev Rogers passed away on October 21, 2004. Over a platter of *tandoor*-baked *naan*, *daal*, and cucumber *raita*, we reminisced about our privileged association with Ev, which began over two decades ago in Los Angeles.

We both began our doctoral work at the University of Southern California's (USC) Annenberg School in Fall 1985—the same year that Ev moved there from Stanford to become the Walter H. Annenberg Professor of Communication and Associate Dean of doctoral students. In our first conversation, we both discovered that we came to USC to explicitly work with Ev Rogers. We chuckled about declining fellowship offers from the Institute of Communication Research at Stanford University upon learning that Ev was moving to USC. Who, in their right mind, would turn down a fellowship and the opportunity to earn a doctoral degree from Stanford? Well, we did. We had hit it off with Ev Rogers, and with each other, from day one, choosing our graduate experiences on the basis of promising personal and mentoring associations rather than just institutional prestige.

At USC, our days with Ev Rogers were heady. Ev nourished and nurtured our interests with the same care and attention that he tended his terraced vegetable garden in the Hollywood Hills (as a bonus, we were both regular beneficiaries of spring onions, radishes, tomatoes, and ground-breaking potatoes from the Rogers garden). We both independently collaborated with Ev Rogers on various projects, found opportunities to jointly travel to overseas locations (India and Egypt, for instance), and at the beginning of each month worked with Liz Lopez, Ev's USC secretary, to divvy up a good deal of his unscheduled time among us. Fortunately for us, Ev had just moved from Stanford to USC with no doctoral advisees in tow. From the first week at USC, we got on his schedule, and he filled ours with op-portunities, projects, and publications.

Remarkably, during our USC years (and the period thereafter), while we both independently (and repeatedly) collaborated with Ev

Rogers, we never wrote anything together. Our research agendas were fairly independent and our research sites different (Arvind worked mostly in overseas contexts, Jim mostly on domestic issues). After attending the USC cap and gown graduation ceremonies with Ev in May 1990, we went our separate ways—Arvind to the School of Communication Studies at Ohio University and Jim to the Department of Communication at Michigan State University. However, in Fall 2003, when Jim joined the faculty at Ohio University—and we became colleagues again—we vowed to find an opportunity to research and write together. It wasn't difficult. When Ev Rogers came to visit us in Athens in mid-October 2003, and noted that we were in neighboring offices on the second floor of Lasher Hall, he winked and said: "I am guessing we will see a lot of Singhal–Dearing collaboration in the near future."

Appropriately, this book—in honor and celebration of our mentor's intellectual legacy—is our first collaborative writing and editing project together. In this first joint enterprise, we are joined by a distinguished cadre of Ev Rogers' collaborators and contemporaries, who write on topics that not only piqued Ev's curiosity, but in which Ev made seminal and lasting contributions: diffusion of innovations (Dearing and Meyer, Chapter 2), communication networks in diffusion (Valente, Chapter 3), innovation generation and technology transfer (Leonard, Chapter 4), social cognitive and social diffusion theories (Bandura, Chapter 5), social marketing (Kotler, Chapter 6), communication and social change in non-Western contexts (Melkote, Chapter 7), strategic extension campaigns (Adhikarya, Chapter 8), and entertainment-education communication strategy and health promotion (Singhal et al., Chapter 9). The concluding chapter by Shefner-Rogers documents Ev's life journey from his modest farm boy beginnings in Iowa, through his distinguished academic career, to his final return to the farmland.

As you read this book, we hope you will get a sense of the diversity of Ev's network—brimming with fascinating people with path-breaking ideas. We invite you to not only learn about their work, but—through association—about Ev, too.

Arvind Singhal and Jim Dearing
Athens, Ohio

1

Communication of Innovations:
A Journey with Ev Rogers

JAMES W. DEARING *and* ARVIND SINGHAL

WHEN WE WERE GRADUATING WITH OUR DOCTORATES IN COMMUNI-
cation, Ev Rogers was amassing papers and laying the groundwork
for what would become his 1994 book, *A History of Communication
Study*. He had a number of other projects ongoing as well, including
a few with us, but there was a special shimmer in his eyes when he was
on the trail of an account or document that he expected might illumin-
ate some forgotten or overlooked aspect of the founding of the field
of communication. Ev had always been keen on history, on names
and places, precedents and consequences, and especially the social
connections that tie people together and might explain aspects of
their character and accomplishments. He'd predictably put his students on the spot publicly ("So Tom, perhaps you could tell our guests
about the correspondence between the fields of statistics and communication as they relate to agricultural science?"). But pulling the
pieces together for his history book was a special self-indulgence for
him. What historically-minded sociologist wouldn't relish weeks in
the library of the University of Chicago? Or rummaging through
the archives of the Rockefeller Foundation? Or interviewing Robert
K. Merton about his first meeting with Paul F. Lazarsfeld and the
genesis of focus group research?

For a writer, even a collaborative and social one like Ev, solitude is
bliss. Ev collaborated so much, with so many students and colleagues
and practitioners, and served in so many group processes with advisory
boards and in consulting and with universities and professional societies, that the opportunity to go away and think and interview and
read and write—by himself—turned into an intellectual treasure hunt

Plate 1.1
The co-editors of this volume, Singhal (left) and Dearing (right), with mentor Ev Rogers
during their Ph.D. graduation at the University of Southern California in 1990
Source: Personal files of author Singhal

almost too good to be true. The unburnished nuggets he'd turn up
and share with his students and colleagues—an insight here, an
explanation there—and his glee in their revelation, made it clear to
us that Ev Rogers would have made a hell of a historian.

Or even a novelist.

Instead, he became a social scientist! A distinguished one!

A positivist

Ev's orientation to social science was positivist in the best sense of
the term. He believed that academics could affect change, not only
study it; he believed that practitioners had much to teach social scientists since practitioners experimented day in and day out in the real
business of social betterment; and he embraced the assumption that
the generalization of lessons across the specifics of communities,

A farm boy who almost never went to college

When Ev Rogers passed away on October 21, 2004, his ashes were returned—according to his wishes—to the family's Pinehurst Farm in Carroll, Iowa, where he was born on March 6, 1931 (see Shefner-Rogers, Chapter 10). In a career spanning 47 illustrious years, Ev wrote 36 books, 138 book chapters, 176 peer-reviewed journal articles, and over a hundred research reports.

Who would now believe that Ev almost never went to college? During a flight between Rio de Janeiro and Sao Paulo in March 2001, Ev told Arvind that he would have stayed home and farmed if it were not for Pep Martens, his high school vocational agriculture teacher. One day in May 1948, Martens packed a bunch of five promising seniors in his car, including Ev, and drove them to Ames, Iowa, the home of Iowa State University. It was Ev's first visit to Ames, located 60 miles from the family farm. Ev liked Ames, and decided to pursue a degree in agriculture.

Iowa State in those years had a great intellectual tradition in agriculture and in rural sociology. Numerous agricultural innovations were generated by scientists at Iowa State. Rural sociologists—including Bryce Ryan and George Beal, Ev's doctoral advisor—were conducting pioneering studies on the diffusion of these innovations, like the high-yielding hybrid seed corn, chemical fertilizers, and weed sprays. Questions were being asked about why some farmers adopted these innovations, and some didn't. These questions intrigued Ev.

Back at his farm, Ev saw that his father loved electro-mechanical farm innovations; but was resistant to biological–chemical innovations. For instance, Ev's father resisted adopting the new hybrid seed corn, even though it yielded 25 percent more crop, and was resistant to drought. However, during the Iowa drought of 1936, while the hybrid seed corn stood tall on the neighbors' farm, the crop on the Rogers' farm wilted. Ev's father was finally convinced. It took him eight years to make up his mind.

These questions about innovation diffusion, including the strong resistances, and how they could be overcome, formed the core of Ev's graduate work at Iowa State University in the mid-1950s. Ev's doctoral dissertation sought to analyze the diffusion of the 2-4-D weed spray (and a bunch of other agricultural innovations) in Collins, Iowa, not far from the family farm. In the review of literature chapter,

CONTINUED ON THE NEXT PAGE

BOX—CONTINUED

Ev reviewed the existing studies of the diffusion of all kinds of innovations—agricultural innovations, educational innovations, medical innovations, and marketing innovations. He found several similarities in these studies. For instance, innovations tend to diffuse following an S-Curve of adoption.

In 1962, Ev published this review of literature chapter, greatly expanded, enhanced, and refined, as the *Diffusion of Innovations* book. The book provided a comprehensive theory of how innovations diffused, or spread, in a social system. The book's appeal was global. Its timing was uncanny. National governments of countries in Asia, Africa, and Latin America were wrestling with how to diffuse agricultural, health, and family planning innovations in their newly-independent countries. Here was a theory that was useful. During the 1960s and 1970s, for every copy of *Diffusion of Innovations* that was purchased in the US, Ev estimated that four were being purchased in the countries of Asia, Africa, and Latin America.

When the first edition of *Diffusion of Innovations* was published, Ev was 31 years old. But he had already become a world-renowned academic figure. "It became my calling card for the next four decades," noted Ev in a lecture at Ohio University in October 2003. According to the Social Science Citation Index, *Diffusion of Innovations* is the second most cited book in the social sciences.

Not bad for a farm boy who almost did not go to college!

populations, times, and topics for the improvement of both scholarly understanding and social conditions was the very purpose of social science. In this, he was a product of those who had come before him and whose ideas formed the basis of his graduate and continuing education: Sir Francis Bacon, who foresaw the policy and social improvement functions that a science of society might fulfill; August Comte, the founder and proponent of sociology and of positivist philosophy; and Georg Simmel, Robert E. Park, and Kurt Lewin, whose ideas and studies of the dependence of the individual on one's immediate network of interpersonal relations foreshadowed the diffusion paradigm's role accorded to local informal opinion leaders and peers.

The influence of George Beal, Ev's dissertation committee chair, was strong on the student's choice of dissertation, which was completed in 1957 as *A Conceptual Variable Analysis of Technological Change*,

Plate 1.2
Between his undergraduate and graduate degrees at Iowa State University, Ev Rogers served in the United States Air Force during the Korean War
Source: Ev Rogers. Copy provided to author Singhal in 2000

chapter two of which became the basis for the 1962 publication *Diffusion of Innovations*. In the dissertation chapter, the giant dwarfing the doctoral candidate-cum-author was Robert K. Merton, whose ideas about the role of theory and testable hypotheses in relation to the accumulation of knowledge were used by Ev to justify the empirical approach taken. The antagonist pitted against Merton was Herbert Blumer, the University of Chicago sociologist and star student of George Herbert Mead, whose critical stance against variable-based analysis for the study of social interaction had been well publicized and debated in departments of sociology and rural sociology. In later years, Ev would come to carry out some of his empirical studies in ways that Blumer would have recognized as similar to symbolic interactionism. Yet Merton's influence on Ev never waned.

Merton's concept of "theories of the middle range" that were not grandiose to the point of being all-encompassing and untestable, nor strictly derived from logical positivism such that data could be devoid of theorizing, captured what Ev Rogers set out to do with abstracting a general model of diffusion based on empirical work from various disciplines. Ev's dissertation committee at Iowa State argued against such extrapolation beyond farmers' adoption of agricultural innovations, but the eventual surprisingly warm reception by practitioners and academics alike to the publication of *Diffusion of Innovations* made a strict delimited disciplinary interpretation of diffusion a mute point. Ev had promulgated an interdisciplinary paradigm of innovation diffusion. Others hovered importantly around the many unresolved issues of the process of diffusion, notably Elihu Katz, James Coleman, Nan Lin, Wilbur Schramm, Bradley Greenberg, Daniel Lerner, Steve Chaffee, Inayatullah, Syed Rahim, Lawrence Green, Vijay Mahajan, Lawrence Mohr, Marshall Becker, Eric von Hippel, Jack Walker, Paul Berman, Paul Deutschmann, and Ithiel de Sola Pool, but Ev's prolific and clear prose, doctoral students (he guided some 150 doctoral dissertations in his career), accessibility, and humbleness put other scholars in the paradigmatic position of often reacting to him when they wrote of diffusion. He worked nonstop, leading and collaborating on studies in international development, rural sociology, and soon, technological adoption and the diffusion of mass mediated news.

Ev's pursuit of generalizable knowledge a.k.a. Merton meant that he needed an intellectual home that was sufficiently broad so that he could study the spread of any type of innovation. Diffusion more than innovation was his focus. The prize question was how well the diffusion process that he along with others were busily codifying mapped across fields and disciplines. The fewer the qualifications that had to be made, the better. More qualifications meant less parsimony, and would reduce the eloquence of the theory. Communication, a derivative field institutionalized by Wilbur Schramm at the University of Illinois in the late 1940s, and then solidified at Stanford University in the mid-1950s, was sufficiently new and undetermined so as to suit the proclivities of such a pursuit. The nascent field had a professional emphasis stemming from journalism and a performance emphasis stemming from rhetoric and speech. Growth of mass communication in the United States and overseas was rapid; new communication technologies full of promise and uncertainty. The largest private foundations were onboard and willing to gamble. The young communication scholars took on the monumental challenges of international development and public health improvement through diffusion-informed communication campaigns. It was a perfect match, even if the results would prove disappointing.

Over the years, Ev would exhibit a knack for joining universities just prior to their crests of communication study prominence (Table 1.1). His arrivals, of course, contributed mightily to the reputation of communication study at Michigan State, University of Michigan, Stanford, University of Southern California (USC), and

Table 1.1
Key events in Ev Rogers' life

March 6, 1931	Born, Carroll, Iowa
1936–44	One-room country school in Carroll, Iowa
1944–48	Carroll High School, Carroll, Iowa
1948–52	Iowa State University, Ames, Iowa, B.S., Agriculture
1952–54	United States Air Force, Second/First Lieutenant, Korean War
1954–57	Iowa State University, Ames, Iowa, MS and Ph.D., Rural Sociology
1957–63	Assistant Professor and Associate Professor of Rural Sociology, Ohio State University
1962	*Diffusion of Innovations* (first edition) published by Free Press
1963–64	Fulbright Lecturer, Faculty of Sociology, National University of Colombia, Bogotá
1964–73	Associate Professor and Professor of Communication, Michigan State University
1973–75	Professor of Population Planning in the School of Public Health, and Professor of Journalism, University of Michigan
1975–85	Janet M. Peck Professor of International Communication, Institute for Communication Research, Stanford University
1981	Fulbright Lecturer, French Press Institute, University of Paris, Paris, France
1985–92	Walter H. Annenberg Professor of Communication, Annenberg School for Communication, University of Southern California
1991–92	Fellow, Center for Advanced Study in the Behavioral Sciences, Stanford, California
1993–2004	Professor and Chair, Regents' Professor and Distinguished Professor, Department of Communication and Journalism, University of New Mexico
1996	Ludwig Erhard Professor, University of Bayreuth, Bayreuth, Germany
1998	Wee Kim Wee Professor of Communication, School of Communication Studies, Nanyang Technological University, Singapore
1999–2000	Visiting Professor, Center for Communication Programs, School of Hygiene and Public Health, Johns Hopkins University
2000–2001	Nanyang Professor, School of Communication Studies, Nanyang Technological University, Singapore
2004	Distinguished Professor Emeritus, Department of Communication and Journalism, University of New Mexico
October 21, 2004	Died, Albuquerque, New Mexico

Source: Ev Rogers' curriculum vitae

Plate 1.3
Ev Rogers conducting a diffusion workshop at CIESPAL, Ecuador, in the late 1960s. Ev was fluent in Spanish since the early 1960s, when he served as Fulbright Lecturer in Bogota, Colombia
Source: Ev Rogers. Copy provided to author Singhal in 2000

University of New Mexico, yet he was an acute judge of potential. He spoke of communication departments and their universities in terms of organizational histories, of their rise and fall, of better times and worse times to be at a particular place. Ev was always eager to share with students his perceptions of a hot department "on the make." Bright students, attention, and resources flowered about him, and followed him when it was time to depart.

Linking macro and micro levels of diffusion

Though Ev Rogers would remain for decades the single most recognizable name associated with the diffusion of innovations, many scholars took up the game. And many diffusion scholars played a game that was different than Ev's. In particular, some working in the paradigm took a macro structural perspective on diffusion, especially those in population planning, demography, economics, and international relations. Anthropologists studying the spread of culture and linguists studying the spread of language also preferred a structural perspective on diffusion, which conceptualized waves of innovations washing over societies. To these structuralists, the study of diffusion was the study of social change writ large. For them, units of adoption were countries or cultures.

This macro orientation to diffusion was highly enticing to scholars because of its deductive and parsimonious potential based in a simple mathematical law of nature that describes a logistic (S-shaped or exponential) growth curve. Marketing scientists, epidemiologists, demographers, and political scientists instantly appreciated the predictive potential and eloquence of the population perspective on diffusion. Mathematical modeling formed the basis of this work, most of which continues today apart from more qualitatively informed micro-level studies of diffusion. A large part of Ev's contribution was to explain how this macro process of system change was linked to micro (individual and group) level processes. And impressively, the explanation offered showed both how micro-level units of adoption (usually people) were influenced by system norms, as well as how system change was dependent on individual action. Diffusion was one of the very few social theories that persuasively linked macro with micro-level phenomena.

But if you grow up watching farmers not adopt new technology as Ev did on an Iowa farm—and in his eyes thus not prosper as they might have done—then sociology comes alive in the study of individual behavior in relation to immediate others. The structural study of abstract systems was not his preference, or at least not what he spent his time doing. Ev focused on community-level phenomena, on interpersonal networks, and on the boundedness of such social systems. They were open systems to be sure—how could that not be acknowledged in the era of television and satellites—but their strength, their resilience to keep out the many worthless innovations and to adapt the few good ones, rested in interpersonal relationships that functioned as very effective filters and gatekeepers. If diffusion is about change and destruction and uncertainty, then interpersonal networks and opinion leaders were about stability, normative influence, and the measured appraisal of new ideas. Though he would go on to study diffusion across nations as well as technology transfer

Ev Rogers' distinguished career

Some of the key recognitions bestowed on Ev Rogers included:

- Paul D. Converse Award of the American Marketing Association for Outstanding Contribution to the Science of Marketing (1975 and 2004).
- Distinguished Service Award, International Communication Division, Association for Education in Journalism and Mass Communication (1986).
- Distinguished Rural Sociologist Award, Rural Sociological Society (1986).
- *Diffusion of Innovations* designated as a Citation Classic by the Institute for Scientific Information, Philadelphia (1990).
- Distinguished Service Award, Association for Education in Journalism and Mass Communication (1993).
- *Diffusion of Innovations* selected by *Inc.* magazine as one of the 10 classic books in business (December 1996).
- Honorary Doctorate in Political Economy, Ludwig-Maximilians Univ. of Munich (1996).
- Wayne Danielson Award for Distinguished Contributions to Communication Scholarship (1999).
- Outstanding Health Communication Scholar Award, International Communication Association/National Communication Association (1999).
- Lifetime Achievement Award, Division of Intercultural and Development Communication, International Communication Association (2000).
- First Fellows Book Award in the Field of Communication (for *Diffusion of Innovations*), International Communication Association (2000).
- *Diffusion of Innovations* named as a Significant Journalism and Communication Book of the Twentieth Century by Journalism and Mass Communication Quarterly (2000).
- National Communication Association (NCA) Applied Communication Division's Distinguished Book (for *Entertainment-Education: A Communication Strategy for Social Change*, with Arvind Singhal) (2000).

CONTINUED ON THE NEXT PAGE

BOX—CONTINUED

- Lewis Donohew Outstanding Scholar in Health Communication Award (2002).
- CHOICE Outstanding Academic Title Award (for *India's Communication Revolution: From Bullock Carts to Cyber Marts*, with Arvind Singhal) (2002).
- Univ. of New Mexico 47th Annual Research Lectureship (2002).
- National Communication Association (NCA) Applied Communication Division's Distinguished Book (for *Combating AIDS: Communication Strategies in Action*, with Arvind Singhal) (2004).

Source: Ev Rogers' curriculum vitae

within firms, it was understanding the social dynamics of community-level systems that was Ev's bread and butter (or *dosa* and coconut *chutney*, as the research site necessitated). In his thinking and approach to the study of innovations, Ev reflected the moral priorities of Amitai Etzioni, that community was a base of strength and support for individuals. Diffusion, Ev saw, could be a means of community capacity building just as it could be a divisive cumulative process by which the haves increasingly left the have-nots behind. To someone who had been a farm boy, the ideas of E. F. Schumacher, Garrett Hardin, and Muhammad Yunus made intuitive sense. Organizing at the community level was key, and the application of diffusion concepts was a means to that end.

Over the years, many observers and acquaintances of Ev's have asked us about him. "How does he do it?" they wanted to know. "How does he write so much? How does he know so many people? How does he know a story about everything?" Ev was a very driven man; driven, perhaps, by early formative experiences of growing up during the American depression, of going without and being hungry. When we knew him he seemingly had it all. But certainly that condition had not characterized his early years. Our best approximation of why he was the way he was harkens back to Max Weber's captivating speech at Munich University in 1918, "Science as a Vocation." In that speech, the great sociologist who would go on to so influence Merton who in turn would go on to so influence Rogers, laid out a compelling and simple formula for progress in the sciences: enthusiasm + hard work = the bright idea. To Weber, the key was intrinsic motivation, genuine interest in a topic under study, what he labeled "the inward calling for science":

> The idea is not a substitute for work; and work, in turn, cannot substitute for or compel an idea, just as little as enthusiasm can. Both, enthusiasm and work, and above all both of them *jointly*, can entice the idea .... Ladies and gentlemen. In the field of science only he who is devoted *solely* to the work at hand has "personality." And this holds not only for the field of science; we know of no great artist who has ever done anything but serve his work and only his work. (Gerth and Mills, 1946: 136–37; italics in the original.)

By Max Weber's definition, Ev Rogers had "personality." And this "personality" was duly recognized by many.

About this volume

Together, the two of us have sometimes marveled at the diversity in perspective that has blossomed in the work of Ev's colleagues and students. The point of his extensive relationships, frequent collaborations, and expert mentoring seems to have been a sort of propagation with natural selection. While some of his students continue to conduct what they explicitly label diffusion research, others have used their interactions with Ev to color and enrich related paradigms, including some that they themselves founded. In both cases, the influence of Ev's work and companionship, as attested to by the contributors to the present volume, is considerable.

Our objective while planning for this book was a volume that would honor the memory and contributions of Ev Rogers. What we have got is something different. The book in your hands achieves its objective but goes considerably further as well. Taken together, the chapters that follow comprise an intellectual landscape about social change that illustrates where Ev's students and colleagues have gone with their own scholarship and practice in communication, management, marketing, development studies, and health promotion. What you will read is a remembrance but more so a starting point; less a stock-taking and more a guide for future scholarship and practice.

Plate 1.4
Ev Rogers (right) on Janpath, the famed shopping street in New Delhi, India, in 1993. Notice his signature leather bag filled with papers, manuscripts, and readings. In a spare moment while shopping, Ev would pull out a manuscript and get to work. In his right hip pocket is his appointment book. He had a PDA (personal digital assistant) but never gave up his appointment book
Source: Personal files of author Singhal

We think Ev would be very pleased with the prospective nature of the result.

How will history treat Ev Rogers? The answer is more obviously positive in cases of prolific scholars who fall centrally within one discipline or field, and are claimed by others working within that tradition as their own. Ev was communication-centric, but this modest field itself is marked by fissures and weak links across sub-specialties. Moreover, Ev was not clearly associated with one of the primary divisions in the field of communication such as mass communication, interpersonal communication, or organizational communication. His main intellectual contribution, the synthesis of the diffusion of innovation paradigm, was fashioned to span and tie together disparate disciplines and fields; thus it was bound to tie together (or fall between) the within-field specialties in communication as well. At a recent talk about diffusion theory, one of us was asked by a natural science participant if anything other than the diffusion of innovations was taught in schools of communication in the United States. To us, the question is of course humorous, for in most communication units diffusion does not constitute its own course, let alone define the unit's purpose. We expect that Ev Rogers and his work will continue to be referred to, cited, and claimed as kin by communication scholars and those in other disciplines and fields. The extensiveness of the network of colleagues and students he worked with would seem to suggest as much. Yet the academy, in particular, is not known for celebrating, rewarding, and remembering inter-disciplinarians.

Thanks Ev, for straddling the lines.

Reference

Gerth, H. H. and C. W. Mills (trans.). 1946. *From Max Weber: Essays in Sociology.* New York: Oxford University Press.

2

Revisiting Diffusion Theory

JAMES W. DEARING *and* GARY MEYER

In productive and successful academic mentor–mentee relationships, the professor is supposed to guide and assist the developing graduate student. Occasionally, the effect is reversed, especially in the case of a new assistant professor being paired with a very bright and experienced graduate student. This situation described my relationship with Gary Meyer at Michigan State University. Gary played key project management roles on several projects with me, and became, through multiple field research trips and advisory visits, a student of Ev's in his own right.

JIM DEARING

In the preface of the fourth edition of Diffusion of Innovations, *published in 1995, Ev named a handful of young "hot shot" diffusion scholars who greatly influenced his thinking and writing on the topic. Foremost among them was Jim. Add Gary to the mix, and you get a dynamic diffusion duo.*

ARVIND SINGHAL

Diffusion theory is not an ideology, but it has been construed ideologically by those who would argue for a "trickle down" approach to economic development. For this reason, the theory has been resisted or ignored by some of those who hold more liberal ideologies. Diffusion theory does not lead to the conclusion that one must wait for the diffusion of a new product or practice to reach the poorest people, assuming that they will be late adopters regardless of the interventions attempted to reach them. In fact, one can accelerate the rate of adoption in any segment of the population through more intensive and more appropriate communication and outreach. (Green, Gottlieb, and Parcel, 1991: 114)

EVERETT ROGERS WAS RIGHT WHEN, IN THE PREFACE TO THE 1995 edition of *Diffusion of Innovations,* he wrote "we do not need 'more of the same' diffusion research." Elihu Katz, in his own way, noted that "there is an apparent paradox at work: the number of diffusion studies continues at a high rate while the growth of appropriate theory is at an apparent standstill" (1999: 145). This chapter is an attempt to respond to the concerns of Rogers (1995) and Katz (1999) by suggesting a route to reaching the potential of this collective literature as concluded by the aforementioned Green, Gottlieb, and Parcel (1991).

We begin this task by providing an example of how most diffusion theorists consider the process of diffusion to work in the case of programs and interventions designed for adoption by service intermediaries such as health care professionals, community outreach workers, environmental managers, and school teachers (we shall refer to this generally-accepted explanation as "the traditional approach"). After identifying the main components of the traditional approach, we then point to alternative ideas about diffusion on several fronts, led by scholars of management, public administration, and sociology. We argue that these divergent attempts to recast the diffusion paradigm share a common emphasis in recasting what it is that potential adopters and actual adopters do in relation to innovations. While the traditional approach to explaining diffusion positions adopters in a reactive role as socially-connected receivers and evaluators of new ideas and objects, new theories about diffusion suggest that adopters do more than alternate as conversationally active and reactive, depending on the innovation in question, in influencing others and being influenced by them. Potential adopters can also be full partners in the creative process of innovating as a result of actively framing the meaning of innovations, trading innovative ideas back and forth as innovation sources and innovation receivers, and by exploiting opportunities and constraints in the information and social environment.

We elucidate the broad multidisciplinary issue of adopter *activity*. Current formulations of adopter activity are mostly relegated to social interaction, and not interaction with an innovation. That is, one's innovation activity is easily and mistakenly conflated with an adopter's activity with other adopters such that one's level of activity is assumed to be defined as where one falls in the normal distribution for the trait innovativeness. Our focus, instead, is on adopters as creators of innovations, a view of democratizing diffusion for public benefit that is strongly analogous to Eric von Hippel's (2005) observation that innovating in multiple sectors is becoming a democratic process that, if recognized and embraced, allows for the capturing of private benefit. Stated differently, while the traditional view of the diffusion of innovations decouples the process of innovation from the process of diffusion, the theoretical perspective we propose here closely weds the two together for the purpose of detailing a means of "making a difference" in social conditions.

The particular context in which we assess adopter activity is the problematic and important multidisciplinary domain of translational research. *Translational research* is the study of how evidence-based practices, programs, and campaigns can best be communicated for adaptation by program staff and intermediaries for the benefit of their constituents. Translational research has become a critical concern of major research institutions and change agencies such as the US National Cancer Institute. While the traditional approach to diffusion scholarship popularized by Katz (Katz and Lazarsfeld, 1956) and Rogers (1962) and since tested and explicated by them and others has applicable concepts and clear implications for advancing translational research, it too is deficient in certain respects. Thus, we advocate a hybrid orientation to the intervention-based study of the diffusion of innovations, one that acknowledges (1) the enduring role that centralized change agencies will continue to play in seeking social betterment; (2) variance among program staff not just as adopters but as innovators, which we conclude is a type of decentralized diffusion; and (3) innovation specificity as a critical concern of program developers and their supporting change agencies in the pursuit of external validity and diffusion. We believe that our approach to the diffusion of innovations as translational research represents a unique niche especially for scholars who consider the field of communication their home.

Diffusion as we know it

How do we understand diffusion to work? Consider the following scenario:

Min Wha has been an assistant professor of chemistry at a California State University campus for two years. She wants to demonstrate her willingness for professional development because her three-year review is only one year away, so Min Wha volunteers to attend a half-day workshop entitled Process Oriented Guided Inquiry Learning (POGIL), an approach to active learning developed by chemistry faculty at Franklin & Marshall College and the State University of New York at Stony Brook and funded by the US National Science Foundation, hosted by her university's center for teaching excellence. The workshop is interesting to Min Wha. She finds POGIL easy to understand, and learns that she can try it out little by little. Yet she decides nothing. Three weeks later she has a chance conversation in the mail room with Rukhsana, a more senior assistant professor whom Min Wha likes. Though she has never seen Rukhsana teach, Min Wha admires her colleague's teaching ability based on students' casual comments about what a good teacher Rukhsana is, and the fact that Rukhsana won a university teaching award. In the mail room, Rukhsana talks as she recycles a flyer about constructivism as a basis for better teaching. Min Wha, alert, listens. She tells Rukhsana about the POGIL workshop. Rukhsana reveals that she too had attended a POGIL workshop and now organizes many of her classes around its approach to classroom learning. Back in her office, Min Wha decides to try POGIL with her chemistry students.

The preceding scenario demonstrates the accepted, traditional approach to explaining the individual decision-process as described and explained via the concepts popularized in *Diffusion of Innovations* through its five editions over 44 years. Knowledge is gained largely through the one-way communication of information. Persuasion occurs through the two-way communication of normally-operating social influence in the form of informal, extant local opinion leadership. Together, communication of information and communication of influence represents a dual-process model of inputs (Bandura, 1986) that can result in a ripple of positive adoption decisions among units of adoption such as teachers to try a new practice. In the preceding scenario, information alone was insufficient to move the individual toward a positive decision or even serious contemplation of innovation costs and benefits when the innovation in question is consequential (perceived to have high relevance to the attainment of personal or collective objectives). Dialogue was the key. Proximity played a role.

And it was not just anyone—a third faculty colleague, for example— who was able to prime Min Wha's memory in a productive way. It was Rukhsana, a person whom Min Wha already believed to be expert and trustworthy. If someone other than Rukhsana had advocated or served as a social model for problem-based learning, Min Wha likely would not have made the decision she did.

The ABCs of diffusion

- When Bob Dylan wrote "The Times They Are A-Changin" he was describing diffusion.
- When Amazon.com invested in a new inventory control system, it was adding to a product's diffusion.
- When the Centers for Disease Control and Prevention promoted its obesity prevention guidelines, it was doing diffusion.
- And when large-scale Columbian coffee farmers decided against planting low-yield, shade grown, high-quality, high return coffee plants, they were limiting diffusion.

Diffusion is a social process by which an innovation is communicated over time among the members of a communication network or within a social sector. Many studies have shown a predictable over-time pattern when an innovation spreads, the S-shaped curve graphed in Figure 2.1.

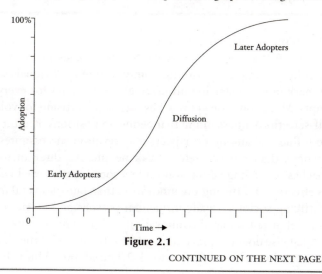

Figure 2.1

CONTINUED ON THE NEXT PAGE

BOX—CONTINUED

An *innovation* can be an idea, knowledge, a belief or social norm, a product or service, a technology or process, even a culture, as long as it is perceived to be new. Innovations are communicated verbally, by one person telling another, and in many other ways such as via magazine advertisements and personal observation. Commonly, we first learn of innovations through impersonal mediated communication channels, but only decide to adopt an innovation for ourselves later, after asking the opinion or observing the behavior of someone whom we know, trust, or consider an expert. Ev Rogers labeled these people "opinion leaders." The social influence of opinion leaders either by talking or by example-setting is what drives the diffusion curve up, giving it its characteristic "S" shape. They are also responsible for innovations *not* diffusing, by ignoring an innovation (passive rejection) or speaking out against it (active rejection). Studies of higher-order aggregates demonstrate opinion leader effects among organizations, counties, states, and nations.

Different people take different amounts of time to adopt innovations. For some, only one or two people in their personal networks or "reference groups" are required to adopt before the focal individual then adopts; for others, nearly all others in their personal networks or reference groups must adopt before the focal individual finally converts. These differences are *thresholds* that vary from person to person for any particular innovation.

Opinion leaders constitute only a small proportion of system members (often about 5 percent). So approaches to spread innovations by seeding them with randomly selected individuals will miss the mark in jump-starting diffusion about 19 times for every 20 attempts. More common approaches such as advertising for volunteers (self-selection), or assuming that people in positions of authority are also influential among near-peers may result in success rates better, or worse, than random selection of people. All three of these approaches of seeding an innovation in a social system are likely to be less effective at diffusing the innovation than one of several means of identifying sociometrically influential persons and recruiting them to model or talk about the innovation with potential adopters.

What else does the preceding scenario tell us about the traditional interpretation of how diffusion works? The adopter, Min Wha, is one in a network of like-professionals. She does not only talk with Rukhsana. She is a teacher who talks with other teachers. Her relations with them are not evenly distributed, but there is a discernable structure to the network in which she is both embedded and to which she contributes. Certain faculty she talks with more and regards more highly; others, less so. This patterned structure is rather topic-specific; in this instance, it is perhaps unique to teaching and learning expertise, though that structure may overlap, sometimes considerably, with related topics, such as chemistry research, university administration expertise, chemistry disciplinary knowledge, or industry consulting expertise. And by extension, we expect Min Wha to talk with students and chemistry professionals.

We can also note that Min Wha is initially prompted to action by an institutional condition: The looming requirement of promotion and tenure review. Institutional rules such as this one are a part of the environmental context within which individuals make decisions. Often, it is an environmental cue that precipitates individual action.

In the scenario, we see how change agencies and their agents of change enter into the information environments and social networks of potential adopters as innovation developers, the funders of their work, and a host intermediary (in this case study, the center for teaching excellence). While adopters may be members of far-flung and loosely-knit communication networks, the formal channels by which innovations are created, defined, tested, refined and communicated are often centralized when obvious interested change agencies are involved. The traditional diffusion perspective is an over-time processual one—communication first occurring through more formal communication channels, from the few to the many—which gives way to interpersonal talk and the possibility of influence in informal channels.

This traditional understanding of diffusion also prominently features the importance of adopters' impressions in leading to their decisions. These attributes of innovations, codified by Rogers as complexity, relative advantage, compatibility, trialability, and observability, constitute perceived benefits and costs of a positive adoption decision. In our example, Min Wha develops a sense that it is easy to understand POGIL, and that she need not make an all-or-nothing commitment to trying it with her classes of students.

Lastly, as the scenario depicts, the innovation in question, POGIL, is a specific entity with multiple components, not so much embedded in physical artifacts as it is a coordinated system of protocols, techniques, and approaches to accomplishing goal-directed objectives, like so many social programs and interventions. It was created by individuals who work at certain institutions, at a particular time. There are books, brochures, web sites, presentations, CD-ROMs, and workshops all devoted to it. Potential adopters learn what POGIL is, the nature of the evidence supporting the workshop claims, how to implement POGIL, and how to get help with its use. Innovation developers are nearly always emotionally and sometimes financially vested in their work. They are the ultimate expert concerning the innovation in question. Because they have worked through many contingencies during the innovation development process, they resist its modification by others, justifiably uncertain that variants on what they have created will still be effective in achieving program objectives.

In summary, the traditional approach to understanding diffusion emphasizes (1) the key generative role of centralized change agencies and those they fund as the sources of innovation, (2) the importance of perceptions by potential adopters of the attributes of an innovation to decrease uncertainty about what the innovation is and can do, and (3) the necessity of personal influence for signaling potential adopters that an innovation should be attended to, that it is consonant with prevailing local social norms, and that it is promising. Our scenario is a rather delimited set of influences on an adoption decision; Wejnert (2002) provides an exhaustive listing of independent variables as either (1) characteristics of innovations, (2) characteristics of innovators, or (3) parts of the environmental context, each of which can affect adoption decisions.

Prevailing beliefs about how diffusion works are just that; related sets of concepts that have been the objects of study, in some cases considerable study. Researchers working in anthropology, agriculture, sociology, education, and other disciplines have over seven decades rarely studied all aspects of the process of diffusion; rather, they have emphasized those concepts most germane to their discipline (Katz, Levin, and Hamilton, 1963). Yet there are still other ways of explaining the spread of new ideas, even if they are less supported yet through empirical research.

Alternatives to traditional explanations of diffusion

A rhetorical perspective on diffusion

Green (2004) proposed a rhetorical explanation for the diffusion of managerial innovations. He argued that through their choices of language, managers increase or decrease the diffusion of new ideas and objects within and across firms, such as Total Quality Management (TQM). The traditional approach to explaining diffusion includes the idea that when diffusion occurs, informational messages precede persuasive messages since potential adopters first have questions about what an innovation is (knowledge-based questions), and then later have questions about the innovation's performance and, in particular, its negative aspects (evaluation-based questions) as they move nearer to making an adoption decision. The traditional explanation also includes the idea that what potential adopters say to each other—and especially what opinion leaders say to near-peers—affects the rate of adoption of an innovation.

In a set of propositions, Green (2004) posited that diffusion rates will vary depending on whether justifications for adopting the innovation are based in pathos (emotion), logos (effectiveness), or ethos (morality). Pathos appeals, he argued, would result in rapid diffusion and rapid discontinuance; logos appeals in moderately rapid diffusion and moderately rapid discontinuance; and ethos appeals in slow uptake and gradual discontinuance. Green reasoned that by combining the three types of justifications in this sequence (pathos arguments, then logos arguments, followed by ethos arguments), diffusion would be both accelerated and prolonged. This formula is different from that in Rogers (2003), where persuasive appeals rich in pathos are understood to be necessary just prior to the time of adopter decision, and after what rhetoricians would consider logical or logos appeals to explain to potential adopters what the innovation is and how it works.

In Green's theorizing about organizations, it is the managers as potential adopters who control the determination of such meaning and its communication. The agency for change within the corporation is placed with the managers as adopters, and less so with the outward-to-inward efforts of change agencies such as consulting firms. While to Green, external change agencies remain the sources of innovation,

Plate 2.1
Ev Rogers (far left) with the San Francisco AIDS research team collaborators Jim Dearing, Geoff Henderson, Gary Meyer, Mary K. Casey, and Nagesh Rao behind Ev's home at the foot of the Sandia Mountains in Albuquerque, New Mexico
Source: Personal file of author Meyer

the meaning of those tools, techniques, and technologies is fomented and negotiated internally, by adopters. To him as well as to others (Strang and Meyer, 1994; Abrahamson and Fairchild, 1999), discourse among adopters determines the fate of managerial innovations. This rhetorical perspective on diffusion is about framing the meaning of innovations. The theory reconceptualizes how we think about innovations; it is a means of explaining how characterizations of innovations influence our adoption of them.

Learning from Ev in the field

Prior to entering into field research, social scientists typically do a lot of thinking about what they want to study, why, and how they will proceed to gather the data they need to test hypotheses or answer research questions. The two present authors spent about two years planning, proposing, and re-proposing what became a federally-funded study of whether social marketing and diffusion of innovation concepts are effective in practice when the adopters in question are highly ostracized, marginal members of cities. Funding in hand, we convened a field research team of about 10 people, one of whom was Ev.

We were excited to do this work because it promised some answers to interesting theoretical questions about marketing and diffusion concepts. Sure, the concepts applied to most people most of the time. But how well did they map onto extreme social situations when the people in question were highly atypical yet also at the highest risk of a dreaded disease?

Accordingly, we took great care to develop and validate measures and instruments. Our methods of data-collection included structured personal interviews. Since we were planning to interview the staff of 20 organizations with five or six two-person teams, we spent considerable time making sure that the interviewers understood the structured interview protocol, and would ask the questions in the same way. Interviews were tape-recorded to enable content analysis of transcripts. Ev was not able to attend our interview training sessions due to his busy schedule, but he was eager to help out with the interviews.

When Ev joined us at the site and we began interviews, the gravity of our mistake hit us squarely in the face. Ev was not following the protocol. He didn't even seem to be looking at the structured set of questions and prompts! It would have been easy to pull a junior team member aside and correct them. But this was Ev Rogers. Later, poring over the transcripts, we felt deflated. His questioning was so different from everyone else's that we resigned ourselves to having to limit the number of organizations in our analysis, excluding the interviews in which Ev had participated.

Then an interesting thing happened. Once we got beyond the odd questioning approach that Ev had followed, we noticed that the number of transcript pages for his interviews was larger than for the rest of us. Analyzing the responses he had generated from interviewees, we were amazed. Ev was eliciting far richer, more detailed responses than

CONTINUED ON THE NEXT PAGE

BOX—CONTINUED

the rest of us. The protocol was more tightly focused on our a priori concepts of interest, but Ev was learning more, including some fascinating, unanticipated results.

Later, after reflection, we concluded that Ev's friendly and sincere style of engaging interviewees in dialogue had produced greater and richer data than had our planned approach, which had been less dialogue and more of a confirmatory questioning.

A trading perspective on diffusion

On the basis of a series of empirical studies, several management scholars have developed the theory that individual adopters employed by competing organizations frequently engage in the informal and asynchronous exchange of proprietary knowledge to solve work-related problems. First postulated by Eric von Hippel (1987) and subsequently further modeled and tested by Carter (1989) and Schrader (1991), "know-how trading" has been shown to ably characterize how engineers and other technical and professional staff learn of process innovations. Though these researchers do not term it as such, know-how trading is an enactment of social capital; adopters access valuable information through extant relational contacts, on a need-to-know basis. Reciprocity is the guiding principle governing information exchanges through these relationships, just as it is with social capital of other types. What you help to solve this week for an acquaintance at a rival firm you will recoup at some unspecified later date. Schrader's study of 294 middle-level managers showed that the diffusion of knowledge through know-how trading benefited both the indi-viduals who were party to the exchanges and their employers.

Traditional theorizing about diffusion strongly suggests a directionality of diffusion, from sources to adopters (receivers). Diffusion researches that incorporate the study of social networks have demonstrated the mediating role of interpersonal relations in speeding or slowing rate of adoption (Coleman, Katz, and Menzel, 1966). The theoretic importance of the trading perspective is its evidence of asynchronous reciprocity; that actors play the roles of sources and receivers at different times, according to the interpersonal request and supply for innovations. The implicit promise of engaging in exchange networks is the attendant obligation for reciprocal behavior, a strongly

Plate 2.2
Ev Rogers and Jim Dearing floating down the River Nile in Egypt in 1989. Even on this dinner cruise, with belly dancers on board, Ev carried out an in-depth personal interview with our host, a representative of the Cabinet of Egypt, on the status of the high-tech industry in Egypt
Source: Personal file of author Dearing

felt norm deriving from informal and tacit agreement. This sense of obligation, of brotherhood or sisterhood, facilitates bilateral diffusion, not just from A to B but from B to C to A. The informality, multiplexity, and strength of interpersonal work-based relationships means that the high value information usually required for successful technology transfer—so-called tacit knowledge—is precisely the type of knowledge that know-how trading facilitates. The trading perspective on diffusion is about the maintaining of important relationships. Whereas the rhetorical explanation for diffusion is about the meanings given to ideas and objects, this trading perspective on diffusion of practices and innovative solutions is about relationships; not what you think but who you know. Know-how trading reconceptualizes how we think about adopters and the activities in which they engage. In know-how trading, adopters are mutually and maximally active. They do not merely reinvent innovations. They are the generative sources of innovative solutions to managerial and technical problems.

An evolutionary perspective on diffusion

Douthwaite, Keatinge, and Park (2002) studied what agricultural adopters did with six post-harvest technologies in the Philippines and Vietnam. They concluded in a cross-case analysis that learning and cycles of adaptation—analogous, they argue, to natural selection in the biological world—characterized how adopters interacted with technologies as a result of their social and work environments. In particular, Douthwaite, Keatinge, and Park identified instances of novelty generation (the creation of differences between adopters, their innovations, or the ways that they use innovations) and the subsequent selection by adopters of the most beneficial "novelties" to best fashion the technology in question. The authors observed that repeated instances of novelty generation and selection of the best-suited novelties led to results (innovations) with "hybrid vigor," innovations that were most able to thrive in use by the adopters in question. The fittest innovations survived from plausible promise to successful adaptation in practice.

In this approach to understanding technological change, innovation and diffusion are inextricably intertwined processes. But unlike the rhetorical perspective that justifications drive diffusion, or the trading perspective that relational obligation drives the spread of innovation, the key force in the evolutionary perspective that determines the adaptations that adopters make to innovations is the environment, which both enables and constrains the prosperity of any one "species" or innovative solution. Adopters change innovations to exploit a perceived niche in which they want to operate. So this perspective reconceptualizes how we think about environmental conditions in relation to diffusion, giving primacy to environmental conditions as a shaping force on innovation and propagation.

This theory suggests that while the environment determines what is possible, the agency necessary to take advantage of that opportunity is the adopters', whose activity is as much defined by a process of innovating as it is by a process of diffusion. The evolutionary perspective on diffusion is about adjusting the innovation-immediate context fit so that an opportunity made possible by the environment can be exploited. The result, according to these authors, is highly tailored innovation, often unique to each individual adopter-user.

Adopter activity as a common thread

While the managerial and agricultural technology explanations for diffusion just reviewed are quite distinct from one another, they have in common a claim that adopters of innovations are by no means passive receivers of innovations. Nor are adopters mere tinkerers or customizers, adapting at the margins of innovations from afar. These three disparate theories of diffusion suggest that adopters are not at all what we have been told they are. Rather, they are creators, inventors, and sources of change. They are, without overstating the case, extremely active in testing, manipulating, jerry-rigging, and doing what it takes to create, both through language and through action, an innovation that precisely addresses the requirements of an acutely felt local problem. If the purpose at hand is to create something radical or wonderful, then the type of adopter activity to which we refer will be of small import. On the other hand, if the purpose is to heighten the utility of a given innovation and hence transform it from something that one will not adopt or use into something that suits a felt need well enough to cause both adoption and implementation, then adopter activity is vital. It is perhaps what Maslow (1959) referred to as *secondary creativity*, individual activity that accounts for the majority of creative if modest outputs "which are essentially the consolidation and exploitation of other people's ideas" (p. 93).

We find it helpful to distinguish two types of adopter activity. Potential adopters can be active in relation to other adopters and potential adopters. They can also be active in relation to an innovation. We discuss activity in relation to others first but then focus on the latter type of activity.

The traditional diffusion perspective is one in which potential adopters actively listen to, read about, and observe others' responses to innovations, and discuss those innovations with others. People are neither passive nor atomized individuals as much communication scholarship has characterized mass audiences. Except for the most venturesome and the most cautious, potential adopters think and act with reference to the social norms that characterize the networks or systems of which they are members. Thus for most people, their activity is of a social type that is normatively guided by prevailing attitudes and values. Their activity is with other adopters and potential adopters, defined more or less by their degree of innovativeness. The earliest adopters ("innovators" in Rogers' categorization) are highly active in scanning information environments, in seeking out new ideas from heterogeneous sources, and in experimentation. Feeling few constraints on their behavior, they act nearly autonomously toward the group, though they often exhibit ties to others outside the immediate group. But innovators comprise only a small proportion (2.5 percent) of the adopters in any social system. The vast majorities of others (early adopters, early majority, late majority, laggards) are less active in how they behave, their activity being more a response to how they perceive others within the group viewing the innovation in question. The last to adopt also exhibit a lesser degree of social integration, though they are more commonly passive rejecters rather than active in relation to others. The essential point is that activity is carried out through social relations. Conceptualizing one's activity as a property of interaction with others dominates both network and structural perspectives on innovation diffusion (see, for example, Burt, 2003).

Adopter activity in relation to an innovation is much less prevalent in diffusion literature. To be sure, there is support from studies that adopters actively change innovations during implementation (Rice and Rogers, 1980; Dearing et al., 1998). But activity of this sort has usually been considered deviant or minor in relation to the original source-defined purpose of an innovation and how it was designed by that source. Rogers (2003) and other scholars labeled such adopter activity *re-invention*. In the present chapter, we maintain along with Green (2004), von Hippel (1987), and Douthwaite, Keatinge, and Park (2002) that adopter activity in relation to innovations is far more important, common, and consequential than reflected in the diffusion literature.

The domain of translational research

For many social problems in the United States, the state of the science (what researchers collectively know about solutions to a given problem) and the state of the art (what practitioners collectively do to help their constituents with a given problem) co-exist more or less autonomously, each realm of activity often having little effect on the other

(Dearing, 2003). This situation has been referred to as a "quality chasm" by the Institute of Medicine, a "problem of translation" by the National Cancer Institute and the Agency for Healthcare Research and Quality, and a challenge of "going to scale" by health policy entrepreneurs (Lenfant, 2003). Explicit calls for using diffusion theory to address problems of translation have been made (Berwick, 2003). By no means are health and health care the only sectors of U.S. society characterized by evidence–practice gaps, yet perhaps in no other sectors are discrepancies so well documented (Committee on Quality of Health Care in America, Institute of Medicine, 2001).

Government agencies and philanthropic organizations have tended to see the closure of evidence–practice gaps as a problem of *doing* dissemination; that is, of distributing information about research results through familiar communication channels such as conferences, workshops, continuing education, proceedings, articles, and increasingly, web sites. A different route to redressing evidence–practice gaps is the funding of research *about* dissemination, or what in certain federal agencies is termed translational research.

Translational research is the study of how evidence-based practices, programs, and campaigns can best be communicated to practitioners for the benefit of their constituents. When translational research strategies are based in diffusion of innovation concepts, the resulting study is a type of *purposive diffusion*.

A *practitioner* is someone who makes decisions about which programs and practices will be implemented to provide information, advice, support, and services to constituents. In organizations such as social service agencies, community-based nonprofits, schools, hospitals, and clinics, practitioners interact directly with constituents by counseling them or instructing them. Many such organizations receive contracts and grants from funders to carry out such programs and practices. For this reason, practitioner organizations are often referred to as *intermediaries*—they mediate and add value to the flow of resources from government and other funding sources to populations of people who need services. We seek to clarify the functional role of practitioners because the outcomes of translational research often focus on them. Their attitudes and behavior in response to the diffusion of innovations is key to eventual constituent outcomes (the percentage of low-income women of childbearing age who smoke goes down) and societal impacts (cancer incidence decreases among low-income women).

Translational research is a form of meta-intervention research in which the domain of action concerns how previously validated interventions can be spread through networks of practitioners who are interconnected through regular, patterned informal communication, or spread through sectors of practitioners who are not knowingly interconnected with each other but who are professionally, geographically, situationally, or behaviorally similar such that they attend to the same sources of information and thus can be reached via the same set of communication channels (the same web sites, the same trade association publications, the same conferences).

Translational research concerns the purposive spread of innovations that have been derived from empirical research and are repackaged for practitioners, for the benefit of the people served by those practitioners. Translation is challenging because the knowledge in question must traverse a heterogeneous divide, from the intellectual and social world of researchers on one side to the intellectual and social world of practitioners on the other. We know from many studies of failed technology transfer, failed knowledge dissemination, and failed research-to-practice that translation cannot be assumed. Researchers and practitioners often exhibit much heterogeneity in education, occupation, interests, and value systems. Practitioners tend to see themselves as members of client systems in which they attempt to gain entrée and intervene on local cultural terms. They often live and work within the same communities that they try to affect. Researchers tend to be outside such systems even when they spend long periods studying them, and are often identified more with change agencies, government departments, and universities. Effective practitioners are considered insiders by the people they try to help; researchers—even effective ones—rarely achieve such status. And while some types of information about effective practices can be communicated effectively and efficiently between heterogeneous groups, other types of information resists easy or rapid translation. People retain some knowledge tacitly, not even knowing what it is that they themselves know and thus what it is that others too need to know. Tacit knowledge is sticky knowledge; it likes to stay where it is (Szulanski, 1996).

While these reasons for the common failure to share effective programs and practices between researchers and practitioners are understandable, conditions are actually worse. The perceptual basis of heterogeneity requires far less to manifest. Effective practices have been shown to require years to diffuse across departments *even within the same organization and even among similarly trained employees* (O'Dell and Grayson, 1998). While a sense of competition can lead people in the same positions but in different organizations to adopt innovations (Burt, 2003), it can also function within the firm as a disincentive on sharing and helping.

A focus on research-to-practice translation is new to many scholars of public health, public affairs, management, education, and other fields. For a behavioral scientist in forestry, for example, studying how the posting of markers along hiking trails may reduce degradation of forests would not be uncommon. But studying how proven practices in trail signage can be spread among forestry managers—a translational research topic—would be uncommon. To water conservation specialists, studies of novel approaches to water reclamation have been common. But studies of failed city to city adoption of evidence-based water reclamation projects—translation—are uncommon. And among disease prevention researchers, studies of hypodermic needle exchange programs for the reduction of HIV have proliferated. But translational studies of how to best encourage city health departments to adopt effective needle exchange programs have been rare.

Where are problems of translation vested? Who is responsible in the many cases when translation fails? Since research evidence in topical domains such as patient care and classroom learning is constantly produced and communicated, a lack of uptake by practitioners such as nurses and teachers is most often conceptualized as their problem; that is, a practitioner problem. The solution in typical dissemination terms is to communicate more, more often, in more ways. The highly publicized disparities in health care have been conceptualized and redressed in this way. If use of the most effective medical care options lag in the American south, medical staff there are blamed for not counseling patients to select those options (Greer et al., 2002). Translation is a problem of practitioners, and as a consequence it is their constituents who lose out.

The problems with this typical view of translation responsibility are twofold: First, solutions to this assignment of blame have not produced more uptake by practitioners. Doctors are blamed for not using a new effective procedure, so content about the procedure is added to continuing medical education modules *in addition to* emailed office alerts, messages to patient support groups telling them to ask their doctors about the procedure, and professional conference presentations. Unfortunately, more communication, more often, in more ways, does not predictably lead to more adoption and implementation of evidence-based practices. We know that practitioners are skilled at ignoring and disavowing the relevance of research to their problems of practice (Dearing et al., 1996). We know that evidence of effectiveness is not a strong predictor of adoption and use (Weiss, 2001). The diffusion literature is replete with ineffective innovations that broadly diffused, and of innovations that rapidly spread without any evidence of their effectiveness. The majority of studies of clinical practice guidelines, which recommend proven practices and procedures for patient conditions, document the difficulty of affecting the decisions of health care providers (Lomas, 1991), and should give pause to anyone with a more-information-is-better view of translation.

Second, researchers can be poor or unconcerned communicators (Dearing, Meyer, and Kazmierczak, 1994); researchers can develop research-based interventions without consideration of practitioner needs or wants; and researchers can mistakenly perceive practitioners as homogeneous sets of professionals ("day care providers", "landlords") who do not have or experience personal, professional, workplace, and client-based variations that would logically lead to diverse practitioner preferences (Greer et al., 2002). In short, there is much to blame researchers for if part of the objective of the research in question is to make a difference among non-academics. In an attempt to sensitize researchers to some of these issues, an increasing number of funders of research have begun suggesting that "if we want more research-based practice, we need more practice-based research" (Orleans, 2004).

To summarize, adopters are conceived in much the same way in translational research as they are in diffusion studies. They are seen as somewhat active in relation to other adopter-practitioners, and mostly passive in relation to communicated intervention programs. The chief difference is that in translational studies the adopters are themselves mediators in the process of change—they are practitioners—who work upstream of their clients, residents, members, and employees. They make adoption decisions about which programs they will implement to benefit their constituents. Unlike many of the constituents to whom public information campaigns and intervention programs are targeted, practitioners in many sectors are highly educated, subject to much outreach and professional information, technically sophisticated, and can be counted on to understand and use advanced communication technologies. For translation strategies, these differences have implications for how and what we choose to communicate with them.

A visit to Lake Lagunita

The Center for Advanced Study in the Behavioral Sciences is a quiet, low-slung row of buildings adjacent to and overlooking the red tiled roofs of Stanford University. The setting is idyllic; perfect for scholarly writing. In the early spring of 1992, we found Ev there, a visiting fellow, writing *A History of Communication Study*. Ev was on sabbatical from the University of Southern California.

With Lake Lagunita shimmering below, the three of us began discussing careers. Ev had clearly been giving some thought to his future. Then we produced the piece of paper we'd clipped out of a recent issue of *The Chronicle of Higher Education* for him. The department of journalism and the department of communication had merged at the University of New Mexico, leading to an advertisement for a chairperson for the joined unit.

"Why don't you apply?" we urged. "They want to start a doctoral program. You've never been a chairperson. And think of the jalapeños you could grow in that long Albuquerque season!" We left the ad with him before beginning our work.

Back in Michigan, a package arrived within days of our return from the West Coast. Ev had written his letter of application, and needed a letter of recommendation.

The active adopter in the process of translation

What adopters and implementers do with innovations has been viewed as a dichotomy. Either they adopt a practice or intervention as is, or they change it to better fit their current workplace or client conditions. Designers of interventions have come to believe that adaptation is either good or bad. For decades in discussions of how to best diffuse or "scale-up" effective educational programs, researchers have kept to this framing of the translational problem (Hutchinson and Huberman, 1993). Adherents of program fidelity believe that working to insure that adopters make as few modifications as possible is key to retaining the success of the original program. If the program is changed, how does one know if it is still effective? On the other hand, adherents of the program adaptation perspective counter that it is only through allowing adopters to change a program to suit their needs that the likelihood of sustainability is increased. If adopters do not feel ownership of the program, how can we insure its persistence in practice? Currently, the same debate is alive and well in disease prevention circles (Backer, 1995; Elliott and Mihalic, 2004).

Our position in this debate is that designing intervention programs to resist modification is futile; the baby may be tossed with the bath water since adopters are free to look elsewhere for workable programs, or they will self-invent by borrowing from what their experience suggests will work and what impresses them from different sources. There is simply too much incentive at the individual or single organizational level to customize, to partly adopt, and to combine innovation components from elsewhere (von Hippel, 2005).

First of all, the adaptation perspective of encouraging sources to enable adopters to change innovations is incomplete. More than an innovation must change if an ideal fit between a program and one's work context is to be achieved. The context, too, should change. If one only changes an adopted program and not the work environment—or vice versa—technical, delivery system, and performance criteria misalignments are likely to characterize implementation. Successful cases of technology transfer are characterized by incremental and over-time ajustments to both an innovation and a work environment (Leonard-Barton, 1988). "Mutual adaptation" of both a new program and of its user environment implies that an awful lot of the action of successful diffusion occurs not at the source nor with the end-user such as a student, but at intermediary organizations such as a school. How practitioners interpret the purpose and promise of a new program will interact with how they choose to make accommodation for it in the workplace. The meanings we make of a new program will contribute to what changes in the workplace we deem useful to best exploit the innovation. Virtually all such user activities would be considered moderating factors in the process of diffusion; in translational research, however, these moderating variables assume center stage and should be given more importance in research designs as outcomes of translation (Glasgow, Lichtenstein, and Marcus, 2003).

Second, adaptation is likely to intensify the meaning of an innovation for users since their actions in accommodation bring the innovation and its work environment more and more into harmony in achieving objectives that are important to each practitioner. Particularly if meaning is personalized and internalized, implementation can be greatly strengthened. Research has shown that people vest certain objects with sacred meaning. The attribution of sacred meaning to objects has been shown to occur across many types of people and across many types of objects. Marketing researchers Belk (1988) and Belk, Wallendorf, and Sherry (1989) argue on the basis of extensive data (Belk, 2005) that in attributing sacred meaning to objects, those objects become much more than possessions. They come to constitute an extended self of the individual. Key to this perspective is the idea that the meanings given are the product of the individual adopter, not of the company, change agency, or marketer selling or promoting the object. We speculate that the assignment of meaning to objects, especially sacred meaning, derives from adopter activity, such as coveting, trying out, learning about, playing with, and especially, changing the object to best attach or create sacred meaning.

We suggest that even seemingly mundane innovations such as a sexually transmitted disease prevention program can become involving and personally meaningful to an adopting practitioner such as a community health outreach worker on the basis of the strong normative beliefs of the people in such positions of helping clients at risk of some dread occurrence. Feedback from representative samples of potential adopters to gather their perceptions of innovation complexity, relative advantage, compatibility, trialability, observability and other relevant attributes prior to communicating can be used in the design of communication materials to heighten the likelihood of positive responses. But all such adjustments must be balanced with the need for effect fidelity. In the face of much adaptation, how can the likelihood of effective outcomes as the result of fielding a program be increased?

Strategies for effective user activity

We begin with the premise that both internal and external validity are important concepts that should be understood and considered by innovation developers and implementers alike. *Internal validity* is the extent to which a causal inference may be made between two or more variables (Campbell and Stanley, 1966; Cook and Campbell, 1979). In other words, internal validity is focused on whether or not program components cause specific and desired program outcomes. In practice, consideration of internal validity is often framed as, "Does the program work?" Internal validity is established through program testing under controlled conditions. The more highly controlled the environment within which a program is tested, the more confidence in the validity of the causal relationship(s) established.

External validity refers to the extent to which the presumed causal inference may be generalized to other populations, settings, treatment variables or measurement variables (Campbell and Stanley, 1966). The more an intervention that was demonstrated and validated in one site can still achieve positive effects when translated in other places, other populations, other times, and other topics, the more externally valid the intervention. So *external validity* is the degree to which a program shown to be effective in an initial demonstration subsequently produces similar outcomes in other contexts. In Guala's (2003) words, "... it [the program] is *externally* valid if A causes B not only in E, but also in a set of other circumstances of interest F, G, H, etc." (p. 4, italics in the original). Consideration of external validity is often framed as, "Does the program work *here*?"

We turn our attention to the application of internal and external validity in purposive diffusion given the premise that the most active users of innovations will be those who modify the innovation to best fit their circumstance and modify their circumstance to best fit the innovation (Leonard-Barton, 1988). Consider first the topic of internal validity. Rather than posing the question, "Does the program work?" perhaps the question can be reframed as "Why does the program work?" or "What are the core components of the program that are thought to be integral to its effectiveness?" Rogers (2003) refers to this as principles knowledge or "information dealing with the functioning principles underlying how an innovation works" (p. 173).

A potential adopter who understands specifically why a program works will be better able to determine those aspects or core components of the program or environment that may be modified with minimal risk to program effectiveness. We suggest that user activity will produce innovations of higher external validity to the extent that core components are known and understood. Developers may tailor communication efforts to explain why or how the program works. Precisely how to do this should not be assumed or guessed at, but rather derive from careful formative evaluation to assess potential adopter needs and wants, and their reactions to successive prototypes of the innovation.

In addition to communicating the conceptual basis for why a program works, developers may communicate in several alternative ways to bring about a desired outcome. Consider, for example, a violence prevention program focused on building self-efficacy as a core component. In other words, increased self-efficacy is determined to be causally related to decreased violent behavior. In this case, developers may provide potential adopters a set of five different options for increasing self-efficacy (one innovation with five examples of how to replicate the desired effect). This gives the practitioner flexibility as well as guidance to adapt the intervention in a fashion most appropriate to the circumstance with little risk to fidelity. Such a strategy emphasizes effect fidelity (the achievement of the source's desired effects in subsequent external validity tests of the program) over program fidelity (exact replication of the program as it was originally demonstrated). Developers can enhance productive user activity by ensuring that users understand the underlying premise for desirable effects, and wherever possible, by providing users with alternative means to achieve the same effect.

Turning to external validity, the question "Does the program work *here?*" may be reframed as, "How are aspects of the circumstance and environment here similar to and different from the circumstance and environment of the demonstration?" This question incorporates two principles identified by Cook (2000) and Shadish, Cook, and Campbell (2002) through which the external validity of specific programs can be assessed. The first relates to the extent to which prototypical characteristics of a model program are like those in second-order sites (what they term "surface similarity") and the second focuses on clarifying which differences between the original demonstration and the subsequent second-order tests are superfluous ("ruling out irrelevancies"). Stated differently, an important related means for communicating the core components that were causally responsible for the internal validity of the program is to also portray the peripheral components that were a part of the original demonstration of the program but determined to not be causally important, as well as the complementary assets of the organizations involved that implemented the program. Peripheral components of a program are those that adopters can be encouraged to change. And the listing of complementary assets or organizational capacities related to fielding the program can give subsequent adopters a strong sense of what it took to successfully implement the program in question.

We suggest that user activity will be relatively more effective if careful thought is given to important similarities as well as important differences between demonstration sites and adopting sites. Developers might, for example, communicate to intermediaries about the subjects used in the demonstration as well as other groups of subjects thought to benefit from the program. At the same time, other groups of subjects to whom the program should not be administered can also be pointed out. Similarities and dissimilarities might also be communicated about program delivery, timing, location, and so forth. With such guidance, intermediaries will be better able to make informed decisions about which aspects of the program or their environment should be changed to achieve the best fit between the two. Of course, some of the responsibility must fall to potential adopters as well to make reasonable determinations concerning the extent and importance of certain similarities and differences between their site and prior test sites.

User activity by a solid waste manager

David has been a manager at a rural solid waste facility in Colorado since receiving bachelor's degrees in resource management and engineering four years ago. He comes from a family of engineers and sees himself as one, too. David prefers working with "things" to working with people; nevertheless, he's become a pretty good "people person," learning by doing on the job. He oversees the work of 12 people. Recently, his supervisor had him attend a workshop in superior–subordinate communication. David was surprised that researchers had studied communication; to him, it just seemed like something you did. Later, after receiving a CD demonstrating effective approaches to managing people, David noticed that a theory for improved communication was clearly explicated for each of the several effective approaches featured on the disk. He learned, for example, that research on superior–subordinate communication indicates that worker performance increases when workers have the opportunity to (1) brainstorm their own solutions to problems, (2) talk about the chemical and other concepts underlying waste management, and (3) discuss ideas with other workers in a structured way.

David had his doubts. The studies reported on the CD were conducted by university researchers; some of the people were not in waste management. And the proven approaches to effective management and productivity had mostly been assessed with production line workers who met for just three shifts per week for 10 weeks whereas his staff worked together five days a week. With all of these differences, he wondered if the research results could be replicated.

David came to the conclusion that although some aspects of his work environment differed from the original sites, the differences were not of sufficient import to suggest that results would differ significantly. And the work team strategies had been validated across a variety of different worksites. He decided to try one of the new approaches but with some changes.

Though he liked the idea of subordinates formulating their own questions and solving problems themselves, David wasn't enamored with the idea of him being put in the role of prompting them and asking questions. He thought that asking workers to discuss ideas with each other as well as to explain waste management concepts with each other were good ideas. He rearranged some furniture in one of the larger rooms to accommodate group discussions.

CONTINUED ON THE NEXT PAGE

BOX—CONTINUED

After several months, David was pleasantly surprised. His staff seemed more satisfied with the work, and happier. Moreover, they had some good ideas for improving conditions at the site, several of which David had helped them to test.

David has been using the principles of participatory management for a few years now. He has tried various combinations of strategies shown to positively affect worker outcomes, hoping to find the most effective mix. He even tried prompting and asking questions of his staff, but isn't yet sold on that specific strategy. David's success was due to the communication of (1) positive research results, which were (2) communicated to him in a way that allowed him to understand their underlying principles, along with (3) alternative strategies for achieving the same results. His willingness to try out the ideas was also due to (4) his understanding of important (and unimportant) similarities and dissimilarities between his circumstance and the original test sites, and (5) his ability to modify his environment as he deemed necessary.

Another promising strategy for increasing the likelihood that adopter–implementers will be able to come to an "ideal fit" of innovation and work environment is the grouping together of several effective innovations in an alternative innovation cluster. Having a delimited set of choices—a few logical alternatives—as a basis for decision making is cognitively appealing. Too many choices, and people often will not decide anything; not having a ready comparison similarly decreases the likelihood of making a selection (Schwartz, 2004). An *alternative innovation cluster* is a set of effective innovations that comprise different means to achieve the same or similar end. The clustering of alternatives is attractive for two reasons. First, change agencies often have catalogues of many interventions of a type, each created by grantees, each of which often addresses the same problem. Piecing together an alternative innovation cluster of effective innovations does not put the change agency in the position of "picking a winner" and runs the risk of seemingly advocating one program at the expense of other effective solutions. Second, clustering enables potential adopters choice from within a set, thus giving them another way to become active participants in both selection and adaptation decisions. Activity is positively related to adoption, implementation, and sustainability of change (Douthwaite, 2002). New technologies allow for vivid side-by-side portrayals of innovations, and enable users to become more active in innovation and the pursuit of mutual adaptation (von Hippel, 2005).

Conclusion

An appreciation of the great and common extent of adopter activity with regard to the mutual adaptation of effective programs from afar and one's immediate work environment requires the acknowledgment that *every practitioner is unique*. We do not make this point to argue for the supremacy of idiographic orientations to knowing over the nomothetic; we fully appreciate the ability to find central tendencies among types of adopters. We emphasize uniqueness because it powerfully underscores the need to develop translational strategies that encourage choice, that acknowledge multiple routes to desired causality, and that provide scenarios and examples of the same principles but of different people and different contexts so that one can see and imagine the creative possibilities of application. We postulate that when practitioners exert creativity in implementation, the meanings they hold of the adapted program will be closer to sacred and less likely ordinary.

What we have argued here is a particular approach to decentralized diffusion. Like other approaches to decentralized diffusion such as those prevalent in the field of international development (Chitnis, 2005), it relies on high degrees of participation from the users of innovations. But there, perhaps, the similarity ends. We are strong believers in the importance and longevity of centralized change agencies in social betterment. Private foundations, international NGOs, and federal agencies will persist and grow. Our approach to decentralized diffusion is one that seeks to marry the advantages of centralized resources and the efficiency of diffusion effects, with good options for individuation at the level of practitioner-adopters. User needs exhibit high heterogeneity (von Hippel, 2005); researchers and others who design the communication of effective programs to practitioners would be wise to heed this fact. We conclude that pursuing a purposive diffusion-based strategy to translation that has as its objective generalized causal inference (a fidelity of effect) rather than program fidelity (replication) is a most promising route to effective translation of research-to-practice.

References

Abrahamson, E. and G. Fairchild. 1999. Management Fashion: Lifecycles, Triggers and Collective Learning Processes. *Administrative Science Quarterly* 44: 708–40.

Backer, T. 1995. Assessing and Enhancing Readiness for Change: Implications for Technology Transfer. In T. Backer, S. David, and G. Soucy (eds), *Reviewing the Behavioral Science Knowledge Base on Technology Transfer*, pp. 21–41. Rockville, MD: National Institute on Drug Abuse.

Bandura, A. 1986. *Social Foundations of Thought and Action: A Social Cognitive Theory*. Englewood Cliffs, NJ: Prentice-Hall.

Belk, R. W. 1988. Possessions and the Extended Self. *Journal of Consumer Research* 15: 139–68.

———. 2005. Possessions, Self, and the Sacred. In A. Griffin and C. C. Otnes (eds), *16th Paul D. Converse symposium*, pp. 46–66. Chicago: American Marketing Association.

Belk, R. W., M. Wallendorf, and J. F. Sherry, Jr. 1989. The Sacred and the Profane in Consumer Behavior: Theodicy on the Odyssey. *Journal of Consumer Research* 16: 1–38.

Berwick, D. M. 2003. Disseminating Innovations in Health Care. *Journal of the American Medical Association* 289: 1969–75.

Burt, R. S. 2003. Social Origins of Good Ideas. Unpublished manuscript. Chicago: Graduate School of Business, University of Chicago.

Campbell, D. T. and J. C. Stanley. 1966. *Experimental and Quasi-experimental Designs for Research*. Chicago: Rand McNally.

Carter, A. P. 1989. Knowhow Trading as Economic Exchange. *Research Policy* 18: 155–63.

Chitnis, K. 2005. Communication for Empowerment and Participatory Development: A Social Model of Health in Jamkhed, India. Ph.D. dissertation, College of Communication, Ohio University.

Coleman, J. S., E. Katz, and H. Menzel. 1966. *Medical Innovation: A Diffusion Study*. New York: Bobbs Merrill.

Committee on Quality of Health Care in America, Institute of Medicine. 2001. *Crossing the Quality Chasm: A New Health System for the 21st Century*. Washington, DC: National Academy Press.

Cook, T. D. 2000. Toward a Practical Theory of External Validity. In L. Bickman (ed), *Validity & Social Experimentation*, pp. 3–43. Thousand Oaks, CA: Sage Publications.

Cook, T. D. and D. T. Campbell 1979. *Quasi-experimentation: Design & Analysis Issues for Field Settings*. Chicago, IL: Rand McNally.

Dearing, J. W. 2003. The State of the Art and the State of the Science of Community Organizing. In T. Thompson, A. Dorsey, K. Miller, and R. Parrott (eds), *Handbook of Health Communication*, pp. 207–20. Mahwah, NJ: Lawrence Erlbaum.

Dearing, J. W., R. S. Larson, L. M. Randall, and R. S. Pope. 1998. Local Re-invention of the CDC HIV Prevention Community Planning Initiative. *Journal of Community Health* 23: 113–26.

Dearing, J. W., G. Meyer, and J. Kazmierczak. 1994. Portraying the New: Communication between University Innovators and Potential Users. *Science Communication* 16 (1): 11–42.

Dearing, J. W., E. M. Rogers, G. Meyer, M. K. Casey, N. Rao, S. Campo, and G. M. Henderson. 1996. Social Marketing and Diffusion-based Strategies for Communicating Health with Unique Populations: HIV Prevention in San Francisco. *Journal of Health Communication* 1: 343–63.

Douthwaite, B. 2002. *Enabling Innovation: A Practical Guide to Understanding and Fostering Technological Change.* London: Zed Books.

Douthwaite, B., J. D. H. Keatinge, and J. R. Park. 2002. Learning Selection: An Evolutionary Model for Understanding, Implementing and Evaluating Participatory Technology Development. *Agricultural Systems* 72: 109–31.

Elliott, D. S. and S. Mihalic. 2004. Issues in Disseminating and Replicating Effective Prevention Programs. *Prevention Science* 4 (1): 47–53.

Glasgow, R. E., E. Lichtenstein, and A. C. Marcus. 2003. Why Don't We See More Translation of Health Promotion Research to Practice? Rethinking the Efficacy-to-Effectiveness Transition. *American Journal of Public Health* 93 (8): 1261–67.

Green, L. W., N. H. Gottlieb, and G. S. Parcel. 1991. Diffusion Theory Extended and Applied. In W. B. Ward and F. M. Lewis (eds), *Advances in Health Education and Promotion*, vol. 3, pp. 91–117. London: Jessica Kingsley Publishers.

Green, S. E. 2004. A Rhetorical Theory of Diffusion. *Academy of Management Review* 29 (4): 653–669.

Greer, A. L., J. S. Goodwin, J. L. Freeman, and Z. H. Wu. 2002. Bringing the Patient Back In: Guidelines, Practice Variations, and the Social Context of Medical Practice. *International Journal of Technology Assessment in Health Care* 18 (4): 747–61.

Guala, F. 2003. Experimental Localism and External Validity. Paper presented at the 2002 Philosophy of Science Association meeting, Milwaukee, WI.

von Hippel, E. 1987. Cooperation between Rivals: Informal Know-how Trading. *Research Policy* 15: 291–302.

———. 2005. *Democratizing Innovation.* Cambridge, MA: MIT Press.

Hutchinson, J. and M. Huberman. 1993. Knowledge Dissemination and Use in Science and Mathematics Education: A Literature Review. NSF EHR/RED report 93–75. Arlington, VA: National Science Foundation.

Katz, E. 1999. Theorizing Diffusion: Tarde and Sorokin Revisited. *The Annals of the American Academy of Political and Social Sciences* 566: 144–55.

Katz, E. and P. Lazarsfeld. 1956. *Personal Influence: The Part Played by People in the Flow of Mass Communications.* Glencoe, IL: Free Press.

Katz, E., M. L. Levin, and H. Hamilton. 1963. Traditions of Research on the Diffusion of Innovation. *American Sociological Review* 28 (2): 237–52.

Lenfant, C. 2003. Clinical Research to Clinical Practice—Lost in Translation? *The New England Journal of Medicine* 349 (9): 868–74.

Leonard-Barton, D. 1988. Implementation as Mutual Adaptation of Technology and Organization. *Research Policy* 17: 251–67.

Lomas, J. 1991. Words without Action? The Production, Dissemination, and Impact of Consensus Recommendations. *Annual Review of Public Health* 12: 41–65.

Maslow, A. H. 1959. Creativity in Self-actualizing People. In H. H. Anderson (ed.), *Creativity and Its Cultivation*, pp. 83–95. New York: Harper and Brothers.

O'Dell, C. and C. J. Grayson. 1998. If Only We Knew What We Know: Identification and Transfer of Internal Best Practices. *California Management Review* 40 (3): 154–74.

Orleans, C. T. 2004. Increasing Physical Activity in Populations: Understanding Diffusion and Dissemination. Oral presentation, the Cooper Institute, Dallas, TX, October 21–23.

Rice, R. E. and E. M. Rogers. 1980. Re-invention in the Innovation Process. *Knowledge* 1: 499–514.

Rogers, E. M. 1962. *Diffusion of Innovations*. Glencoe, IL: Free Press.

———. 1995. *Diffusion of Innovations*. New York: Free Press.

———. 2003. *Diffusion of Innovations*. New York: Free Press.

Schrader, S. 1991. Informal Technology Transfer between Firms: Cooperation through Information Trading. *Research Policy* 20: 153–70.

Schwartz, B. 2004. *The Paradox of Choice: Why More is Less*. New York: HarperCollins.

Shadish, W. R., T. Cook, and D. T. Campbell. 2002. *Experimental and Quasi-experimental Designs for Generalized Causal Inference*. Boston, MA: Houghton Mifflin.

Strang, D. and J. W. Meyer. 1994. Institutional Conditions for Diffusion. In R. W. Scott and J. W. Meyer (eds), *Institutional Environments and Organizations: Structural Complexity and Individualism*, pp. 100–111. Thousand Oaks, CA: Sage Publications.

Szulanski, G. 1996. Exploring Internal Stickiness: Impediments to the Transfer of Best Practice within the Firm. *Strategic Management Journal* 17: 27–43.

Weiss, C. H. 2001. What Kind of Evidence in Evidence-based Policy? Paper presented at the Third International, Inter-disciplinary Evidence-based Policies and Indicator Systems Conference, University of Durham.

Wejnert, B. 2002. Integrating Models of Diffusion of Innovations: A Conceptual Framework. *Annual Review of Sociology* 28: 297–326.

3

Communication Network Analysis
and the Diffusion of Innovations[1]

THOMAS W. VALENTE

In some graduate programs, the selection committees for evaluating and selecting new doctoral students include current doctoral students as student-members of the committees. I was the student member on the graduate admissions committee at the University of Southern California's (USC) Annenberg School the year that Tom applied. He was so obviously an outstanding choice that little discussion ensued. I telephoned him in Japan and gave him the good news. Tom's unfolding career is proof that committees can—on occasion—make very wise decisions.

JIM DEARING

In 1988, within a year of Tom joining the Annenberg School Ph.D. program, the International Association for Mass Communication Research met in Barcelona, Spain. Both Tom and I, along with several other Annenberg School faculty members, were in attendance. In a gala conference reception, overflowing with over a thousand delegates, held in the gardens of a royal palace, Ev drew my attention to Tom, who was holding court among a group of attendees. "Hey Arvind, Tom has star quality," Ev whispered in my ear. A moment later, he added: "Mark my words, Tom will be star in our field someday." Ev was a pro at spotting (and nurturing) potential.

ARVIND SINGHAL

I STARTED MY DOCTORAL WORK AT USC'S ANNENBERG SCHOOL FOR Communication in 1987 while Ev Rogers held the Walter H. Annenberg Chair. I was interested in diffusion of innovations as well as social network analysis and Ron Rice was my advisor. After Ron left USC

[1] Support for this research was provided by National Institute on Drug Abuse (NIDA) grant P50–DA16094.

in 1989, Ev became my advisor. Ev helped me clarify my interests and focus my energies. He connected me to other important scholars working on network models of diffusion and helped me see the forest rather than the trees. We also collaborated on understanding information theory and, most importantly, health communication, which became one of my areas of specialization.

This chapter provides a cursory review of communication network models developed to understand how innovations diffuse through communication and social networks (Table 3.1). We begin with early models (type 1) proposed by Rogers (1962), Coleman, Katz, and Menzel (1966), and Becker (1970) on the influence of opinion leadership on adoption of innovations. Type 1 models also propose that greater density and connectedness are associated with faster diffusion. We then turn to structural models (type 2) that focuse on how key bridges or structural characteristics of a whole network affected diffusion. Type 3 models espouse a "critical points" view, proposing that critical times or critical thresholds trigger widespread diffusion. Finally, a fourth type of model focuses on the dynamic interplay between network position and adoption/diffusion. The chapter closes by describing a fifth type of model that can be used to design interventions that accelerate diffusion of innovations.

Diffusion and interpersonal influence (type 1)

Diffusion theory has its roots in anthropology, economics, geography, sociology, marketing, among other disciplines (Brown, 1981; Hägerstrand, 1967; Robertson, 1971; Rogers, 2003), and has in some ways been adapted from epidemiology (for example, Bailey, 1975; Morris, 1993). The premise, confirmed by empirical research, is that many new ideas and practices spread through interpersonal contacts largely consisting of interpersonal communication (Beal and Bohlen, 1955; Katz, Levine, and Hamilton, 1963; Ryan and Gross, 1943; Rogers, 2003; Valente and Rogers, 1995; Valente, 1995, 2005).

We read Rogers' *Diffusion of Innovations* (any edition) and are struck by the elegance and comprehensiveness of the theory. We digest its principles: adoption occurs in stages, diffusion takes a long time, the

Table 3.1
Lineage of diffusion network models

Concept	Description	Publication
Social factors	Social factors such as media exposure, discussion with friends are more important than economic ones such as wealth.	Ryan and Gross, 1943
Integration	People well connected to the social system adopt innovations earlier than those on the periphery.	Coleman, Katz, and Menzel, 1966
Opinion leaders	People who are sought out by others for advice adopt earlier and influence others to adopt.	Rogers and Cartano, 1962; Rogers, 1962
Norms	Community norms affect whether opinion leaders will be early or later adopters.	Becker, 1970
Weak ties	Weak ties—links that connect otherwise disconnected groups—facilitate diffusion.	Granovetter, 1973
Thresholds	People adopt based on how many others they see adopting.	Granovetter, 1978
Structural equivalence	People are influenced in their adoption decisions by others who occupy similar positions in the network.	Burt, 1987
Structural holes	Gaps in the network.	Burt, 1992
Small worlds	Networks characterized by high levels of clustering yet overall short distances between people.	Travers and Milgram, 1969; Pool and Kochen, 1978; Watts, 2002
Critical mass, tipping point	Diffusion reaches a distinct point where behavior is self propelling and it would be difficult to stop.	Marwell, Oliver, and Prahl, 1988; Markus, 1987; Schelling, 1978; Gladwell, 2000
Network thresholds	Thresholds can be calculated at the social network level.	Valente, 1995
Dynamic models	Using event history analysis, susceptibility to the influence of others, and infectiousness, the ability to influence others can be measured.	Strang and Tuma, 1993; Myers, 2000
Interventions	Using network data to identify change agents to promote behavior change.	Valente et al., 2003

pattern of diffusion follows an S-shaped curve, perceived character-istics of the innovation affect its adoption/diffusion, and social struc-ture affects diffusion. Early diffusion studies generally recognized the importance of interpersonal communication in the adoption/diffusion process. In Rogers' dissertation research, he interviewed many farmers who told him that they relied on communication with other farmers when making their adoption decisions. Rogers either knew about social network methods, or was smart enough to record exactly who farmers talked to when making adoption decisions. Social network methods entail recording the communication linkages between every-one in a community. Thus, Rogers collected social/communication network data in this dissertation and a few subsequent studies, creating a marriage of method, theory, and application.

Ryan and Gross (1943) pioneered the study of diffusion of innov-ations by investigating when and how farmers decided to adopt hybrid corn seed. Hybrid seeds were being developed in laboratories across the US and Europe in the early 20th century (Crabb, 1948). Hybrids outperformed the alternative (so-called open pollinated seeds) but required that farmers buy seeds from seed companies rather than using seed from their own crops. This was a radical change in behavior for the farmers to adopt. The US Department of Agriculture established an extension service to help diffuse these new hybrid seeds (and other innovations) to farmers throughout the country (different hybrids were created for different climates).

During my conversations with Everett Rogers we noted that the Ryan and Gross study contained most of the variables known today as the diffusion of innovations paradigm (Valente and Rogers, 1995). But Rogers noted that Ryan and Gross did not collect information amenable to social network analysis. Ryan and Gross were concerned about interpersonal influence, and they measured sources of informa-tion including extension agent contact, bulletin readership, and radio audience. Ryan and Gross could have collected sociometric infor-mation because they interviewed all the farmers who lived in one county in Iowa. Sociometric information would have entailed record-ing who communicated with whom within the area of study. But the study of formal social network analysis was in its infancy when Ryan and Gross conducted their study (Freeman, 2004) and they were not aware of this methodology.

Rogers, however, measured who *specifically* each farmer talked to and thus used the sociometric method (Scott, 2000; Valente, 1995; Wasserman and Faust, 1994). He told me, however, that he didn't know how to analyze the data. Computer programs for network analysis were not available and so he could not simply read the data into a computer and calculate a network indicator. He used tennis balls and yarn in an attempt to lay-out a sociogram, but found this uninformative. He did tally the number of nominations each farmer received and used this as an indicator of opinion leadership, but it did not figure prominently in his dissertation, or writings which emerged from his dissertation data.

But Rogers knew the who-to-whom data was important. When he connected with James Coleman, Elihu Katz and Herbert Menzel, he learned that they too had collected sociometric information on interpersonal communication behavior of physicians.

Coleman, Katz, and Menzel's (1966) approach had been to classify physicians as those who were integrated into the flow of communication and those who were not. They classified physicians as receiving no nominations, one to three, and four or more. They then graphed the diffusion curves for these three different groups and showed how the diffusion curve accelerated exponentially (snowballed) for highly integrated physicians, yet accelerated slowly for non-integrated physicians (those who received no nominations). Figure 3.1 graphs diffusion curves for three groups of physicians from one community (Peoria) of the CKM study; those who received three or more nominations, and those who received one or two, and those who received none.

Rogers (1962) recognized the CKM analysis as a social interaction effect and quotes Ryan and Gross (1943), "There is no doubt but that the behavior of one individual in an interaction population affects the behavior of his fellows. Thus, the demonstrated success of hybrid seed on a few farms offers a changed situation to those who have not been so experimental. The very fact of acceptance by one or more farmers offers new stimulus to the remaining ones" (p. 23; Rogers, 1962: 215). The interaction effect was also called a "chain reaction," and later Rogers called it the "diffusion effect." Essentially, these early scholars described contagion, the process by which an infected person infects an uninfected person or the process by which an adopter

The Coleman, Katz, and Menzel medical innovation study

In the mid-1950s James Coleman, Elihu Katz, and Herbet Menzel were colleagues at the Bureau of Applied Research at Columbia University. Based in the Sociology Department, these scholars were interested in how ideas and practices spread. Coleman was a mathematical sociologist and had a burgeoning interest in social network analysis (he later conducted a large study of adolescent school-based networks). Menzel had conducted a pilot study of physician networks in one New England town and felt they could explain physician behavior. Pfizer, the pharmaceutical company, contacted Coleman, Katz, and Menzel (CKM) to ask them to evaluate their marketing efforts, including their use of "detail agents" (a practice still common today), pharmaceutical company representatives hired to visit physician offices and persuade them to use their products.

CKM agreed and suggested that the inclusion of social network information would enhance their study. The researchers identified four small cities in Illinois within which to conduct the study: Peoria, Bloomington, Galesburg, and Quincy. Attempts were made to interview all physicians in the four communities, and about half were successfully interviewed. The final sample consisted of 125 physicians: Peoria, 62; Bloomington, 24; Galesburg, 21; and Quincy, 18. The study is noteworthy because the researchers inspected prescription records at local pharmacies in four study communities to get an objective measure of time of adoption. Most diffusion studies at that time (as still is the case) relied on respondent recall of adoption time. The average time of adoption was in the sixth month and the study ended data collection in the seventeenth month. By the end of the study, CKM published their results in a 1957 publication (Coleman, Menzel, and Katz, 1957) showing that tetracycline, a new antibiotic, diffused through these physician networks.

persuades a non-adopter. An interesting philosophical question has always been: Is contagion necessary for diffusion? Most scholars have described diffusion as any behavior change process, not just that induced by person-to-person contact.

In addition to the diffusion effect, Rogers was intrigued by the role of the opinion leader. In contrast to other early scholars on diffusion, Rogers felt the opinion leader played an important role and he

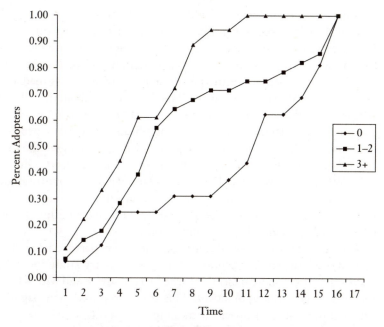

Figure 3.1
Diffusion was faster among integrated physicians (those receiving three or more nominations) than among isolated ones (those receiving no nominations)
Source: Data from Coleman, Katz, and Menzel, 1966

was particularly interested in using social network data to measure opinion leadership. Rogers used in-degree—a count of the number of nominations received—as a measure of opinion leadership in his early studies. In an influential paper published in 1962 (Rogers and Cartano, 1962) he compared sociometric measures of opinion leaders (through the number of nominations received, or being nominated by a neighbor as a source of advice) with two other measures: key informant designation as opinion leader and self designation as an opinion leader. He found the three measures to be moderately but statistically significantly correlated.

During the 1960s there was very little research on social networks and diffusion. The Coleman, Katz, and Menzel (1966) book was released but the major findings from this study had been published in a journal article in 1957 (Coleman, Menzel, and Katz, 1957). Rogers

conducted some sociometric studies in the US (in Ohio) and a significant project in three villages/communities in Colombia (during a
Fulbright year) (Rogers and Cartano, 1962) but the analytic methods
for social network analysis remained underdeveloped. Instead, researchers were focused on the power and role of the mass media in
social change. Marshall McLuhan (1964) had written about the "global
village" and "the medium is the message" and most researchers were
convinced that television was the most significant influence on people's
lives (indeed, this may have been in part why Rogers changed the title
of *Diffusion of Innovations* to *Communication of Innovations*). During
the 1960s, Rogers oversaw a large USAID funded three-country study
on factors associated with the diffusion of innovations among farmers
in three countries (India, Nigeria, and Brazil) using multiple waves
of data and studying multiple innovations.

Rogers' interest in social networks, however, persisted, and the
second wave of data collection in the three-country study included
survey questions on who farmers turned to for advice and with whom
they discussed farming practices. This study produced many significant publications and provided training for countless graduate students (at both the masters and doctoral level). Of the many farming
innovations studied, few diffused. None of the innovations diffused
in India or Nigeria. In Brazil, hybrid corn seed diffused slowly and at
different rates in the 11 village studied.

Marshall Becker conducted a significant study of diffusion networks,
expanding on Rogers' work by studying opinion leadership. Becker
(1970) hypothesized that opinion leaders would be early adopters of
innovations that were compatible with the culture of the community,
but would delay adoption if the innovation was seen as incompatible.
Becker interviewed public health officers in three states (Michigan,
Ohio, and New York) asking them about their adoption of two innovations: Diabetes screening, which had low adoption potential and
measles immunization, which had high adoption potential. As hypothesized, public health officers who received many nominations
(as opinion leaders) were earlier adopters of measles immunization
and later adopters of diabetes screening.

This first group of early studies (Becker, 1970; Coleman, Katz, and
Menzel, 1966; Rogers, 1962; Ryan and Gross, 1943) posited that being
connected in the community led to earlier adoption by individuals.

Communities/networks that were more integrated would have faster diffusion. The CKM (1966) study is most typical of this perspective, but as is Becker's hypothesis that group norms influence opinion leader decision-making.

Structural models (type 2)

During the 1970s, Marc Granovetter wrote one of the most significant articles on the role of networks and diffusion by arguing that weak ties were critical for diffusion to occur (Granovetter, 1973). Granovetter posited that social systems lacking weak ties had longer paths connecting everyone in a network and thus it took a long time for information to spread. Granovetter (1978) also wrote an influential paper introducing the concept of thresholds in innovation diffusion, arguing that the distribution of thresholds (the number of prior adopters needed for a person to adopt) affects the diffusion of innovations. Rogers collaborated with Granovetter in both of these papers.

In the early 1970s, during a visit to the East–West Center at the University of Hawaii, Rogers began collaboration with colleagues from the Seoul School of Public Health who were launching a study of mothers' clubs in Korea and the clubs' role in the diffusion of family planning ideas and practices. Rogers saw this as another opportunity to collect social network data and see if he could map the diffusion of contraception through women's networks. Data were collected in 1973 and over the next few years this data was analyzed and presented at some meetings of a small band of scholars interested in social network analysis. Rogers focused again on opinion leadership and found that the adoption behavior of the sociometric opinion leaders in these communities was mimicked by other women in the communities (Rogers and Kincaid, 1981).

The data provided the basis for a book on communication networks, co-authored with Larry Kincaid (ibid.) which set the stage for a burgeoning new paradigm using social network data to understand behavior. Figure 3.2 depicts one of the villages from the Korean family planning study that shows social network linkages in one Korean village among women of reproductive age. Data were derived by asking each respondent who they went to for advice about family planning

Plate 3.1
Three generations of diffusion scholars. Tom Valente (right) with his Ph.D. advisor
Ev Rogers (center), in turn with his Ph.D. advisor, George Beal (left) , in Hawaii in
May 1991. Tom and Ev traveled to Hawaii to meet with George Beal to reminiscence
about the early diffusion studies
Source: Personal files of author Valente

and interviewing all the residents of the village. Lines indicate advice
seeking with arrows showing the direction of this advice seeking.
Woman number 13 was the founder of the mothers' club in her village.
Her high degree of connectedness suggests that she was influential
in spreading information about family planning in her village.

In many ways, Rogers' had accomplished a major ambition with the
publication of *Communication Networks: A New Paradigm for Research*—
the visualization of social networks and how innovations spread within
that structure. He was active in the early development of the social
network community: the International Network for Social Network
Analysis, which held an annual meeting referred to as the "Sunbelt"
conference. Rogers attended the early meetings and was its keynote
speaker in 1987 and organized/hosted the conference in 1990. By the
mid-1990s, however, his interests and commitments were so widespread it was difficult for him to keep abreast of the burgeoning specialty area of social network analysis.

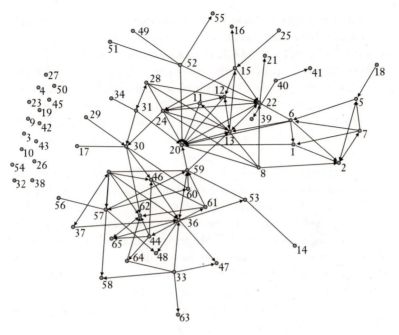

Figure 3.2
Social network data for one village of the Rogers and Kincaid (1981)
study of the diffusion of family planning in Korea

Diffusion network research continued to grow in the 1980s with a significant publication and research effort by Ron Burt, then at Columbia University. Burt (1987) posited that structural equivalence, the degree to which two people occupy the same position in the network, affects their tendency to imitate each other's behavior and hence affects the diffusion of innovations. Burt (ibid.) acknowledged that cohesion (direct contact) was important, but that in many situations, people monitor the behavior of those in similar positions and will engage in behaviors if others in their same position do so. This might be particularly true for firms in the same industry as they are in competitive positions and so must monitor each other's behavior. To test his hypothesis, Burt ventured into the basement of his Columbia University building and found the original surveys from the Coleman, Katz, and Menzel (1966) study and re-entered the data. He also created a specialty computer software program called STRUCTURE which calculated exposure to adoption behavior by peers and structurally equivalent others. Burt also did a huge service to the diffusion network community by making the CKM data available to other scholars.

Burt followed up his work on structural equivalence with the observation that people who bridged structural holes in a network occupied key positions in the network (Burt, 1992). Structural holes are gaps in a network that increase the distance between everyone in the network. Burt (ibid.) defined "brokers" as those who span structural holes.

Another structural model that has received considerable attention recently is the small world. Stanley Milgram (1967; Travers and Milgram, 1969) pioneered research on the small world by conducting an innovative study to show that everyone is connected to everyone else by an average of six steps (see box: "The Milgram Small World Experiment"). The term "small world" comes from the well-known phenomenon that occurs when two people meet for the first time and discover they have a friend or acquaintance in common (Pool and Kochen, 1978). Usually this discovery is accompanied by the statement "Wow, it's a small world." The phrase has also come to be associated with the idea that everyone is connected to everyone by only a few intermediaries.

Duncan Watts (2002) rejuvenated interest in the small world phenomenon, leading to new models for the diffusion of innovations. Watts proposed that many networks found in the biological, physical, computer and social worlds could be characterized as "small world" networks if they were highly clustered (almost everyone in a group or clique knows one another) and had relatively short distances connecting everyone in the network. Typically, highly clustered networks have few bridges connecting groups and so it takes many steps to link any two people chosen at random. Small world networks, on the other hand, have a lot of clustering, yet have short distances overall between any two people in the network, even those in different clusters (groups). One particularly relevant observation made by Watts was that non-small world networks could be "rewired" to make them small world networks. In fact, we could find those links that would provide the best rewiring by finding which tie should be added to the network to create the greatest decrease in average distance between nodes.

For example, we calculated distances—the number of steps between each node—for the women in the Korean family planning

The Milgram Small World Experiment

When two people meet for the first time they might learn they have a place or event in common. A person might say "I lived in such and such town" or "I used to work at a certain place or went to a particular school." If the other person happens to know someone who lived in that town or went to that school, he or she might ask, "Oh do you know so and so?" At times people discover that they have an acquaintance in common or both know the same person. This discovery is often accompanied by the remark "Gee, what a small world." Many of us have our favorite small world story or a story about seeing someone we know in a strange or different place.

The small world phenomenon can be generalized as a social structural phenomenon and generalized with the following research question: What is the likelihood that two people, chosen randomly are connected via 1, 2, 3,... K intermediaries? To answer this question, Stanley Milgram, a social psychologist at Harvard University,[2] conducted experiments.

In one study, he selected a "target" recipient who was a Boston stockbroker and then selected three random samples of about 100 people each: randomly selected Nebraska residents; randomly selected Nebraska residents who owned blue chip stocks; and randomly selected Boston residents. Study participants received a packet they were asked to send to the ultimate target by giving it to a friend or someone they knew. Once people sent the packet to a friend they could mail in a postcard with data about themselves and who they passed the packet to.

Of the 296 packets, 217 (73.4 percent) were passed to at least one person. Of these 217, 64 (29.5 percent) made it eventually to the Boston stockbroker (a 21.6 percent completion rate). The average number of steps for the completed chains was 5.2. The average length of completed chains for those who used professional links (passing the packet to another stockbroker) was 4.6; but it was 6.1 for those who passed the packet to acquaintances based on geography (getting it to someone who knew someone in Massachusetts). This data, coupled with one of Milgram's earlier studies, led to the popular conception that only six steps separate everyone in the world; that is, "six degrees of separation."

[2] Milgram is perhaps better known as the scientist who conducted experiments on how people respond to authority. He had confederates pretend to administer

network shown in Figure 3.2. The average distance between women was 30.54 steps; of course we have substituted N–1, the maximum possible distance between unreachable nodes. This greatly inflates the distances but is the best choice from a theoretical perspective.[3] To create a better connected network, one with shorter distances overall between nodes, we could add links to shorten the average distance between any people. The most optimal link to add would be from woman 20 to woman 8. This link shortens the average overall distance by 3.56 steps because woman 8 sent many nominations but was not nominated by anyone.[4] Adding a link back to her, by someone as well connected as 20, reduces distances considerably and makes the network more efficient. If there was an innovation we wanted to speed through this network and it was an innovation we felt would diffuse more quickly if there was more communication in the network, we would want to add this link to the network by creating a tie from 20 to 8. In this example then, the bridge which makes the network a smaller world network is one which creates a reciprocal link where before it was unidirectional.

The structural argument requires information from the entire network to find structural properties of the network which facilitated or deterred diffusion. These structural properties were most frequently concerned with bridges and structural holes which signified the presence of individuals or links that provided strategic advantage to the network's ability to diffuse an innovation. Granovetter's (1973)

---

electric shocks to other confederates at the command of the study subjects. Study subjects were able to tell the confederates to increase the dosage to near lethal levels. Milgram discovered that people were quite willing to give orders which caused considerable pain and suffering to others.

[3] Mathematically, unconnected nodes would get a distance of infinity, but then mathematical operations on the network are not possible, thus some assumption about the distance between unconnected nodes must be made. One could substitute 1 + the maximum distance calculated from the connected part of the network and this would provide a more realistic average distance of about 8 between nodes. The trouble with this choice is that network changes will change the maximum distance and thus distances between networks are no longer comparable.

[4] Conversely, deleting the link from 59 to 13 would cause the most disruption to the network by increasing overall distances between nodes by an average of 3.3 steps.

strength of weak ties is most indicative of this hypothesis. Granovetter's (1978) threshold model is also a structural argument because it posits that the distribution of thresholds and having people with certain thresholds in certain positions affects diffusion. Burt's (1987; 1992) structural equivalence and structural holes arguments also hypothesize that structural positions and the behavior of individuals in key positions are also structural in nature.

Critical mass, tipping points, and thresholds models (type 3)

The next significant development in diffusion network models was a focus on the critical mass. Scholars had long recognized that the diffusion curve (or any growth curve for that matter) contained *inflection points*, times where the curve accelerated or decelerated dramatically (Mahajan and Peterson, 1985). Marwell, Oliver, and Prahl (1988) wrote persuasively about the importance of the critical mass for achieving collective action. Once critical mass was reached, momentum toward achieving collective goals would propel the social movement forward. Markus (1987) argued that interdependent innovations (telephones, faxes, email) were particularly prone to critical mass effects because once a technological medium was adopted by a large enough number of people it would be too difficult for them to defect to another medium and there were inherent advantages to subsequent adopters to adopt the technology.

The notion of a critical mass and particularly the notion of interdependence and the interaction of agents was insightfully investigated by Schelling in his 1978 book *Micromotives and Macrobehavior*. Schelling showed how complex and sometime counterintuitive outcomes can arise from individuals acting in response to their neighbors' (defined theoretically) behaviors. For example, the distribution of racism can affect white flight—the process by which whites leave neighborhoods based on the percentage of blacks that move into their neighborhood.

Malcolm Gladwell popularized the notion of a tipping point in his book *The Tipping Point: How Little Things Add Up to Make a Big Difference* (2000). Gladwell showed how opinion leaders can have a strong influence on others' behavior and can make the difference between a product having no sales or taking off. Gladwell's contribution to diffusion network models was to show how the concepts could be scaled up to a population level. While many scholars had been focusing on behavior within small self-contained communities, Gladwell generalized these principles on a large, national, and international scale, and to a wider range of behaviors.

First elucidated by Schelling (1978) and subsequently adapted and investigated by many scholars, the tipping point or critical mass is that moment when diffusion momentum was at its greatest. Mahajan and Peterson (1985) identified inflection points in the many growth curves used to model diffusion and mathematicians describe inflection points as the moments when the first and second derivatives equal zero (Valente, 1993). Valente (1995; 1996) showed that individuals have thresholds to adoption calculated by measuring the proportion of adopters in their networks required for them to adopt. Critical point hypotheses of diffusion emphasize that once a critical point is reached, either for an individual or system, diffusion is likely to be self-sustaining.

Dynamic models (type 4)

Another significant re-analysis of the CKM data was conducted by Marsden and Podolny (1990). These researchers reshaped the CKM data so that each observation consisted of person–time data. That is, each record in the reshaped dataset was a physician and one year in which he or she did not adopt and a final record for the year he or she adopted. Thus, in a dataset with 62 physicians and an average adoption time of year six, the reshaped data would have 372 observations (62*6). Marsden and Podolny (ibid.) conducted event history analysis of the CKM data to compare cohesion and structural equivalence to see if they could replicate Burt's (1987) findings using the event history framework. They found very weak effects for cohesion, and none for structural equivalence.

Strang and Tuma (1993) modeled what they called spatial and temporal heterogeneity in network effects on adoption. Strang and Tuma (ibid.) posited that modeling diffusion over time could include analysis of whether people were more susceptible to adopting the innovation based on their position in the network, and if others were more likely to adopt after people in certain network positions adopted. Thus, two significant variables were created; susceptibility, the degree a person is more likely to adopt based on their network position (outdegree) and infectiousness, the degree a person influences others to adopt based on their network position (indegree) (Myers, 2000). Scholars could then not only pose the question: Do networks influence a person's likelihood of adoption? but also: How is network position associated with greater susceptibility or infectiousness during diffusion?

Type 4 models, dynamic ones, are currently being debated in the field, and considerable effort is being expended to develop appropriate statistical models to account for changes in network and behavior at the same time (Snijders, 2005). Marsden and Podolny (1990) were the first to use the event history analysis framework for analyzing diffusion of innovations dynamically with a network exposure model. Valente (1995) replicated this approach expanding the number of datasets (including the Korean family planning and Brazilian farmers studies) and the scope of the network exposure definitions (including ties of ties, flow matrix, structural equivalence, etc.). The dynamic models were enhanced by Strang and Tuma's (1993) and Myers' (2000) construction of network-weighted indices over time. These models posit that network characteristics and adoption behavior interact. Specifically, susceptibility is measured by calculating whether persons with high outdegree are more likely to adopt an innovation and infectiousness as persons with high indegree influence others' adoption.[5]

Network-based interventions (type 5)

A final (fifth) type of network model has been to use social network information to design behavior change programs. The most common model has been to use social network data to locate opinion leaders within communities and use them as change agents (Valente and Davis, 1999). Valente and Pumpuang (forthcoming) located over 20 studies

[5] Valente (1995) constructed a similar term which he called the critical mass index calculated as the proportion of adopters over time weighted by individual centrality scores.

that used social network data to find people in the organization or community most frequently cited as ones that others go to for advice or consultation. These individuals are then recruited and trained to promote a particular behavior. Some studies have used network data to find naturally occurring sub-groups and then find leaders within those sub-groups (Buller et al., 1999) or identify leaders and construct groups based on the social network data around them (Valente et al., 2003). Broadhead et al. (1998) and Latkin (1998) have demonstrated the utility of networks for recruitment into behavioral change programs in a snowball manner. Note that this first group of interventions builds on the type 1 model innovation diffusion, namely an integration/normative model.

A second approach (type 2 models) to accelerating innovation diffusion is to change the network so that structural holes are spanned by adding bridges to the network. Thus, we change the network to shorten the overall path lengths between people in the network. Adding bridges shortens the distance information has to travel to reach everyone and accelerates the speed the innovation can traverse the network. Finding the best bridges to add would be a process of calculating reduced overall distances in the network based on the hypothetical addition of links.

A third approach (type 3 models) would be to capitalize on information regarding critical points such as critical mass, thresholds, and tipping points. At the micro level, diffusion can be accelerated by targeting promotions for behavior change to those with low thresholds. By getting the low threshold adopters to adopt early a chain reaction process can be started to accelerate diffusion. At the macro level, diffusion can be accelerated by using promotions for behavior change until critical mass (the tipping point for the system) is reached. Once critical mass is reached, no further promotions will be needed because diffusion will self-sustain. One variant of the critical mass approach is to focus promotional programs on network-defined sub-groups in order to reach critical mass among this subset. The sub-group becomes a source of social support and behavioral reinforcement not available if behavior change is spread out among people in the larger group. Critical mass is more likely to be achieved in the sub-group than in the community as a whole.

Finally, dynamic models (type 4 models) suggest an integration of social network methodology with monitoring and evaluation of behavior change programs. As scholars discover how networks affect behavior change, and behavior change affects networks, specification of how diffusion occurs in any one setting can inform whether promotions are working. Specifically, diagnostic tools can be developed that indicate whether diffusion rates for different sub-groups (defined demographically, geographically, or socio-economically) vary, and whether adoption occurs via network exposure, whether certain individuals display susceptibility, infectiousness, and the early shape of the threshold distribution. These diagnostics will help promoting organizations tailor their promotions more effectively and focus their activities more on who gets the message, and who delivers it rather than what the message says.

It should be noted that many, perhaps all, of the network models focus specifically on the interpersonal connections, without addressing how media influences simultaneously affect adoption behavior. In a telling reanalysis, Van den Bulte and Lillien (2001) supplemented the CKM data with data on marketing efforts at the time of the CKM study. Indeed, Pfizer, the study sponsor, originally solicited the CKM team to evaluate their marketing efforts, not to study the diffusion of tetracycline through the physician network. Van den Bulte and Lillien (ibid.) showed that adoption of tetracycline in CKM was driven by marketing effort, not social networks. The social network threshold model accounts for media influence by showing that individuals with low thresholds are more likely to report media influence (Valente, 1995; Valente and Saba, 1998).

Summary

In this chapter, significant models to explain how innovations diffuse through networks have been presented. Rogers' role in the early studies of diffusion networks was highlighted. The chapter continued with a presentation of other significant models including strength of weak ties, thresholds, structural equivalence, critical mass and tipping point models, and dynamic models. We classified the diffusion network approaches into four types: integration, structural, critical points, and dynamic. Integration models posit that being connected facilitates diffusion. Structural models posit that being in a particular position and the presence (or absence) of key linkages affects diffusion. Critical points posit that critical moments at both the micro and macro levels trigger accelerated adoption/diffusion. Finally, dynamic models investigate the role of network characteristics and behavior over time.

The chapter then suggested a fifth type of network model concerned with using network data to accelerate behavior change. Rogers provided considerable input to all of these models and was a life long proponent of using science to improve the human condition. He would be excited about the new developments taking place in the communication network analysis field today; his data still informs our thinking and his writings and research have provided the foundation needed for us to go forward.

References

Bailey, N. T. J. 1975. *The Mathematical Theory of Infectious Diseases and Its Applications*. London: Charles Griffen.

Beal, G. M. and J. M. Bohlen. 1955. *How Farm People Accept New Ideas*. Cooperative Extension Service Report 15. Ames, IA.

Becker, M. H. 1970. Sociometric Location and Innovativeness: Reformulation and Extension of the Diffusion Model. *American Sociological Review* 35: 267–82.

Broadhead, R. S., D. D. Hechathorn, D. L. Weakliem, D. L. Anthony, H. Madray, R. J. Mills, and J. Hughes. 1998. Harnessing Peer Networks as an Instrument for AIDS Prevention: Results from a Peer-driven Intervention. *Public Health Reports* 113 (S1): 42–57.

Brown, L. 1981. *Innovation Diffusion: A New Perspective*. New York: Methuen.

Buller, D. B., C. Morrill, D. Taren, M. Aickin, L. Sennott-Miller, M. K. Buller, L. Larkey, C. Alatorre, and T. M. Wentzel. 1999. Randomized Trial Testing the Effect of Peer Education at Increasing Fruit and Vegetable Intake. *Journal of the National Cancer Institute* 91: 1491–500

Burt, R. S. 1987. Social Contagion and Innovation: Cohesion versus Structural Equivalence. *American Journal of Sociology* 92: 1287–335.

———. 1992. *Structural Holes: The Social Structure of Competition*. Cambridge, MA: Harvard University Press.

Coleman, J. S., E. Katz, and H. Menzel. 1966. *Medical Innovation: A Diffusion Study*. New York: Bobbs Merrill.

Coleman, J. S., H. Menzel, and E. Katz. 1957. The Diffusion of an Innovation among Physicians. *Sociometry* 20: 253–70.

Crabb, R. 1948. *The Hybrid Corn Makers: Prophets of Plenty*. New Brunswick, NJ: Rutgers University Press.

Freeman, L. 2004. *The Development of Social Network Analysis: A Study in the Sociology of Science*. Vancouver, BC: Empirical Press.

Gladwell, M. 2000. *The Tipping Point: How Little Things Add Up to Make a Big Difference*. Boston, MA: Little, Brown.

Granovetter, M. 1973. The Strength of Weak Ties. *American Journal of Sociology* 78: 1360–80.

———. 1978. Threshold Models of Collective Behavior. *American Journal of Sociology* 83 (6): 1420–43.

Hägerstrand, T. 1967. *Innovation Diffusion as a Spatial Process* (trans. A. Pred). Chicago, IL: University of Chicago Press.

Katz, E., M. L. Levine, and H. Hamilton. 1963. Traditions of Research on the Diffusion of Innovation. *American Sociological Review* 28: 237–53.

Latkin, C. 1998. Outreach in Natural Setting: The Use of Peer Leaders for HIV Prevention among Injecting Drug Users' Networks. *Public Health Reports*, 113 (S1): 151–59.

Mahajan, V. and R. A. Peterson. 1985. *Models of Innovation Diffusion*. Newbury Park, CA: Sage Publications.

Markus, M. L. 1987. Toward a "Critical Mass" Theory of Interaction Media: Universal Access, Interdependence and Diffusion. *Communication Research* 14: 491–511.

Marsden, P. V. and J. Podolny. 1990. Dynamic Analysis of Network Diffusion Processes. In J. Weesie and H. Flap (eds), *Social Networks through Time*, n.p. Utrecht: ISOR.

Marwell, G., P. Oliver, and R. Prahl. 1988. Social Networks and Collective Action: A Theory of the Critical Mass. III. *American Journal of Sociology* 94: 502–34.

McLuhan, M. 1964. *Understanding Media: Extensions of Man*. New York: McGraw-Hill.

Milgram, Stanley. 1967. The Small World Problem. *Psychology Today* 22: 561–67.

Morris, M. 1993. Epidemiology and Social Networks: Modeling Structured Diffusion. *Sociological Methods and Research* 22: 99–126.

Myers, D. J. 2000. The Diffusion of Collective Violence: Infectiousness, Susceptibility, and Mass Media Networks. *American Journal of Sociology* 106 (1): 173–208.

Pool, I. S. and M. Kochen. 1978. Contacts and Influence. *Social Networks* 1: 5–51.

Robertson, T. S. 1971. *Innovative Behavior and Communication*. New York: Rinehart and Winston.

Rogers, E. M. 1962. *Diffusion of Innovations* (1st ed.). New York: Free Press.

———. 1995. *Diffusion of Innovations* (4th ed.). New York: Free Press.

———. 2003. *Diffusion of Innovations* (5th ed.). New York: Free Press.

Rogers, E. M. and D. G. Cartano. 1962. Methods of Measuring Opinion Leadership. *Public Opinion Quarterly* 26: 435–41.

Rogers, E. M. and D. L. Kincaid. 1981. *Communication Networks: A New Paradigm for Research*. New York: Free Press.

Ryan, R. and N. Gross. 1943. The Diffusion of Hybrid Seed Corn in Two Iowa Communities. *Rural Sociology* 8 (1): 15–24.

Schelling, T. 1978. *Micromotives and Macrobehavior*. New York: Norton.

Scott, J. 2000. *Network Analysis: A Handbook* (2nd ed.). Newbury Park, CA: Sage Publications.

Snijders, T. A. B. 2005. Models for Longitudinal Network Data. In P. Carrington, J. Scott, and S. Wasserman (eds), *Models and Methods in Social Network Analysis*. New York: Cambridge University Press.

Strang, D. and N. B. Tuma. 1993. Spatial and Temporal Heterogeneity in Diffusion. *American Journal of Sociology* 99: 614–39.

Travers, J. and S. Milgram. 1969. An Experimental Study of the Small World Problem. *Sociometry* 32: 425–43.

Valente, T. W. 1993. Diffusion of Innovations and Policy Decision-making. *Journal of Communication* 43 (1): 30–41.

———. 1995. *Network Models of the Diffusion of Innovations*. Cresskill, NJ: Hampton Press.

———. 1996. Social Network Thresholds in the Diffusion of Innovations. *Social Networks* 18: 69–89.

———. 2005. Models and Methods for Innovation Diffusion. In P. Carrington, J. Scott, and S. Wasserman (eds), *Models and Methods in Social Network Analysis*. New York: Cambridge University Press.

Valente, T. W. and R. L. Davis. 1999. Accelerating the Diffusion of Innovations Using Opinion Leaders. *The Annals of the American Academy of the Political and Social Sciences* 566: 55–67.

Valente, T. W., B. R. Hoffman, A. Ritt-Olson, K. Lichtman, and C. A. Johnson. 2003. The Effects of a Social Network Method for Group Assignment Strategies on Peer-led Tobacco Prevention Programs in Schools. *American Journal of Public Health* 93 (11): 1837–43.

Valente, T. W. and E. M. Rogers. 1995. The Origins and Development of the Diffusion of Innovations Paradigm as an Example of Scientific Growth. *Science Communication: An Interdisciplinary Social Science Journal* 16 (3): 238–69.

Valente, T. W. and P. Pumpuang. Forthcoming. *Identifying Opinion Leaders to Promote Behavior Change*. Transdisciplinary Drug Abuse Prevention Research Center, University of Southern California.

Valente, T. W. and W. Saba. 1998. Mass Media and Interpersonal Influence in a Reproductive Health Communication Campaign in Bolivia. *Communication Research* 25: 96–124.

Van den Bulte, C. and G. L. Lillien. 2001. Medical Innovation Revisited: Social Contagion versus Marketing Effort. *American Journal of Sociology* 106: 1409–35.

Wasserman, S. and K. Faust. 1994. *Social Networks Analysis: Methods and Applications*. Cambridge, UK: Cambridge University Press.

Watts, D. 2002. *Small Worlds: The Dynamics of Networks between Order and Randomness*. Princeton, NJ: Princeton University Press.

4

Innovation as a Knowledge Generation and Transfer Process

DOROTHY A. LEONARD

In the late 1980s, Ev drove me to a management conference where we presented a paper about technology transfer. I was excited because I would get to see both Rolf Wigand and David Gibson, two of Ev's favorite scholars studying issues of information flow, communication technology, and distributed organizations. We entered a darkened hotel cocktail lounge and found Rolf and Dave. Then, to my delight, Ev introduced Dorothy, whose work about diffusion and opinion leadership and the implementation of innovations I had read and reread and cited and admired very much. She was gracious and didn't seem to mind indulging the many questions of an eager graduate student.

JIM DEARING

I have yet not met Dorothy in person although during my two decades long association with Ev, I heard him talk about her several times. When I first corresponded with Dorothy about the prospect of contributing to this volume, she was kind, gracious, and enthusiastic—qualities that reminded me of Ev.

ARVIND SINGHAL

THE DOCTORAL STUDENTS AT THE STANFORD INSTITUTE FOR Communication Research in 1978 had an "unobtrusive" (but infallible) measure of whether Professor Ev Rogers was out of town: How full our mailboxes were. Whenever he returned from his frequent travels around the world, his large leather briefcase bulged with articles he had ripped out of journals for our edification, clippings from newspapers and magazines and hand-written notes to be stuffed into those waiting mailbox mouths. Among the detritus of those early career

Plate 4.1
Ev Rogers in discussions with dairy farmers of the Kolhapur Milk Union in India's Maharashtra state. Ev was a tireless globetrotter, averaging 8–10 overseas visits a year. India was one of his cherished destinations
Source: Personal file of co-editor Singhal

days I recently found such a clipping about California living styles, relevant to the study Ev and I were conducting on "voluntary simplicity." Attached to the clipping was a note in Ev's small, neat handwriting: "Look what I found—in Japan!"

A prodigious networker, Professor Rogers used his office as a kind of salon for idea-sharing. The doctoral student ushered in (a halfhour after the appointed time) usually found the office populated by visitors from the prior couple of appointments. Ev integrated the newcomer into the on-going discussion with a brief personal introduction and a description of the issue under debate. The topic might not be relevant to the doctoral student's research, and indeed the student often left Ev's office without obtaining answers to the questions she went in with, but she emerged instead with serendipitous interpersonal connections and exposure to foreign lands and perspectives. I doubt Ev ever turned away a person wishing to meet him; he always expected to learn as well as teach through the connection and his door was open to the most humble researchers.

Plate 4.2
Ev Rogers during his Stanford days
Source: Ev Rogers. Provided to co-editor
Singhal in 2000

Everett Rogers embodied the communications of innovation theory he taught, gathering and diffusing knowledge like an intellectual Johnny Appleseed. He was ahead of his time in understanding the power of personal networks and the role of serendipity in innovation. And most of the other concepts about which he was the acknowledged reigning expert have continued relevance today. This chapter addresses just a very few of those topics.

Innovation as bundles of knowledge

Many of the thousands of researchers writing today about innovation—especially in business—would be surprised to find how many of their ideas hearken back to some idea in the prodigious output of Ev Rogers' fecund brain. A single chapter provides inadequate space in which to connect all the dots. I therefore narrow the focus by adopting a particular perspective born of my own intellectual wanderings. I discuss innovation—both its generation and its diffusion—as a process of knowledge generation and transfer.

In this chapter, innovations (whatever their outward form) are considered to be essentially bundles of *knowledge*, including know-how and sometimes know-who, that must be generated and then transferred from origin to users in order for the organization to implement the new product, service, process, methodology, philosophy or capability. This perspective has much in common with the traditional one of innovation generation and diffusion. However, the reader will find that the chapter focuses heavily on *learning processes*, that is, how the innovator garners knowledge for the creation of the innovation, and then how the adopter(s) absorb enough knowledge to implement the innovation. Of course, the innovator often learns from the adopters, so the learning process is reciprocal and iterative. Moreover, as discussed later in the chapter, diffusion and implementation inevitably involve creativity and innovation. So the distinction between the two stages of generation and diffusion is an artificial one—but useful for drawing upon somewhat separate research traditions.

Types of knowledge

Any innovation embodies different types of knowledge. If the innovation is a physical product (software or hardware), embedded in that artifact is the knowledge of its creators, just as a coral bed preserves the structure of its former organic inhabitants. To the extent that the product can be reverse engineered, that knowledge can be discovered and duplicated. Today it is often difficult to tell the original from its copy. In fact, a report on global counterfeiting notes that "[M]any fakes are getting so good that even company execs say it takes a forensic scientist to distinguish them from the real McCoy" (Balfour, 2005). Especially in China, products from shoe polish to medicines to motorcycles are being reproduced to look like (if not always perform as well as) originals.

Processes that are extremely well documented can likewise be replicated. For example, Intel is known for its Copy Exactly! policy for transferring semiconductor manufacturing procedures from the first factory to produce a particular chip to subsequent production facilities (Szulanski and Winter, 2002) and pharmaceutical companies have to prove to the US Federal Drug Administration that they can exactly and reliably reproduce the production process in order to obtain a license for distribution. However, often the most important part of an innovation is know-how associated with its invention or use that is *tacit*, or unarticulated. The learning that is associated with creating, adopting, adapting or using an innovation is therefore an essential part of organizational innovation (Nonaka and Takeuchi, 1995; Leonard, 1995; 1998). In fact, some innovations are entirely undocumented and even so difficult to describe that would-be adopters are unable to implement the innovation in their own environment.

In the 1980s, the US auto industry was challenged by the Japanese, who initiated an amazing innovation: a reliable, relatively energy efficient automobile. An amusing but telling cartoon of the period shows a group of auto workers outside their plant vigorously bashing in a Japanese car. When the car has been almost crushed, one of the workers suddenly realizes, "Now, how are we going to get home?" Replies his compatriot: "Don't worry. These babies always start up."

How did the Japanese do it? After auto executives had spent days in flight back and forth between Detroit and Tokyo, they came to a surprising conclusion: at the end of World War II, the Japanese not only listened to a quality advocate named Deming—but actually implemented his ideas. The Japanese workers, inculcated with the revolutionary notion that poor quality was unnecessary, contributed their brain power daily and hourly to a process of continuous improvement. One of the most striking aspects of this innovation was the reliance upon ideas from everywhere in the company. Even assembly line workers were assumed to have good, innovative ideas.

US companies have for many years attempted to emulate the idiosyncratic capabilities of the famous Toyota production system (TPS). Even after all the visible elements of the system were transferred (the kanban inventory control, the rules of continuous improvement, quality circles), a gap in performance remained between the role model and the would-be imitators. Steven Spear (2002; 2004) argues that the major factor underlying the TPS is a mind-set favoring constant hypothesis-testing that permeates the organization, its workers, and their routine behaviors. Mind-sets are not easily transferred, because so much of the know-how is unconscious, or at least tacit.

Even otherwise easily described innovations, however, often include tacit aspects that are recognized only through use and that are not captured in manuals, presentations or even conversations. Tacit knowledge is, by definition, not readily expressed by those who possess it. A central dilemma for managers interested in organizational innovation, therefore, is *how to create and transfer the knowledge that is essential to any particular innovative undertaking*. In this chapter, I discuss that dilemma and offer some suggestions about how to address it. Let us begin by considering the generation of innovations as a process of identifying, accessing, and fusing knowledge from different sources. In the second segment of the chapter, I will turn to the issue of implementation or diffusion as a transfer of knowledge.

Generating innovations: Where do innovative ideas come from?

The original premise of the diffusion literature was that experts working in a laboratory invented an innovation that was subsequently diffused to a less technically sophisticated populace. This premise was challenged over the years by a number of realizations. First, the innovation literature was applied to non-technical fields. In the late 1970s and early 1980s, Ev Rogers studied such social and policy innovations as the "Dial-a-Ride" effort to wean Californians away from personal cars to shared transportation, and the spread of family planning. Second, one of the most important realizations—that many innovative ideas could come from factory or office workers—was forced on the US by the advent of the Total Quality movement that grew out of the Japanese challenge to the auto industry, as previously described. And finally, the role of the industrial laboratory waned, and business organizations began to seek other sources of new products, processes, and services. Industrial laboratories in the US were increasingly required to tie their inventions to the bottom line of the company sponsoring them. "Relevance" became the mantra for research and parallel to the reduction of large laboratories such as AT&T's famous Bell laboratories was a stronger focus on small companies, and the often young people founding them, as a source of invention (Chesbrough, 2003).

Innovation, it seemed, could originate anywhere.

While specific functions in organizations continue to have innovation generation as their primary job—research and development, engineering design, industrial design, among others[1]—increasingly company leaders are asking *all* their employees to contribute creative thinking, i.e., to generate innovations. For example, in the last part of the 1990s David Whitwam, then CEO of Whirlpool, came to the conclusion that Whirlpool would begin to fade as a vibrant company if the company could not distinguish itself in the appliance business from the rest of the competitors in the "sea of white" washing machines, dryers and dishwashers. He therefore set out to forge such a strong relationship with customers that they would always ask for Whirlpool when they entered a store. And the way he hoped to achieve that aim was through innovation. He wished to permeate the company with a spirit and drive for innovation.

By the time Whitwam retired, the remake of the organization was incomplete—but well underway. One example of the innovations that originated outside research or engineering, was the rugged Gladiator line of appliances intended for use by men (instead of the traditionally targeted female consumers). The Beer Box and Freezerator (both designed to withstand extremes of temperature) and the Gearwall workshop modules, were all designed for use in the garage. This product line moved from concept to prototype in an unprecedented six months and was touted by some as Whirlpool's first major new brand in 50 years. It was expected to generate sales of $300 million by 2007. CEO David Whitwam was so pleased with this project's results that he increased the company's "skunk-works" budget by 60 percent to $80 million (Parks, 2003).

Managers can increase the probability that their organization or group will be able to generate innovations by enhancing knowledge flows, both among the members of the group and also from outside the organizational boundaries. The first step is to consider the composition of the group—the degree to which its members are intellectually homophilous or heterophilous.[2]

---

[1] Rogers (2003: 137–40) calls attention especially to the roles of Research and Development.

[2] For a thorough examination of the creative process in organizations, see Leonard and Swap, 1999.

Creative abrasion: Intellectual diversity

In the *diffusion* of innovations, homophily, that is, the degree to which individuals are alike, eases communication and hence the spread of the new concept, and heterophily is often a barrier (Rogers, 2003: 305–306). However, in the *generation* of innovations, heterophily is actually helpful. Birds who flock together (to subvert the old saying) become more of a feather—and this increasing similarity of thought can screen out novelty. Research has consistently found that groups of people that are intellectually heterogeneous are more creative than homogeneous ones. Creative ideas come at the intersection of different planes of thought. While a Leonardo de Vinci may not have needed to gather a group of diverse thinkers to come up with his endless creations, most of us do not have in our heads what scientists have called "requisite variety," i.e., enough different options from which to choose at least one that is likely to be novel. Moreover, today's products, processes and services are so complex that their design usually draws upon and merges different disciplines and functions.

Therefore, in the initial stages of an innovation, intellectual diversity is highly productive. Such diversity arises from personal background, education, personality, and work experience. Although Xerox's famous Palo Alto Research Center (PARC) was among those industry-sponsored research facilities that failed to provide their mother companies with enough direct financial payback to justify their size and expense, it has always been a hotbed of creativity. Many of today's computer innovations, including the mouse and the icons on our screens, can trace their roots back to this organization. PARC threw anthropologists together with artists and computer scientists, intermingling intellectual bloodlines to stimulate originality.

Today's scientific innovations often require the merging of diverse bodies of expert knowledge. For example, chemical engineer Robert Langer joined forces with noted surgeon and cancer researcher Judah Folkman to test Folkman's theory that cancer tumors could be killed by inhibiting the proteins that recruited blood supplies feeding the tumors' growth. Each man had specialized knowledge to contribute. Langer invented tiny plastic capsules that entrapped the proteins long enough to study them for the first time and verify Folkman's theory. The history of science is rife with such examples. The Japanese have even institutionalized such creative abrasion by building the city of Tsukuba as a planned community of scientists from various disciplines who are co-located in a relatively isolated place (Dearing, 1996).

As these examples suggest, the notion of a lone inventor is largely a myth. While contemporary media and much of history written since, glorifies Thomas Edison as a "solitary genius" revolutionizing the world with such inventions as the light bulb, in truth Edison worked with some 14 other individuals—and he didn't invent the light bulb. One of his co-workers, Charles Batchelor, was so essential to transforming Edison's ideas into working prototypes that he shared 50:50 with Edison in all profits. As Andrew Hargadon (2003) explains, Edison's true genius was his ability to design an innovative work group, merge existing technologies and exploit his ties in industry.

Such interaction is not without friction, as the term "creative *abrasion*" implies.[3] People have difficulty separating *intellectual* from *personal* conflict. However, so long as the friction is anticipated and therefore the group members can depersonalize the conflict and recognize its potential worth, the abrasion is productive. It falls to managers within the organization both to design work groups for creative abrasion, and to then manage that creative friction for light rather than heat.[4] To the degree that leaders manage this process well, the organization will generate more innovation.

Accessing innovative ideas from the marketplace

Of course, many innovations originate outside organizational boundaries. The strongest influence on generating innovations in recent years in the business setting has been the increasing emphasis on learning from the market what is desired. However, the marketplace can inform innovation in many ways besides the obvious one of asking potential or actual users what characteristics they want (and will pay for). Let us consider some of the sources of innovation available to

---

[3] The term was coined by Jerry Hirshberg (1998). See also prior discussions of the concept as reported in Leonard (1995; 1998). Hagel and Brown (2005) extend the concept to business partnering.

[4] Specific suggestions for managers may be found in Leonard and Swap (1999).

the developer. New ideas for products, processes or services, originate from many sources, and vary along at least two dimensions: the extent to which the innovation aligns with the organization's current customer base versus addresses a new market, and the degree to which the technical or methodological design itself is mature (see Figure 4.1).

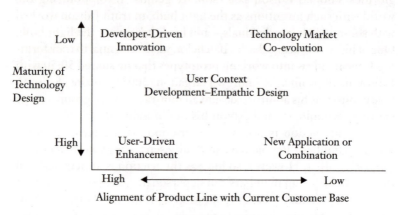

Figure 4.1
Sources of new products, processes, and services
Source: Adapted from Leonard, 1998

The most common sources of new product ideas, if one includes relatively incremental innovations in that description, are specific requests and suggestions from users and clients (bottom left of Figure 4.1). Consumers invited in to so-called usability laboratories to test drive software or hardware in the presence of product developers identify problems requiring minor changes to the design. Such laboratories may be physical, as when Fisher-Price invites children in to play with new toys, or virtual, as when selected Microsoft Word users are asked to comment on new features. And of course, traditional market research through surveys, interviews and other systems of customer inquiry, yield improvement suggestions. Second (top left of Figure 4.1), developers or classes of users who are themselves capable of innovating, often do so in response to a personal—or organizational—need. The ubiquitous roll-on suitcase, for example, was designed by an airline pilot who was tired of lugging his suitcase around the world, and von Hippel (1988) documents many cases of lead users in industrial settings. In recent years, users as innovators in the Open Source software movement have built products and services that rival mighty Microsoft and model a radically new innovation strategy (Grand et al., 2004). Third, as technology and markets co-evolve (top right of Figure 4.1) new products and services emerge from the interaction. Increased high speed, capacious bandwidth stimulates the growth of new services delivered via Internet, for example. Fourth (bottom right of Figure 4.1), products or services designed for one purpose and market often have application in another. The sportsman's "fish locator" is an adaptation of sonar technology developed during World War II to display objects under water. Henry Ford's innovative continuous flow assembly of the Model T was actually a transfer of methods from a number of other unrelated industries, including cigarette and cereal making (Hargadon, 2003).

Empathic design: Accessing users' tacit knowledge

The Holy Grail for innovators is to get inside the heads of potential users and access not just the needs, wants and desires that users can describe, but those that they cannot. An increasing source of innovations is user-context development (center of Figure 4.1). Specially trained teams of designers immerse themselves in the environment of their potential customers in order to mentally assume the perspective of the users, in a process I have termed "empathic design."[5] Because these teams *observe behavior* more than just *interview* the populations they wish to serve, the observers almost always originate innovations that the populations themselves would not. The observers (usually trained in anthropology, psychology or other disciplines steeped in ethnographic traditions) discover barriers to comfort, performance or satisfaction that the users experience but can't (or won't) articulate. Or the observers see opportunities for innovation that would not occur to the general populace. Product development company IDEO (see box on IDEO) is particularly good at this kind of innovation. Their designers use the full complement of possible innovation sources suggested in Figure 4.1, but they are especially

---

[5] This process has been described in greater detail in: Leonard and Swap (1999; 2005) and Leonard and Rayport (1997).

IDEO—the premier design company in the US[6]

IDEO, a design company based in Palo Alto, California, has won more awards and received more publicity for its innovativeness than any other similar company. Originally a merger of an industrial design company and an engineering design company, IDEO retains the flavor of both. The company is noted for its informal but hard-working culture, its endless creativity and for its design processes, which have been widely emulated.

Their process sounds straightforward:

1. Understand the market, the client, the technology, and the innovation opportunity.
2. Use empathic design methods to uncover unarticulated needs.
3. Visualize possible solutions and futures, through simulation or other prototyping methods.
4. Evaluate and refine prototypes.
5. Implement the innovation for commercialization.

In 1999, almost 10 million people viewing the US television show *Nightline* got a front-row seat to watch IDEO go through this process in order to address the toughest design challenge that the ABC team could think of: to redesign the supermarket shopping cart in just five days. The IDEO team first researched statistics and facts about shopping carts and discovered some key issues such as child safety (many children hospitalized after falls from carts). Team members spread out to local supermarkets to immerse themselves in the product environment. Interviewing shoppers, supermarket workers and managers, they discovered design considerations such as the economic importance of theft—people stealing the carts to use as personal luggage carriers or barbeque stoves. They took pictures of folks shopping and watched how professional shoppers left the cart in a particular spot and sped around the supermarket to the different shopping sections, returning with small burdens to unload into the cart, whereas the average shopper held on to the cart all the time and maneuvered it awkwardly around in crowded aisles. After a day in the field, the team members regrouped

CONTINUED ON THE NEXT PAGE

[6] Besides the television show mentioned and my own interviews and interactions with the company, this description of IDEO draws upon Kelley (2001) and Hargadon (2003).

to share what they had learned and to brainstorm solutions. They next divided into smaller teams to prototype several different carts, each optimized to address a particular design issue: safety, shopping, checkout and finding what you are looking for. The next step was to select the very best features from each of the prototypes and blend them into a final design.

That final design was radically different from extant carts. The main basket, for example, was replaced by an open frame into which six standard small handbaskets fit. The shopper would take the small baskets around to fill at dairy, produce, dry goods, etc., stations, and leave the large open frame as a home base, parked in some convenient spot. The cart could be pushed sideways as well as forward and included an electronic scanner for shoppers to use to record items as they placed them in the basket. Although the whole show was intended to demonstrate the innovation *process* rather than sell a new design, a number of the innovations have since been incorporated in supermarkets. At many places, customers can now electronically scan their purchases, pay for them electronically and avoid the checkout line entirely.

IDEO's special talent is in combining all the aforementioned sources of knowledge into a new product or service. Researched information on the product category is combined with what users *say* they want, with what designers as users themselves would like, with observed unarticulated needs, with aesthetic considerations, with capabilities enabled by evolving technologies and with ideas from other industries.

Because IDEO designs everything from yachts to medical equipment to toys to new services, its employees are particularly good at combining ideas from different applications—what Andrew Hargadon calls "technology brokering" and describes as a strategy that, "[r]ather than producing fundamentally novel advances in any one technology or dominating any one industry, ... involves combining existing objects, ideas and people in ways that ... spark technological revolutions" (2003: 12).

skillful at developing innovations based on the unarticulated needs of users that they discover through intensive research in the user context. IDEO's Jane Fulton Suri, for example, helped NEC overcome their difficulties in the computer laptop market by following salespeople around in Japan. She noticed the difficulties these salespeople had in taking their laptops on the road and displaying product lines to customers. From her insights came specifications enabling the user to swap out a floppy drive for an extra battery on long trips and a screen that could be swiveled to direct the screen towards the customer, while the salesperson manipulated the keyboard. The Versa product line won international awards and, more important, doubled NEC's US market share in its first six months (Kelley, 2001: 38–39). The salespeople had not *asked* for such improvements because they were so accustomed to routines that worked around their difficulties.

Empathic design is responsible for product ideas as critical as a screen suspended before the eyes of a physician, imaging the surgery site and guiding her through delicate procedures in real time, to the profitable but not life-saving innovation of pull-up diapers for toddlers that relieve both child and parent of the (unspoken) embarrassment of late toilet training. The process of ethnographic research and subsequent analysis of observed behavior has also proven very fruitful for non-physical innovations and the redesign of organizations. In 2001, an insurance company strategically repositioned themselves with the help of a consulting company. The consultants used ethnographic research to establish that consumers were less concerned about getting the maximum amount of payout than they were to have help in resuming their normal life after an accident. So, for example, dropping off a rental car at their home after an auto accident would be highly appreciated. The researchers also helped the company determine how the innovation of a virtual work environment for claims would affect the social capital within the firm.

Innovation diffusion as a process of learning

The literature on diffusion of innovations among individuals and organizations that Rogers dominated, and studies on the transfer of knowledge, share a common underlying assumption: that the ideas, processes, products and services invented in one site can be re-used— albeit with alterations—in another. As the previous discussion suggests, innovation always requires the combination of knowledge from diverse sources, that is, the transfer of knowledge from brain to brain. Put another way, innovation always requires learning, both in its generation and its diffusion or implementation. The more explicit, structured, documented and visible is the knowledge, the more easily it is packaged up and delivered to another site, another group of people or another mind. The more tacit knowledge content in the innovation, the more difficult the fusion involved in its generation and the more problematic its adoption or implementation.

Among Rogers' famous five characteristics of an innovation (relative advantage, compatibility, complexity, trialability, observability), the last two reflect a concern for the extent to which an innovation includes tacit knowledge. It is difficult to try out an innovation that cannot be completely observed and is still largely in someone else's head, or in multiple heads. In fact, a high degree of tacit knowledge protects valuable innovations from unwanted diffusion. The CEO of Chaparral Steel, a mini mill renowned for its innovative capability, invited competitors at the height of its success to come view its operations, because he was confident that they could never duplicate the culture that underlay its performance. He knew that much of Chaparral's advantage lay in the innovative capability, the heads and hands, of his long-time employees.

In the next segments of this chapter, I consider the diffusion process as one of transferring knowledge. While this perspective has much in common with the sociological one, it owes more to the field of cognitive psychology. The emphasis is less on how adopters become cognizant of an innovation and on their adoption decision-making processes than on how adopters learn the skills necessary to implement the innovation.

Entrepreneuring in cyberspace as an innovation

The focus and examples in the following discussion draw heavily upon a multi-year, multi-method international study of the spread of Internet-based business models. At the end of the 1990s and spilling over into the first years of the new century, the world was witness to an extensive experiment in new ventures based on a series of technological innovations that had rather suddenly coalesced into a new territory of unexplored business opportunity. Unprecedented numbers of new companies based on the promising technology of the Internet were born (and died) within the period of a few years. It seemed as if there were aspiring CEOs in every college dormitory room and garage or their equivalents. Walter Swap and I studied entrepreneurs and the investors who were coaching them in 35 startup companies in the US, India, Singapore, and Hong Kong, in order to understand the transfer of entrepreneurial knowledge between the relative experts and novices (Leonard and Swap, 2005).

The innovation that was diffusing was as much social and methodological as technological. The mostly young people around the globe hastening to set up businesses usually had a good grasp of the technical workings of cyberspace, but were woefully unprepared to set up even the most basic and mundane aspects of a new venture—much less to lead the formulation of strategy or to manage employees and boards of directors. The young venture founders had gone through the stages of adoption at warp speed (knowledge, persuasion, adoption, and implementation), having learned about the promise of the Internet through the Internet itself, and through the media that touted early Internet heroes. One of the entrepreneurs studied, for example, had a magazine photograph of Netscape's Mark Andreessen pinned up on the wall of his home in India, as a role model and inspiration. Implementation was the problem. The diffusion of Internet ventures thus depended upon the ability of these novice entrepreneurs to learn a whole set of essential business skills—fast. They learned from as many sources as possible, all at once: courses, the media and peers as well as from their own experimentation. However, among the most important sources of knowledge about how to set up a new business were startup coaches.

The "knowledge coaches," as we came to describe them (because, unlike at least some classes of mentors, these advisors had specific skills and know-how to impart to their protégés), were either cashed-out entrepreneurs working independently ("mentor capitalists") or venture capitalists who were in the business of investing in and helping startups. These coaches had years of experience in the most routine business essentials of accounting, taxes, and labor laws—all highly explicit and well-documented knowledge. But more important, they had built up judgment and decision-making skills that were, by this time, based on "intuition," and were therefore mostly tacit knowledge, for example how to find the "sweet spot" in the market for a promising technology, or how to decide on whom to hire.

For the ventures to succeed, both explicit and tacit knowledge had to be learned, and of course the latter transfer was much more difficult.

The empty vessel hazard

Even highly explicit knowledge can fail to transfer, however, if the mind of the intended recipient has no receptors. A counterpoint to the empty vessel fallacy (the belief that the potential adopter's mind is a blank) is what we might think of as the empty vessel hazard—the possibility that the potential adopter's mind does not contain the mental hooks and structures to make sense of the innovation. Consider the question: What three-dimensional avatar would you like to have in the next Multi-User-Domain (MUD) you enter? If you are not a gamer, i.e., someone who plays interactive games, the query makes no sense. It is just a string of words. However, if you have experience playing in MUDs, the question is not only comprehensible, but the words stimulate a host of associations, mental pictures, specific memories and even emotions. Gamers have the mental *receptors* to process the question. They have constructed three-dimensional representations of themselves for use in cyberspace and have a host of experiences that will inform their response to the question. Comedian Robert Dubac points out the difference between information and knowledge. Information is understanding that the toilet and the shower share a common cold water pipe feed. Knowledge is based on experience: when you hear the toilet flush, *get out of the shower—quick!*

In order to construct knowledge out of information, people need to have some mental scaffolding, some "hooks" to which they can attach the stimulus they are receiving, be it text, images, observed behavior or audio signals. Skilled teachers and coaches know that they cannot start imparting their knowledge using language or concepts for which the students are totally unprepared. This same caution applies to any attempts at knowledge transfer or innovation implementation. The targeted recipient must have receptors that allow him to construct knowledge out of information. Such receptors are constructed either from instruction or direct experience. Increasingly, online education offers the opportunity to develop receptors and build the mental structures that give form and meaning to experience (see box on WIDE).

The case of WIDE

The Harvard Graduate School of Education offers an online (web-based) professional development program for kindergarten to grade 12 teachers and administrators from—at last count—64 countries. WIDE (Wide-scale Interactive Development for Educators) World instructors include researchers from Harvard's "Project Zero" and Educational Technology Center, where the pedagogical framework known as "Teaching for Understanding" was developed. The framework emphasizes developing learners' understanding through active learning, clear goals and ongoing assessment and coaching. The objective of WIDE World is to help educators design curricula that integrate new technologies and improve their skills in assessment, attention to multiple intelligences, and teaching for understanding.

WIDE courses enable busy educators to interact with each other as well as with the instructors. And the program has an additional, highly personal aspect—coaches have been designed in as an essential part of the course. The coaches are drawn from the population of students. After taking the course themselves at least once, they sometimes go through it a second time as an "apprentice coach." In this second pass through the course, they focus more on observing the coaching process than on course content. There is also a special online course for coaches, which focuses on coaching techniques as well as content. After this training, the coaches are ready to take responsibility for 10–12 teachers in a study group. One of the coach's tasks is to moderate online discussions, a responsibility that includes modeling productive interaction with participants as well as keeping the discussion on point. Coaches also give individual feedback to learners and summarize the progress, concerns and themes expressed by learners for the instructors. And they serve as peer consultants for fellow coaches.

One of the primary benefits to WIDE is access. As the global nature of the project illustrates, the WIDE experts transfer their pedagogical frameworks and development techniques to teachers who would otherwise be unable to obtain this professional training, because of geography or resource constraints. The principal type of the knowledge transferred is explicit, as the learning exchanges are mostly textual. However, WIDE co-principal investigator Stone Wiske maintains that online discussions have an advantage over classroom interaction, in that the web-based interactions are captured in forms that can be re-visited.

In the Internet business models study, the entrepreneurs who were on their second or third venture had plenty of receptors. The ones who had studied business in school had some. But the company founders who came straight out of engineering school or whose credentials for starting a company were strictly technology-based, had none. The first chore for the advisors, therefore, was to determine what receptors existed, and to base their coaching on those—using a variety of knowledge transfer methods.

Knowledge transfer methods

All forms of teaching *should* equate to knowledge transfer, but they don't. The wag who described lectures as a process in which the notes of the teacher pass to the notes of the student—without passing through the heads of either—was correct in many cases. Knowledge is more than information, and as discussed earlier in this chapter, includes tacit dimensions that its possessor may not be able to articulate. As Figure 4.2 suggests, there is a hierarchy of methods for transferring knowledge, ranging from quite passive reception to active learning. All of these modes of knowledge transfer are useful, but towards the bottom of the hierarchy, the principal result of interaction between the source of knowledge and the learner (whether that pair be teacher and student, coach and actor, parent and child, or innovator and adopter) is the creation of receptors in the minds of the learners. That is, at this extreme, the transfer of knowledge is very incomplete. The more the pair use modes towards the top of the hierarchy, the more mental and physical activity is demanded of the learner and the more the result of the interaction is a replication of knowledge, including its tacit dimensions. It is never possible for people to completely transfer all the knowledge they have to another being, but the more that the learners focus on learning by doing, the more they recreate the knowledge possessed by the knowledge source.

Knowledge coaches as change agents

The knowledge coaches in the entrepreneurship study were a form of change agents, both advising the real adopters, the entrepreneurs,

Active
Learning

- Learning by Doing
  - Experience Guided by Coaches

Increasing
Growth of
Tacit Knowledge

- Simulation
- Socratic Questioning
- Stories with a Moral
- Rules of Thumb
- Directives/Presentations/Lectures

Passive
Reception

Figure 4.2
Modes of knowledge transfer
Source: Leonard and Swap, 2005

and helping with the implementation of the innovation. Most of the small Internet-based ventures ultimately failed, if independent growth is used as a measure of success. However, many of them were sold to larger companies and a few of them grew to challenge established business models. For example, the startup NetFlix which sends through the mail an unlimited number of movies on DVD to subscribers for a monthly fee, has threatened the business model of the highly successful Blockbuster rental stores. A large number of failures could be attributed to the naïveté of both entrepreneurs and their would-be coaches about the basic nature of the innovation they were attempting (see box on "Internet incubators").

The knowledge coaches whom we studied used the entire menu of knowledge transfer modes illustrated in Figure 4.2, with the exception of simulations. The more experienced the knowledge coaches, the more that they recognized the need to stimulate their protégé's thinking and require some real action on the part of the (mostly novice) entrepreneurs. The less experienced coaches were at best able to pass along some "best practices" that they had learned from others, such as to get the highest profile advisors possible on the board of the fledgling enterprise. More experienced coaches could deliver rules of thumb and stories to back them up. The knowledge coach who told his protégés, "be careful about sequencing" could also tell stories about the inexperienced managers who hired a large sales force before the

Internet incubators: Failed innovation?

In 1995, there were only a dozen or so incubators devoted to helping companies start-up. According to one report, by 1999, there were 63 and halfway through 2000, 348! (Veverka, 2002). While some of these entrepreneurial nests for new ventures offered only space, shared office support, and technology, others claimed to be "full-service." In addition to access to venture capital, the major service proffered in these incubators was knowledge: about management, recruiting, shaping the business proposition, communications training—anything and everything that a hopeful entrepreneur would need to launch a business.

There were several problems with the notion, not the least of which was that the incubators could remain financially solvent only if their protégé businesses went public quickly enough to pay for the investment. Given that in 1995, 5 million shares of Netscape issued at $28 had sold for $74.75 when the company went public (making founder Marc Andreessen immediately worth more than $50 million), the hopes for fast profits seemed at least feasible. But many, if not most, of the incubator managers lacked much entrepreneurial experience. What rationale did they have for setting themselves up as knowledge coaches? Many considered their Rolodex enough, since their personal networks tapped into possible funding sources among wealthy acquaintances. Others viewed themselves as intermediaries between the inexperienced entrepreneurs and older people who *did* have experience. But some simply had boundless (and foundation-less) self-confidence. In evaluating an incubator at the request of an entrepreneur, I asked about the manager's prior experience. I was stunned to find that his *only* entrepreneurial experience was in setting up the incubator!

Operating on a flawed business model and with little knowledge to offer, almost all the incubators failed. Of the nine incubators in the entrepreneurship study, by 2004, six had shut down completely, one became a barely surviving venture firm, one merged with a venture firm and one became an investment bank. They had been set up so fast that there was no opportunity to experiment—or to learn from others' failures.

product was really ready for commercialization. Stories are effective in that they are remembered longer than dry facts (Swap et al., 2001). Experienced coaches also used meetings with the novice entrepreneurs to probe their protégés' understanding through Socratic questioning: "Why do you think that your competitors are not investing in their own web sites?"

Simulations (the next higher form of active learning) need not be computerized to be useful ways of teaching. Case studies are a form of simulation, in that they reproduce a real-world situation. In the hands of a skillful instructor who asks students to role play the reactions of case study characters, such studies can approach verisimilitude. However, the extremely realistic, interactive simulations now possible in cyberspace offer more immersive opportunities to learn. Training in many fields, from military to medical, now includes simulated experience. While the coaches in our study often referred to real life situations as examples, they had neither the time nor the inclination to put their protégés through simulated experience. Rather, the learners were plunged into real life situations, the responses to which determined their future.

Kanwal Rekhi, the first Indian-born CEO in Silicon Valley, coached dozens of small venture founders from his Santa Clara office during the Internet boom. He gave them advice about specific actions to take and then invited them back to report on the results. However, if they could not report at least trying to do what he advised, he would not meet with them a third time. There were too many would-be entrepreneurs lined up outside his office to spend time on those who were not receptive to coaching.[7]

Knowledge chains: Silicon Valley to Bangalore and Delhi

One of the interesting aspects of the diffusion of the Internet business models was that the prevailing Gold Rush mentality set a premium on speed. There was a sense that while the opportunities to exploit the Internet territory were vast; would-be occupants were numerous. Moreover, no one had years of experience in designing successful

[7] Towards the end of the original entrepreneurship study, we tested our findings in research about intrapreneuring inside large organizations such as Best Buy and NASA's Jet Propulsion Laboratories. We found that the same hierarchy of knowledge transfer methods applied and the role of the knowledge coach was essentially the same.

Internet business models. In the jostling for space among many competitors, the entrepreneurs sought advice from anyone who had even
the slightest superior experience, including fellow entrepreneurs who
were somewhat ahead of them on the path to implementing a new
business.

A chain of knowledge exchanges linked the US-based hotbeds of
entrepreneurial activity to those in India, China and other parts of the
world. So, for example, after Kanwal Rekhi sold his company Excelan
to Novell in 1989, he started helping other entrepreneurs. Two of his
beneficiaries were K. B. Chandrasekhar and B. V. Jagadeesh, founders
of Exodus Communications. Chandrasekhar, in turn, coached fledgling
entrepreneur Rajesh Reddy, who was in India building a company
called Unimobile based on wireless technology. Even after he moved
to the US, Reddy kept in contact with friends in India, and advised
28-year-old Saumil Majmudar, who was setting up QSupport, a technical support company for personal computing. To our surprise,
Majmudar was coaching three other start-ups in India! Knowledge
flowed along this chain from Rekhi to Majmudar's protégés, although
at each successive link, the coach had less experience-based "deep smarts"
to pass along. Thus the innovation flowed through an accelerated diffusion process that was highly efficient in terms of communication—
but deeply flawed by the incomplete understanding of implementation
requirements. Towards the end of the chain, the "coaches" had such
fragmentary knowledge that they were mostly passing along the rules
of thumb that they had been given by their coaches.

Communities of practice and horizontal diffusion

The communities of entrepreneurs and their coaches furiously ex-
changing experiences around the globe resembled somewhat a phenomenon that has recently garnered much attention: Communities
of Practice (CoP). Such CoPs are defined as "groups of people who
share a concern, a set of problems, or a passion about a topic, and who
deepen their knowledge and expertise in this area by interacting on
an ongoing basis" (Wenger, McDermott, and Snyder, 2002: 4).

Interest in CoPs has grown for a number of reasons. First, and
perhaps most important, has been the growing recognition of one of

the issues touched upon in this chapter, namely the importance of experience in creating knowledge. Second, organizations have been increasingly pressed to re-use extant knowledge—both that already existing within their boundaries and that in organizations that they benchmark—rather than constantly re-create it. Third, technology enables people in diverse geographies to communicate not only through text and verbal exchanges but with photographs and other visuals. CoPs have been credited with greatly aiding not only the spread of knowledge, but its creation.

Interestingly, Ev Rogers and I wrote about "horizontal diffusion," which we characterized as differing from the classical diffusion model in having "relatively more user innovation" and "innovation dissemination among and by peers," over 25 years ago (Leonard-Barton and Rogers, 1981). Unfortunately, it was an idea that neither of us pursued enough to stimulate research. Certainly many of the observations we made continue to apply to CoPs today. We contrasted the horizontal diffusion process with the vertical one epitomized by the US Agricultural Extension Services in several ways. The greatest differences lay in the origins of the innovation (users rather than research laboratories), the legitimization process (users, through adoption, rather than experts), the diffusion process (users instead of a centralized authority) and the modes of diffusion (through personal contact among users rather than through a hierarchical, structured system).

All of those characteristics would sound familiar to those working with communities of practice. In 1980, there were even fledgling computerized systems that enabled individuals to seek advice from peers. For example, a "Legitech" system allowed state legislators to solicit suggestions from other states for solving a problem such as how to clean up toxic waste sites. The possible benefits and dangers in horizontal diffusion were also already apparent. The advantage of credible, practical information was balanced against the lack of a central quality-control authority.

Today, many communities of practice thrive—in businesses, in non-profit organizations, internationally and locally. Wenger, McDermott, and Snyder (2002) identify four principal types of CoPs: Helping (peer groups connected in forums to share knowledge), Best-practice (focused on developing, validating and diffusing specific methodologies or processes), and Knowledge-stewarding (organized to structure,

World Bank thematic groups

On October 1, 1996, at the Annual Meeting of the World Bank, President James Wolfensohn announced a new vision for his organization: it was to become "The Knowledge Bank." This speech signaled a significant shift from the Bank's historical emphasis on providing loans for developing nations. Instead of loaning money to build physical infrastructure such as highways and dams, the Bank would become a clearing house for knowledge about development. It would collect and disseminate information about challenges and potential solutions, connecting those who needed knowledge with those who had it. Drawing upon the increasing attention paid to communities of practice, in 1998 the Bank diverted $15 million to support "thematic groups." At the time, a few informal groups existed, such as one focused on highways, whose members had exchanged ideas for 15 years. The monetary support spurred the formation of many more such groups, and by late 1999, there were 124 of them.

By 1999, the Bank had progressed in knowledge management far enough to invite evaluation by outside experts. The report they submitted pointed out problems common to communities of practice, such as the heavy dependence upon volunteer leadership, uneven and inconsistent organizational practices, and concerns about how to verify information, assure high quality, and organize information for easy access and use. However, the outside consultants also called the thematic groups the "heart and soul of knowledge management in the Bank."

The groups, which varied tremendously in formality and effectiveness, were organized around such themes as urban poverty. The Thematic Group on Services to the Urban Poor, set up in 1997, found that their website was less compelling than face-to-face conferences. They set up meetings attended by regional directors, managers and workers in Latin America and Asia, and a "pilot slum immersion" for practitioners from Latin America and the Caribbean region, was open to anyone working on upgrading slums. The World Bank continues to support many such thematic groups, and in recent years has begun to leverage what it has learned about communities of practice to help its clients set up their own. For example, mayors from capital cities in Central America and the Caribbean have begun meeting every quarter, with consulting help from the Bank.

Sources: Fulmer (2001); Wenger, McDermott, and Snyder (2002); Leonard and Swap (2005)

upgrade and distribute knowledge their members use routinely). The fourth, Innovation Communities, are specifically designed to "foster unexpected ideas and innovations" and "intentionally cross boundaries to mix members who have different perspectives" (2002: 77). An example is Daimler Chrysler's Austauschgruppe connecting 240 experts around the world whose tasks include assessing new directions in research. The champions of CoPs point out that such communities cannot be forced into being. They are social systems that depend upon willing, interested, motivated members. They *can* be aided through the provision of resources—especially those that enable and support communication.

Communities of Practice both *generate* innovations (often through creative abrasion) and *diffuse* innovations. Such communities have the potential to capitalize on the benefits of both homophily (rapid communication because of shared interests and motives) and of heterophily (different perspectives born of geographic or functional disparity).

Ev Rogers as knowledge coach

We hadn't coined the term until very recently, but in retrospect, Ev Rogers was a knowledge coach. He used the entire menu of knowledge transfer mechanisms featured in Figure 4.2, but his preference was always on the methods towards the top—active learning. His use of stories was legendary, as he understood the power of narrative to teach. And he was very good at asking the embarrassing Socratic question: "Why?" I also recall his patience during some late night joint problem-solving exercises, when we had an overdue report to deliver to the state of California. But what I appreciate the most was his providing me with experiences—often before I felt ready for them.

Invited to a very small prestigious workshop on solar energy, he sent me instead. At the time, having focused my dissertation research on energy conservation in Palo Alto, California, I knew, in agonizing detail, the attitudes and behavior (as verified by household energy bills) of a very small population towards conservation and solar energy. How, I wondered, could I possibly contribute to the aggregate knowledge of a group of very senior researchers from this meager base? "Don't worry," Ev said, when I confessed my trepidations. "You know

Plate 4.3
Ev Rogers, the knowledge coach,
listening to Ev Rogers, Jr.
Source: Personal file of co-editor
Dearing

more than you think." It turned out that because there were so few empirical studies of actual behavior at the time, my research was very useful in building models. From this experience I learned an extremely valuable lesson—the contribution that deep understanding, even if it is very narrow in scope, can make to the whole.

Ev had what I think of as "equality of expectations." He expected everyone to perform well and to learn quickly. These are tremendously motivating characteristics in a knowledge coach.

References

Balfour, F. 2005. Fakes! *Business Week*, February 7. Web version: www.businessweek.com/magazine/content/05_06/b3919001_mz001.htm.

Chesbrough, H. W. 2003. *Open Innovation: The New Imperative for Creating and Profiting from Technology*. Boston, MA: Harvard Business School Press.

Dearing, J. 1996. *Growing a Japanese Science City: Communication in Scientific Research*. New York: Routledge.

Fulmer, W. 2001. *The World Bank and Knowledge Management: The Case of the Urban Services Thematic Group*. Harvard Business School Case 9-801-157.

Grand, S., G. von Krogh, D. Leonard, and W. Swap. 2004. Resource Allocation Beyond Firm Boundaries: A Multi-level Model for Open Source Innovation. *Long Range Planning* 37 (6): 591–610.

Hagel, J., III and J. S. Brown. 2005. Productive Friction: How Difficult Business Partnerships Can Accelerate Innovation. *Harvard Business Review*, February (Reprint #R0502D).

Hargadon, A. 2003. *How Breakthroughs Happen: The Surprising Truth about How Companies Innovate*. Boston, MA: Harvard Business School Press.

von Hippel, E. 1988. *The Sources of Innovation*. New York: Oxford University Press.

Hirshberg, J. 1998. *The Creative Priority: Driving Innovative Business in the Real World*. New York: Harper Business.

Kelley, T. 2001. *The Art of Innovation: Lessons in Creativity from IDEO, America's Leading Design Firm*. New York: Doubleday.

Leonard, D. 1995, 1998. *Wellsprings of Knowledge: Building and Sustaining the Sources of Innovation*. Boston, MA: Harvard Business School Press.

Leonard, D. and J. Rayport. 1997. Spark Innovation through Empathic Design. *Harvard Business Review* 75 (6): 102–13 (Reprint #97606).

Leonard, D. and W. Swap. 1999. *When Sparks Fly: Igniting Group Creativity*. Boston, MA: Harvard Business School Press.

———. 2005. *Deep Smarts: How to Cultivate and Transfer Enduring Business Wisdom*. Boston, MA: Harvard Business School Press.

Leonard-Barton, D. and E. M. Rogers. 1981. Horizontal Diffusion of Innovations: An Alternative Paradigm to the Classical Diffusion Model. Massachusetts Institute of Technology Working Paper 1214–81.

Nonaka, I. and H. Takeuchi. 1995. *The Knowledge-Creating Company: How Japanese Companies Create the Dynamics of Innovation*. New York: Oxford University Press.

Parks, B. 2003. 25,000 Minds are Better than One: Executives at Stagnating Appliance-maker Whirlpool Turned to Employees to Find Entirely New Market. *Business 2.0 Media Inc.* May 20.

Rogers, E. M. 2003. *Diffusion of Innovations* (5th ed.). New York: Free Press.

Spear, S. J. 2002. The Essence of Just-in-Time: Embedding Diagnostic Tests in Work-systems to Achieve Operational Excellence. *Production Planning & Control* 13 (8): 754–67.

———. 2004. Learning to Lead at Toyota. *Harvard Business Review* 82 (5): 78–86.

Swap, W., D. Leonard, M. Shields, and L. Abrams. 2001. Using Mentoring and Storytelling to Transfer Knowledge in the Workplace. *Journal of Management and Information Systems* 18 (Summer): 95–114.

Szulanski, G. and S. Winter. 2002. Getting it Right the Second Time. *Harvard Business Review* January: 62–69 (Reprint #R0201E).

Veverka, M. 2002. Pied Piper of the 'Net: How John Doerr Sparked the Internet Boom and Brought Home Big Profits. *Barron's* June 10: 19–22.

Wenger, E., R. McDermott, and W. M. Snyder. 2002. *Managing Organizational Knowledge through Communities of Practice*. Boston, MA: Harvard Business School Press.

5

On Integrating Social Cognitive
and Social Diffusion Theories[1]

ALBERT BANDURA

In the days before the Internet and pdf files, one of the signs that someone, somewhere, read the arcane and tortured texts that we call scholarship, was the postcard. Active scholars kept a stack of them nearby in case they saw a reference to a journal article that they wanted to read. I distinctly remember the heady feeling when two of Al Bandura's handwritten request cards showed up in my faculty mailbox within a couple of weeks of each other. My work couldn't be completely without worth, I reasoned, if Al Bandura saw fit to request a copy.

JIM DEARING

Once Ev got me enthused about entertainment-education, Al Bandura's work loomed large. No matter where one looked, Al's pioneering work on modeling, identification, and efficacy, drove the research and practice agenda in entertainment-education and health promotion. In a published interview in 1980, Al noted: "The worth of a theory is ultimately judged by the power of the change it produces." By this metric, Al's social cognitive theory and Ev's work on diffusion would rank close to the top.

ARVIND SINGHAL

HOW LUCKY WE WERE TO HAVE EV ROGERS AS A COLLEAGUE AND FRIEND, and how deeply he will be missed by the countless people for whom his work has made a major difference. Ev epitomized the consummate scholar and scientist who brought a special blend of broad vision,

---

[1] Some sections of this chapter include revised, updated, and expanded material from *Social Foundations of Thought and Action: A Social Cognitive Theory* (Bandura, 1986).

innovativeness, and fresh insights to fundamental issues regarding human adaptation and change. Ev was a delightful person and during his tenure at Stanford University from 1975 to 1985 and thereafter, we had many opportunities to explore ideas. One evening in Palo Alto, while we were nursing a bottle of the noble grape, I was reflecting on the fortuitous character of life. Some of the most important determinants of life paths, I noted, often occur through the most trivial of circumstances. I cited examples of how people are often inaugurated into new life trajectories, marital partnerships, and occupational careers through fortuitous circumstances.

A couple of weeks later Ev sent me a section from a volume authored by David Fischer (1994) documenting the concatenating social processes triggered by fortuitous events around the alarm sounded by Paul Revere on April 18, 1775 warning that a British military force was approaching. Revere and a fellow revolutionary, William Dawes set forth from Boston to sound the alarm. Revere had the faster horse and found himself on a route he had not planned to go by that brought him to Medford Massachusetts. Once in the village, he alerted the commander of the local minutemen who triggered the town's alarm system and sent other riders rapidly spreading the alarm throughout the countryside. Dawes, traveling a longer distance on a slower horse, met up with Revere in Lexington Massachusetts about three hours later. Revere got immortalized as the midnight rider who alerted the populace to the impending British attack. For want of a speedier horse and a more fortuitous choice of route, Dawes has remained in relative obscurity. Ev unearthed this revealing bit of historical serendipity before the era of the mighty Google search engine. This is but one example of his extraordinary breadth and depth of scholarship.

Ev was deeply bonded to his Iowa rural roots. His doctoral studies at Iowa State University on the social diffusion of agricultural innovations shaped the course of his professional career. Although Ev traveled in international circles in the course of his diverse program of research, he maintained his rooted ties to his beloved farm in Carroll. It was here that he went for rest and relaxation from a hectic academic life. Upon joining the faculty at Stanford, Ev promptly added to this urbane academy a notable rural touch graced with lavishly productive vegetable gardens and prolific domestic fowl. In the following box, Henry Breitrose, who was Ev's colleague at Stanford, vividly remembers the experience.

On the ruralization of Stanford

The cliché is that you can take the boy out of the country, but you can't take the country out of the boy, and Ev Rogers was the "ideal type" that classical sociologists, rural or otherwise, might point to in order to support the accuracy of that statement. Ev bought a house on the Stanford campus in the faculty housing area. Not long after he moved in he acquired a pick-up truck, and became immersed, figuratively and literally, in the Santa Clara adobe clay.

Rather than concentrating on adobe as a virtually indestructible construction material, Ev was fixated on its nutritive qualities, and how to exploit them by preventing the adobe clay from setting up solid as a rock. The cure, he announced, was "amendment" and compost. "Amendment" was a portmanteau word for compost, and manures, fresh and aged, from a variety of animals. In a few months, Ev's garden bloomed with all manner of garden crops. The neighbors, having endured the manuring of Ev's plot, gladly benefited from the foison of Ev's field.

Then there were the chickens. Over a weekend, an unplanted area evolved into a chicken coop. There was some discussion among the neighbors about whether the chickens were legal. Ev's logic was impeccable. The chickens were Bantams, and didn't need much space. They produced eggs, for human consumption, and chicken manure in impressive quantities, which was excellent fertilizer. The only problem was the rooster. To egg the chickens on, as it were, it was necessary to have a rooster, and Ev's Bantam rooster was a leather-lunged beast who greeted each dawn with a vociferous cock-a-doodle-doo. It appeared that Ev took a certain pride in the rooster. He allowed as how this was a "macho" bird, and that the ear-splitting cock-a-doodle-doo was a testament to the rooster's virility.

Ev tried to placate the neighbors with fresh eggs, noting how they were a joint enterprise of chicken and rooster, but all to no avail, and eventually, to the considerable relief of his neighbors, the rooster and the chickens were dispatched to a happier place.

Plate 5.1
Ev in front of the famous garage close to the Stanford University campus where Bill Hewlett and Dave Packard started the Hewlett-Packard Company in 1938. During his Stanford years, Ev's interests went beyond adobe, compost, chickens, and roosters to include silicon chips, microcomputers, and the high-tech culture of Silicon Valley. In the early 1980s, he co-authored a best selling book titled *Silicon Valley Fever*
Source: Personal file of co-editor Singhal

Core features of a social cognitive theory of social diffusion

The present chapter centers on the integration of social cognitive theory with Ev's pioneering theorizing and research on social diffusion of innovation. Social cognitive theory distinguishes among three separable components in the social diffusion of innovation. This triadic model includes the determinants and mechanisms governing the acquisition of knowledge and skills concerning the innovation; adoption of that innovation in practice; and the social networks through which innovations are promulgated and supported (Bandura, 1986).

Acquisitional determinants

Psychological theories have traditionally emphasized learning from the effects of one's actions. If knowledge and skills could be acquired only by repeated trial and error experiences, human development would be greatly retarded, not to mention exceedingly tedious and hazardous. Moreover, the constraints of time, resources, and mobility impose severe limits on the situations and activities that can be directly explored for the acquisition of new knowledge. However, humans have evolved an advanced cognitive capacity for observational learning that enables them to abbreviate the acquisition process by learning from the informative examples provided by others. A special power of psychological modeling is that it can simultaneously transmit knowledge of wide applicability to vast numbers of people in dispersed locales through symbolic modes of communication. By drawing on these modeled patterns of thought and behavior, observers can transcend the bounds of their immediate environment. Because of the growing primacy of the electronic media, observational learning from the symbolic environment is playing an increasingly powerful role in people's everyday lives.

Symbolic modeling usually functions as the principal conveyer of innovations to widely dispersed areas. This is especially true in the early stages of diffusion. Newspapers, magazines, radio, television, and Internet-based sources of influence inform people about new practices and their likely risks or benefits. Early adopters, therefore, come from among those who have had greater access to media sources of information.

The revolutionary advances in communications and Internet technologies are transforming acquisitional and social diffusion processes. The Internet is swift, wide-reaching and free of institutional controls. It alters how people communicate, educate, work, relate to each other, and conduct their business and daily affairs. Video systems feeding off of telecommunications satellites have become the dominant vehicle for disseminating symbolic environments. New ideas, values, and styles of conduct are now being rapidly diffused worldwide in ways that foster a globally distributed consciousness.

Observational learning is governed by three subfunctions. These include attentional, representational, and productive processes. *Attentional processes* determine what people selectively observe in the profusion of modeling influences and what information they extract from ongoing modeled events. Included among the factors influencing observational learning are the cognitive skills, preconceptions, and value preferences of the observers. These pre-existing orientations influence the types of models individuals select, what they look for, how they interpret and organize the information generated in dealings with their environment, and what they retrieve from their memory representation. Differences in the knowledge and skills that particular innovations require produce variations in rate of acquisition.

Modeling political change

Global broadcasts now show socio-political conflicts as they are happening. This makes televised modeling an especially influential vehicle for political and social change. The speed with which Eastern European rulers and regimes were toppled by collective action beginning in the late 1980s was greatly accelerated by televised modeling. The tactic of mass action modeled successfully by East Germans was immediately adopted by others living under oppressive rule (Braithwaite, 1994). The timing and form of collective action is better predicted by the force of modeling than by social structural conditions.

A mass uprising by citizens of the Ivory Coast in 2001 dislodged the military dictator Guei who declared himself a winner of an election he was losing in the ballot count. The protestors modeled the militant strategy after the popular revolt against Milosevic in Yugoslavia who tried to annul an election in which he was defeated (Onishi, 2000). In commenting on the influential role of televised modeling in the popular uprising, a student protestor remarked, *"The mistake Guei made was to let us watch scenes from Belgrade."*

Televised modeling of civic strife in contests of power is a double-edged sword, however. It can fortify social control as well as promote social change depending on the depicted consequences of militant socio-political action. In 1989, during the Tiananmen Square uprising, the Chinese populace watched on CNN the militia breaking down doors and arresting student activists. Live portrayal of brutal arrests helped to curb the spread of the uprising.

Innovations that are difficult to understand and use receive more reluctant consideration than simpler ones (Tornatzky and Klein, 1982).

Other factors are the attractiveness and functional value of the modeled activities. Successful modes of behavior command more attention than do less effective ones. The way in which societies are socially organized along age, gender, racial and class lines largely determines the types of models to which its members have ready access. When television models new practices on the screens in virtually every household, people in widely dispersed locales can learn them. Not all innovations are promoted through the mass media, however. Some rely on informal personal channels. In such instances, physical proximity determines which innovations will be repeatedly observed and thoroughly learned.

People cannot be much influenced by observed events if they do not remember them. A second subfunction governing observational learning concerns cognitive *representational processes*. Retention involves an active process of transforming and restructuring information about modeled events into rules and conceptions for generating new patterns of behavior. Preconceptions and emotional states can bias how observed information is transformed into memory codes. Similarly, recall involves a process of reconstruction of past experiences rather than simply retrieval of registered past events.

In the third subfunction in observational learning—the *production processes*—symbolic conceptions are transformed into appropriate courses of action. This is achieved through a conception matching process in which conceptions guide the construction of behavior patterns and enactments are modified as necessary to achieve close correspondence between conception and action. The richer the knowledge and repertoire of subskills that people possess, the easier it is to integrate them to produce the new forms of behavior.

Modeling is not simply a process of response mimicry as commonly believed. Modeled judgments and actions may differ in specific content but embody the same underlying principle. For example, a model may deal with moral dilemmas that differ widely in the nature of the activity but apply the same moral standard to them. Modeled activities thus convey principles for generative and innovative behavior. This higher level learning is achieved through abstract modeling. Once observers extract the principles underlying the modeled activities they can generate new behaviors embodying the principles that go beyond what they have seen or heard.

Creativeness rarely springs entirely from individual inventiveness. Indeed, selective modeling is often the mother of invention. People adopt modeled beneficial elements, improve upon them, synthesize them into new forms, and tailor them to their particular circumstances (Bolton, 1993; Gist, 1989; Harris and Evans, 1973).

Modeling affects acquisition and receptivity to innovations in several ways. It instructs people about new ways of thinking and behaving by demonstration or description. Models motivate as well as inform. People are initially reluctant to embark on new undertakings that involve costs and risks until they see the advantages that have been gained by early adopters. Modeled benefits accelerate diffusion by weakening the restraints of the more cautious potential adopters. As acceptance spreads, the new ways gain further social support. Models also display preferences and evaluative reactions, which can alter the observers' values. Changes in evaluative standards affect receptivity to the innovation being modeled. Models not only exemplify and legitimate innovations, they also serve as advocates for them by directly encouraging others to adopt them.

It has been commonly assumed in the theory of mass communication that modeling influences operate through a two-step diffusion process. Influential persons pick up new ideas from the media and pass them on to their followers through personal influence. This dual-link view that diffusion is exclusively a filter-down process is disputed by a large body of evidence concerning modeling influences (Bandura, 1986). Human judgment, values, and styles of behavior can be altered by televised modeling without having to wait for an influential intermediary to adopt and model what has been shown.

There is no single pattern of social diffusion. Social cognitive theory not only posits a multi-pattern diffusion, but specifies how the different functions of modeling operate, in concert with other sources of influence, in the various components of the process of social diffusion. The media can implant ideas for change either directly or through adopters. In some instances the media both teaches new forms of behavior and creates motivators for action by altering people's preferences, perceptions of personal efficacy, and outcome expectations. In other instances, the media teaches, but other adopters provide the motivation to perform what has been learned observationally. In still other instances, the effect of the media may be entirely socially mediated. People who have had no exposure to it can be influenced by adopters who have had the exposure and then, themselves, become the transmitters of the new ways.

Social cognitive theory adopts an agentic perspective to self-development, adaptation, and change (Bandura, 2001, 2006). To be an agent is to intentionally influence one's functioning and life circumstances. In this view, people are self-organizing, proactive, self-regulating, and self-reflecting. They are contributors to their life circumstances; not just products of them. The theorizing and research on human agency has centered almost exclusively on personal agency exercised individually. Social cognitive theory distinguishes among three different modes of human agency: individual, proxy, and collective. In personal agency exercised individually people bring their influence to bear on their own functioning and on environmental events. In many spheres of functioning, people do not have direct control over conditions that affect their lives. They exercise socially-mediated agency. They do so by influencing others who have the resources, knowledge, and means to act on their behalf to secure the outcomes they desire. People do not live in isolation. They have to work together to manage and improve their lives. In the exercise of collective agency, people pool their knowledge, skills, and resources, and act in concert to shape their future. Everyday functioning requires an agentic blend of individual, proxy, and collective efficacy.

With the dawn of the electronic era in this third millennium, people worldwide are becoming increasingly enmeshed in a cyberworld that transcends time, distance, place and national borders. By enabling individuals to transcend their environment, these information technologies are placing a premium on the exercise of personal and collective agency. Individuals can now access an unlimited variety of modeled attitudes, values, beliefs, and styles of behavior in the comfort of their homes. Through Internet postings, blogging, and podcasting, they not only have unrestricted boundless access to modeling in virtually every aspect of life, but they can have a voice in this new media by participating in it.

The Internet provides an avalanche of information in diverse sources of varying quality. It requires a robust sense of efficacy and self-directive capabilities to access, process, and evaluate the glut of information. Individuals who are assured in their efficacy to manage the Internet technology are the ones who take advantage of this expansive environment (Bandura, 2002). Social cognitive theory provides guides for building the personal efficacy and cognitive skills needed to use the Internet productively and creatively (Debowski, Wood, and Bandura, 2001).

Internet technology does more than just expand access to vast bodies of information. It also serves as a convenient vehicle for building social networks for creating shared knowledge through collaborative learning. Through interactive electronic networking, people link together in dispersed locales, exchange information, share new ideas, and work collaboratively on projects (Staples, Hulland, and Higgins, 1998). In the social and political arena, Internet technology gives people an instrument of global reach, free of centralized institutional controls and gatekeepers who reign over the mass media. It provides vast opportunities to participate directly in social and political matters of concern, and a ready vehicle for mobilizing grassroots activity to promote desired changes in social practices and policies. It is being used to connect disparate groups to one another in pursuit of a common cause. By coordinating and mobilizing decentralized, self-organizing groups, participants can meld local networks into widespread collection action. Human agency does not come with a built-in value system, however. The Internet is a double-edged tool. Internet freelancers can also use this unfiltered and unfettered forum to propagate hate and to mobilize support for detrimental social purposes.

Adoption determinants

The acquisition of knowledge and skills regarding innovations is necessary, but not sufficient for their adoption in practice. The second major component in the triadic model specifies the factors that determine whether people will adopt in practice what they have learned. Unless people believe that they have the efficacy to do what is needed to gain the benefits of a given innovation they have little incentive to adopt it or to stick with it in the face of difficulties. Perceived self-efficacy is, therefore, one key factor governing adoption of innovations.

Innovations that are difficult to understand and use are given less consideration than simpler ones (Rogers, 1995; Tornatzky and Klein, 1982). Perceived difficulty is a relational attribute rather than solely an inherent one. Personal efficacy largely determines how complex things look. Activities that exceed perceived capabilities appear complex, whereas those that fall within the bounds of perceived capabilities are viewed as doable.

The influential role of people's beliefs in their personal efficacy is verified across diverse types of innovations. For example in community-wide campaigns designed to promote health, both people's pre-existing beliefs in their self-regulatory efficacy and the efficacy beliefs instilled by the media campaigns increase adoption and diffusion of healthful habits (Maibach, Flora, and Nass, 1991; Rimal, 2000; Slater, 1989). The perceived efficacy of organizational decision makers influences their receptivity to new technologies and practices (Jorde-Bloom and Ford, 1988). The perceived efficacy of employees likewise affects how readily they embrace those that are organizationally instituted (Hill, Smith, and Mann, 1987; McDonald and Siegall, 1992). Efficacy-fostered adoption of new technologies, in turn, alters the organizational network structure and confers influential status on early adopters within an organization over time (Burkhardt and Brass, 1990).

Innovations require innovators. Turning visions into realities requires heavy investment of time, effort, and resources in ventures strewn with many hardships, unmerciful impediments, and uncertainties. A resilient sense of efficacy provides the necessary staying power in the tortuous pursuit of innovations. Indeed, perceived self-efficacy predicts entrepreneurship and which patent inventors are likely to start new business ventures (Chen, Greene, and Crick, 1998; Markman and Baron, 1999).

Perceived self-efficacy influences the adoption of new technologies for household and leisure products as it does for innovations in the workplace. Efficacy beliefs operate at both pre-purchase and post-purchase phases. People shy away from products they believe exceed their efficacy to use them (Stern and Kipnis, 1993). As most readers would testify, the opaque product operational manuals further weaken perceived efficacy to use the products (Celuch, Lust, and Showers, 1995).

Adoptive behavior is also highly susceptible to incentive influences. In social cognitive theory (Bandura, 1986) the incentive motivators take three forms—material, social, and self-evaluative. Some of the motivating incentives derive from the inherent utility of the adoptive behavior. The greater the tangible benefits provided by an innovation, the higher the incentive to adopt it (Downs and Mohr, 1979; Ostlund, 1974; Rogers and Shoemaker, 1971). But benefits cannot be experienced until the new practices are tried. Promoters, therefore, strive to get people to adopt new practices by altering their preferences and beliefs about likely outcomes, mainly by enlisting vicarious incentives. Advocates of new ideas and technologies create outcome expectations that the innovations offer better solutions than the established ways. Modeled benefits increase adoptive decisions. Modeling influences can, of course, impede as well as promote the diffusion process (Midgley, 1976). Modeled negative reactions to a particular innovation, as a result of having had disappointing experiences with it, dissuade others from trying it. Even modeled indifference to an innovation in the absence of any experiences with it, will dampen the interests of others.

Many innovations serve as a means of gaining social recognition and status. Indeed, status incentives are often the main motivators for adopting new styles and tastes. In many instances, the innovative styles do not provide better natural benefits or, if anything, they are the more costly ones. Status is thus gained at a price. People who strive to distinguish themselves from the common and the ordinary adopt new styles in clothing, grooming, recreational activities, and forms of conduct, thereby achieving distinctive social standing. As the popularity of the new behavior grows, it loses its status-conferring value until eventually it, too, becomes commonplace. It is then discarded for a new form.

Adoptive behavior is also partly governed by self-evaluative reactions to one's own behavior. People adopt what they value, but resist innovations that violate their social and moral standards or that conflict with their self-conception. The more compatible an innovation is with prevailing social norms and value systems, the greater its adoptability (Rogers and Shoemaker, 1971). However, self-evaluative sanctions do not operate in isolation from the pressures of social influence. People are often led to behave in otherwise personally devalued ways by strategies that circumvent negative self-reactions. This is done by changing appearances and meanings of new practices to make them look compatible with people's values (Bandura, 1986).

The amenability of an innovation to brief trial is another relevant characteristic that can affect the ease of adoption. Innovations that can be tried on a limited basis are more readily adoptable than those that have to be tried on a large scale with substantial effort and costs. The more weight given to potential risks and the costs of getting rid of new practices should they fail to live up to expectations, the weaker is the incentive to innovate. And finally, people will not adopt innovations even though they are favorably disposed toward them if they lack the money, the skills, or the accessory resources that may be needed. The more resources innovations require, the lower is their adoptability.

Analysis of the determinants and mechanisms of social diffusion should not becloud the fact that not all innovations are useful, nor is resistance to them necessarily dysfunctional (Zaltman and Wallendorf, 1979). In the continuous flow of innovations, the number of disadvantageous ones far exceeds those with truly beneficial possibilities. Both personal and societal well-being are ably served by initial wariness to new practices promoted by unsubstantiated or exaggerated claims. The designations "venturesome" for early adopters and "laggards" for later adopters are fitting in the case of innovations that hold promise. However, when people are mesmerized by alluring appeals into trying innovations of questionable value, the more suitable designation is gullibility for early adopters and astuteness for resisters. Rogers (1995) has criticized the prevalent tendency to conceptualize the diffusion process from the perspective of the promoters. This tends to bias the search for explanations of nonadoptive behavior in negative attributes of non-adopters.

Social networks and flow of diffusion

The third major component that affects the diffusion process concerns the structure and function of social networks. People are enmeshed in networks of relationships that include occupational colleagues, organizational members, kinships, and friendships, just to mention a few. They are linked not only directly by personal relationships, but because acquaintanceships overlap different network clusters, many people become linked to each other indirectly by interconnected ties. Social structures comprise clustered networks of people with various ties among them, as well as persons who provide connections to other clusters through joint membership or a liaison role. Clusters vary in their internal structure, ranging from loosely knit ones to those that are densely interconnected. Networks also differ in the number and pattern of structural linkages between clusters. They may have many common ties or function with a high degree of separateness. In addition to their degree of interconnectedness, people vary in the positions and status they occupy in particular social networks which can affect their impact on what spreads through their network. One is more apt to learn about new ideas and practices from brief contacts with causal acquaintances than from intensive contact in the same circle of close associates. This path of influence creates the seemingly paradoxical effect that innovations are extensively diffused to cohesive groups through weak social ties (Granovetter, 1983).

Information regarding new ideas and practices is often conveyed through multilinked relationships (Rogers and Kincaid, 1981). Traditionally, the communication process has been conceptualized as one of unidirectional persuasion flowing from a source to a recipient. Rogers emphasized the mutuality of influence in interpersonal communication. People share information, give meaning by mutual feedback to the information they exchange, gain understanding of each other's views, and influence each other. These transactional events embody the acquisitional and adoptive influences of the triadic model. Specifying the channels of influence through which innovations are dispersed provides greater understanding of the diffusion process than simply plotting the rate of adoptions over time disembodied from psychosocial influences.

There is no single social network in a community that serves all purposes. Different innovations engage different networks. For example, birth control practices and agricultural innovations diffuse through quite different networks within the same community (Marshall, 1971). To complicate matters further, the social networks that come into play in initial phases of diffusion may differ from those that spread the innovation in subsequent phases (Coleman, Katz, and Menzel, 1966). Adoption rates are better predicted from the network that subserves a particular innovation than from a more general communication network. This is not to say that there is no generality to the diffusion function of network structures. If a particular social structure subserves varied activities, it can help to spread the adoption of innovations in each of those activities.

People with many social ties are more apt to adopt innovations than those who have few ties to others (Rogers and Kincaid, 1981). Adoption rates increase as more and more people in one's personal network adopt an innovation. The effects of social connectedness on adoptive behavior may be mediated through several processes. Multi-linked relations can foster adoption of innovations because they convey more factual information, they mobilize stronger social influences, or possibly because people with close ties are more receptive to new ideas than those who are socially estranged. Moreover, in social trans-actions, people see their associates adopt innovations as well as talk about them. Multiple modeling increases adoptive behavior (Bandura, 1986; Perry and Bussey, 1979).

If innovations are highly conspicuous, they can be adopted directly without requiring interaction among adopters. Television and Internet technology are being increasingly used to forge large single-link struc-tures, in which many people are linked directly to the media source, but they may have little or no direct relations with each other. For example, television evangelists attract loyal followers who adopt the transmitted precepts as guides for how to behave in situations involv-ing moral, social, and political issues. Although they share a common bond to the media source, most members of a virtual community may never see each other.

Political power structures are similarly being transformed by the creation of new constituencies tied to a single media source, but with little personal interconnectedness. Mass marketing techniques using computer identification and mass mailings, create special-interest constituencies that bypass traditional political organizations in the exercise of political influence. However, with increasing interactivity through blogging and podpostings, Internet technology is intercon-necting people globally in the virtual social networks of the cyber-world. This enables people to exercise control by not only creating their own site in the cyberworld, but having a central voice in it. In the socio-political arena, the existence of a multiplicity of voices in the cyberworld does not necessarily give rise to diversity of influ-ence at the individual level. All too often, people select sites promoting their particular ideologies. Selectivity fuels social polarization.

The evolving information technologies will increasingly serve as a vehicle for building social networks. Online transactions transcend the barriers of time and space (Hiltz and Turoff, 1978; Wellman, 1997). Through interactive electronic networking, people link together in widely dispersed locales, exchange information, share new ideas, and transact any number of pursuits. Virtual networking provides a flexible means for creating diffusion structures to serve given purposes, expanding their membership, extending them geographically, and disbanding them when they have outlived their usefulness.

As previously noted, structural interconnectedness provides potential diffusion paths, but psychosocial factors largely determine the fate of what diffuses through those paths. In other words, it is the transactions that occur within social relationships rather than the ties, themselves, that explain adoptive behavior. The course of diffusion is best understood by considering the interactions among psychosocial determinants of adoptive behavior, the properties of innovations that facilitate or impede adoption, and the network structures that provide the social pathways of influence. Sociostructural and psychological determinants of adoptive behavior should, therefore, be treated as complementary factors in an integrated comprehensive theory of social diffusion, rather than be cast as rival theories of diffusion.

Productive partnership in theoretical integration in global applications

The conceptual integration of social cognitive theory and social diffusion theory is not just an academic endeavor. It also involves an implementational partnership. I had the honor and pleasure of interacting with Ev in connection with the extraordinary applications of enabling media to alleviate some of the most urgent global problems. These include soaring population growth, especially in less developed nations; pernicious gender inequity in which women are subjugated, marginalized and denied aspirations and their liberty and dignity; and the spreading AIDS epidemic. Some societies present unique problems that require special social themes tailored to their cultural practices. They include female genital mutilation that subjects about 130 million women in Africa to this brutal procedure; child trafficking that sells children from large impoverished families for slave labor under inhumane conditions; and the detrimental effects of dowry systems.

Long running serial dramas serve as the vehicle to alleviate such problems and to improve the quality of people's lives. They inform, enable, motivate, and guide viewers towards personal and social changes that improve their life conditions. These dramatic productions are not just fanciful stories. They portray people's everyday lives. They help viewers see a better life and provide the strategies and incentives that enable them to take the steps to realize it. The storylines model family planning, women's equity, spouse abuse, environmental conservation, AIDS prevention and a variety of life skills.

To change deeply held beliefs and social practices requires strong emotional bonding to enabling models who provide a vision of a better future. Hundreds of episodes allow people time to form emotional bonds to the characters. They become emotionally engaged in the evolving lives of the models and identify with their aspirations, perseverance, and the steps they take that advance them toward the future they want to realize.

The productive partnership in this global endeavor is grounded in the essential components of a psychosocial model for affecting society-wide changes. The first component is a *theoretical model* that specifies the determinants of psychosocial change and the mechanisms through which they produce their effects. This knowledge provides the guiding principles. The second component is a *translational and implementational model* that converts theoretical principles into an innovative operational model by specifying the content, strategies of change, and their mode of implementation. The third component is a *social diffusion model* on how to promote adoption of psychosocial programs in diverse cultural milieus. It does so by making functional adaptations of the programs to different sociostructural circumstances, providing enabling guidance, and enlisting the necessary resources to achieve success.

It is of limited value to motivate people to change if they are not provided with appropriate resources and environmental supports to realize those changes. Enlisting and creating environmental supports is an additional and especially helpful feature for promoting personal and social change (Bandura, 2004). To foster large-scale changes, the dramatic productions are designed to operate through two pathways. In the direct pathway, the serials promote changes by informing, enabling, motivating, and guiding viewers. In the socially-mediated pathway, media influences are used to connect viewers to social networks and community settings. These places provide continued personalized guidance, as well as natural incentives and social supports for desired changes. For example, serial dramas aimed at stemming a nation's burgeoning population growth linked viewers to family planning services. A serial aimed at promoting national literacy linked viewers to reading service centers. Programs designed to raise the status of women linked viewers to women's support groups. At a more informal level, media influences lead viewers to discuss and negotiate important matters with others. In the informal mode of social mediation, the media set in motion transactional experiences that further shape the course of change. Socially-mediated influences can have stronger impacts than direct media influence.

We often cite examples in the natural and biological sciences where knowledge pursued for its own sake has unforeseen human benefits. The knowledge gained regarding social modeling in the early Bobo Doll experiments[2] contributed through interdisciplinary partnership unimagined global applications designed to enable people to change their lives for the better. One morning in the mid-1970s, I received a call from Miguel Sabido, a creative dramatist at Televisia in Mexico City, explaining that he had created a generic media model to promote social change based on the modeling principles he extracted from the Bobo Doll research (Bandura, Ross, and Ross, 1961; 1963). He visited Stanford with video clips from a serial drama he had created to inform, motivate and guide the general public to enroll in a national self-study literacy program. It was a masterful translation of theory into practice.

---

[2] In the Bobo Doll experiment, young children watched a film of an adult role model punching and kicking the Bobo doll. When hit, the Bobo doll falls backward and immediately springs upright as if offering a counter punch. Then children were let into a playroom with several attractive toys including a Bobo doll. Interestingly, children who watched the film imitated the media model's behavior.

Plate 5.2. Miguel Sabido (left) and Al Bandura (right) at the University of Southern California campus in Los Angeles in the early 2000s. Sabido masterfully translated Bandura's social learning and social cognitive theories to produce pro-social soap operas in Mexico, inspiring many other countries to follow suit
Source: Miguel Sabido

Four basic sociocognitive principles serve as guides for constructing the dramatic serials. The first is *contrast modeling*. The episodes include positive models exhibiting beneficial lifestyles, negative models exhibiting detrimental lifestyles, and transitional models changing from detrimental to beneficial styles of behavior at a gradual and believable pace. Contrasting modeling highlights the personal and social effects of different lifestyles. Viewers draw inspiration from seeing others change their lives for the better. The second principle enlists *vicarious motivators*. Unless people see modeled lifestyles as improving their welfare, they have little incentive to adopt them. The benefits of the favorable practices and the costs of the detrimental ones are vividly portrayed. Depicted outcomes provide incentives for change.

A third principle guiding the creation of the dramatic productions concerns the *attentional and emotional engagement* of viewers. There are several elements that serve this purpose. The most powerful one is functional relevance. The dramas mirror the realities of people's everyday lives, the impediments with which they struggle, and model ways by which they can enhance their personal development and improve their life conditions. Personally relevant story lines with functional modeling command attention and high interest. Melodramatic embellishments of engrossing plot lines with emotive musical accompaniments give further dramatic intensity to the episodes. Ongoing engagement in the evolving lives of the models provide numerous opportunities to learn from them and to be inspired by them.

The power of storytelling through emotional bonding

Unlike brief exposures to media presentations that typically leave most viewers untouched, extended dramatizations that reflect viewers' life experiences get audience members deeply involved in the lives of mass media models and emotionally attached to them.

In 2003, a formerly illiterate teenager in India's Bihar state who was inspired by Taru, a lead character in a popular radio serial, to pursue her education described the depth and power of emotional bonding: "There are moments when I feel that Taru is directly talking to me, usually at night. She is telling me, 'Usha, you can follow your dreams.' I feel she is like my elder sister ... and giving me encouragement."

In the mid-1980s in India, 400,000 viewers of *Hum Log*, a highly popular television serial, sent letters supporting, advising, or criticizing various models in the drama. In Tanzania, women spotted a negative model from the serial drama at a market and drove him out under a rain of tomatoes and mangoes.

In Brazil, 10,000 people showed up for a virtual filming of a marriage of two of the characters in a serial drama.

In *Ven Conmigo*, a serial drama produced by Miguel Sabido in Mexico to promote enrollment in a national literacy program, a day after a popular actor in an epilogue encouraged viewers to take advantage of it, approximately 25,000 people descended on the distribution center in Mexico City to obtain the primers.

To control the transmission of HIV infection in Ethiopia spread heterosexually by long-distance truckers, audiocassettes from a serial drama on this theme were distributed to truck drivers and commercial sex workers. They waited in long lines to receive each new episode.

The fourth principle addresses the enlistment and creation of *environmental supports* for personal and social changes. Environmental guides and supports are provided to expand and sustain the changes promoted by the media. Epilogues, often presented by culturally celebrated figures, provide contact information to relevant community services and support groups.

We profit little from our successes in the social sciences. This is because we lack effective social diffusion models. Based on Miguel Sabido's notable success in accomplishing society-wide changes in Mexico using televised serial drama, Population Communications International (PCI) in New York served as the social diffusion system (Poindexter, 2004). In close collaborative partnership with the host nation, PCI advises the country's media personnel on how to create engrossing serial dramas, tailors the media productions to fit different cultural circumstances, and provides enabling guidance and the

---

System-level effects

The serial dramas promote changes at the social system level as well as individually (Law and Singhal, 1999). In a radio serial drama, *Taru*, broadcast in India during 2002–2003, with a listenership of about 25 million, a mother challenges restrictive cultural norms for her daughters and enrolls them in a school. *Taru* inspired ardent teenage listeners who had no access to education to become avid readers and raise their academic aspirations. Four teenage girls in Abirpur village of India's Bihar state started a school for a large group of poor children through classes held regularly around the village water well. In the neighboring Kamtaul village, the mother of one of the teenagers also began a school for illiterate women. The teenagers fought against gender and class discrimination and early forced marriages. Their efforts produced changes in community norms. The elders in the community acknowledged the need to alter their social practices to fit the changing times. Parents relaxed restrictive norms for their daughters.

One of the teenagers explained the power of enabling modeling to inspire listeners to work for social change: "When Taru and her mother can fight harsh circumstances, why can't we?" Another teenager describes poetically how her revered model transformed her life: "Before Taru there was darkness. Now there is light."

technical and financial resources needed to achieve success. The Population Media Center (under Bill Ryerson) also serves as the social diffusion system.

Many worldwide applications of this creative format in Africa, Asia, and Latin America are promoting personal and society-wide changes that are bettering people's lives (Bandura, 2004; Singhal and Rogers, 1999; Singhal et al., 2004).

In closing

Ev Rogers was not only an important contributor to these global applications that integrated social cognitive and social diffusion theory; he and his colleagues also conducted stringent evaluations of the diverse personal and social changes fostered by this approach (Rogers et al., 1999; Vaughan et al., 2000; Vaughan and Rogers, 2005). Ev took advantage of the unique experimental opportunity provided by Tanzania because it contains regions with separate broadcast transmitters. Using experimental and control regions with a reversal design and multiple controls for other possible determinants, Ev verified the substantial impact of the serialized dramatizations on increased use of family planning services, adoption of contraceptive methods, and condom use to curtail the spread of the AIDS virus (Rogers et al., 1999). To successfully implement a reversal of experimental and control conditions across national regions was no small feat.

Ev Rogers left behind a wonderfully rich legacy of scholarship that will have a lasting impact. We give thanks by our remembrance of his inspiration and the creativeness and wisdom he brought to the field of social change.

References

Bandura, A. 1986. *Social Foundations of Thought and Action: A Social Cognitive Theory*. Englewood Cliffs, NJ: Prentice-Hall.

———. 2001. Social Cognitive Theory: An Agentic Perspective. *Annual Review of Psychology* 52: 1–26.

———. 2002. Growing Primacy of Human Agency in Adaptation and Change in the Electronic Era. *European Psychologist* 7: 2–16.

Bandura, A. 2004. Social Cognitive Theory for Personal and Social Change by Enabling Media. In A. Singhal, M. J. Cody, E. M. Rogers, and M. Sabido (eds), *Entertainment-Education and Social Change: History, Research, and Practice*, pp. 75–96. Mahwah, NJ: Lawrence Erlbaum.

———. 2006. Toward a Psychology of Human Agency. *Perspectives on Psychological Science* 1: 164–80.

Bandura, A., D. Ross, and S. A. Ross. 1961. Transmission of Aggression through Imitation of Aggressive Models. *Journal of Abnormal and Social Psychology* 63: 575–82.

———. 1963. Imitation of Film-mediated Aggressive Models. *Journal of Abnormal and Social Psychology* 66: 3–11.

Bolton, M. K. 1993. Imitation versus Innovation: Lessons to be Learned from the Japanese. *Organizational Dynamics* 21 (3): 30–45.

Braithwaite, J. 1994. A Sociology of Modeling and the Politics of Empowerment. *British Journal of Sociology* 45: 445–79.

Burkhardt, M. E. and D. J. Brass. 1990. Changing Patterns or Patterns of Change: The Effects of a Change in Technology on Social Network Structure and Power. *Administrative Science Quarterly* 35: 104–27.

Celuch, K. G., J. A. Lust, and L. S. Showers. 1995. An Investigation of the Relationship between Self-efficacy and the Communication Effectiveness of Product Manual Formats. *Journal of Business and Psychology* 9: 241–52.

Chen, C. C., P. G. Greene, and A. Crick. 1998. Does Entrepreneurial Self-efficacy Distinguish Entrepreneurs from Managers? *Journal of Business Venturing* 13: 295–316.

Coleman, J. S., E. Katz, and H. Menzel. 1966. *Medical Innovation: A Diffusion Study*. New York: Bobbs-Merrill.

Downs, G. W., Jr. and L. B. Mohr. 1979. Toward a Theory of Innovation. *Administration and Society* 10: 379–408.

Debowski, S., R. E. Wood, and A. Bandura. 2001. Impact of Guided Exploration and Enactive Exploration on Self-regulatory Mechanisms and Information Acquisition through Electronic Search. *Journal of Applied Psychology* 86: 1129–41.

Fischer, D. H. 1994. *Paul Revere's Ride*. Oxford: Oxford University Press.

Gist, M. E. 1989. The Influence of Training Method on Self-efficacy and Idea Generation among Managers. *Personnel Psychology* 42: 787–805.

Granovetter, M. 1983. The Strength of Weak Ties—A Network Theory Revisited. In R. Collins (ed.), *Sociological Theory 1983*, pp. 201–33. San Francisco, CA: Jossey-Bass.

Harris, M. B. and R. C. Evans. 1973. Models and Creativity. *Psychological Reports* 33: 763–69.

Hill, T., N. D. Smith, and M. F. Mann. 1987. Role of Efficacy Expectations in Predicting the Decision to Use Advanced Technologies: The Case of Computers. *Journal of Applied Psychology* 72: 307–13.

Hiltz, S. R. and M. Turoff. 1978. *The Network Nation: Human Communication via Computer*. Reading, MA: Addison-Wesley.

Jorde-Bloom, P. and M. Ford. 1988. Factors Influencing Early Childhood Administrators' Decisions Regarding the Adoption of Computer Technology. *Journal of Educational Computing Research* 4: 31–47.

Law, S. and A. Singhal. 1999. Efficacy in Letter-writing to an Entertainment-education Radio Serial. *Gazette* 61: 355–72.

Maibach, E. W., J. Flora, and C. Nass. 1991. Changes in Self-efficacy and Health Behavior in Response to a Minimal Contact Community Health Campaign. *Health Communication* 3: 1–15.

Markman, G. D. and R. A. Baron. 1999. Cognitive Mechanisms: Potential Differences between Entrepreneurs and Non-entrepreneurs. Paper presented at the Babson College/Kauffman Foundation Entrepreneurship Conference, May.

Marshall, J. F. 1971. Topics and Networks in Intravillage Communiction. In S. Polgar (ed.), *Culture and Population: A Collection of Current Studies*, pp. 160–66. Cambridge, MA: Schenkman Publishing Company.

McDonald, T. and M. Siegall. 1992. The Effects of Technological Self-efficacy and Job Focus on Job Performance, Attitudes, and Withdrawal Behaviors. *The Journal of Psychology* 126: 465–75.

Midgley, D. F. 1976. A Simple Mathematical Theory of Innovative Behavior. *Journal of Consumer Research* 3: 31–41.

Onishi, N. 2000. Popular Uprising Ends Junta's Rule Over Ivory Coast. *The New York Times* October 26: A1.

Ostlund, L. E. 1974. Perceived Innovation Attributes as Predictors of Innovativeness. *Journal of Consumer Research* 1: 23–29.

Perry, D. G. and K. Bussey. 1979. The Social Learning Theory of Sex Differences: Imitation is Alive and Well. *Journal of Personality and Social Psychology* 37: 1699–712.

Poindexter, D. O. 2004. A History of Entertainment-Education, 1958–2000: The Origins of Entertainment-Education. In A. Singhal, M. J. Cody, E. M. Rogers, and M. Sabido (eds), *Entertainment-Education and Social Change: History, Research, and Practice*. Mahwah, NJ: Lawrence Erlbaum Associates.

Rimal, R. N. 2000. Closing the Knowledge–Behavior Gap in Health Promotion: The Mediating Role of Self-Efficacy. *Health Communication* 12: 219–37.

Rogers, E. M. 1995. *Diffusion of Innovations* (4th ed.). New York: Free Press.

Rogers, E. M. and D. L. Kincaid. 1981. *Communication Networks: Toward a New Paradigm for Research*. New York: Free Press.

Rogers, E. M. and F. Shoemaker. 1971. *Communication of Innovations: A Cross-cultural Approach* (2nd ed.). New York: Free Press.

Rogers, E. M., P. W. Vaughan, R. M. A. Swalehe, N. Rao, P. J. Svenkerud, and S. Sood. 1999. Effects of an Entertainment-Education Radio Soap Opera on Family Planning Behavior in Tanzania. *Studies in Family Planning* 30: 192–211.

Singhal, A. and E. M. Rogers. 1999. *Entertainment-Education: A Communication Strategy for Social Change*. Mahwah, NJ: Lawrence Erlbaum.

Singhal, A., M. J. Cody, E. M. Rogers, and M. Sabido (eds). 2004. *Entertainment-Education and Social Change: History, Research, and Practice*. Mahwah, NJ: Lawrence Erlbaum.

Slater, M. D. 1989. Social Influences and Cognitive Control as Predictors of Self-Efficacy and Eating Behavior. *Cognitive Therapy and Research* 13: 231–45.

Staples, D. S., Hulland, J. S., and C. A. Higgins. 1998. A Self-Efficacy Theory Explanation for the Management of Remote Workers in Virtual Organizations. *Journal of Computer-Mediated Communication* (online) 3 (4): http://jcmc.indiana.edu/vol3/issue4/staples.html.

Stern, S. E. and D. Kipnis. 1993. Technology in Everyday Life and Perceptions of Competence. *Journal of Applied Social Psychology* 23: 1892–902.

Tornatzky, L. G. and K. J. Klein. 1982. Innovation Characteristics and Innovation Adoption–Implementation: A Meta-analysis of Findings. *IEEE Transactions of Engineering and Management* EM-29: 28–45.

Vaughan, P. W. and E. M. Rogers. 2005. The Role of Two Entertainment-Education Radio Dramas in Family Planning in Tanzania during the 1990s. Unpublished manuscript.

Vaughan, P. W., E. M. Rogers, A. Singhal, and R. M. Swalehe. 2000. Entertainment-Education and HIV/AIDS Prevention: A Field Experiment in Tanzania. *Journal of Health Communication* 5: 81–100.

Wellman, B. 1997. An Electronic Group is Virtually a Social Network. In S. Kielser (ed.), *Culture of the Internet*, pp. 179–205. Mahwah, NJ: Lawrence Erlbaum.

Zaltman, G. and M. Wallendorf. 1979. *Consumer Behavior: Basic Findings and Management Implications*. New York: Wiley.

6

Social Marketing and the Broadening of Marketing Movement

PHILIP KOTLER

Along with a crack team of young scholars, Ev and I studied the extent to which social marketing and diffusion concepts were actually used by community-based health improvement practitioners on the streets of San Francisco. We paired social marketing and diffusion because of their obvious similarities. Once one tried to use diffusion concepts in the way that a marketing scientist uses theory-based concepts to affect rates of product penetration, marketing and diffusion looked a lot alike. That study was subsequently replicated in Thailand by Peer Jacob Svenkerud and Arvind Singhal. The conceptual basis for our understanding of social marketing was Phil Kotler's work. Phil wrote with the same easy, confident authority about social marketing as Ev did about diffusion.

JIM DEARING

Some decades ago, in the remote jungles of New Guinea, British physician Tim Black saved the life of a dying baby by performing a difficult operation under the village tree. When he proudly presented the still-sedated baby to the mother, who already had four young children to feed, he saw disappointment in her eyes. She had wished that the sick baby not live through the operation. Shocked and confused, Black came to an important realization: "Preventing a birth could be as important as saving a life" (Black, quoted in Harvey, 1999: 19). Believing that "every child should be wanted," Black co-founded (with Phil Harvey) Population Services International, a global organization to promote social marketing of contraceptives. While Black and Harvey (and others) were busy launching field-based social marketing programs in developing countries, Phil Kotler and his colleagues led the scholarship in systematizing and synthesizing these experiences.

ARVIND SINGHAL

EVERETT ROGERS HAD A PROFOUND INFLUENCE ON MY MARKETING thinking and writing. I wrote the first edition of *Marketing Management* in 1967. In preparing a first-time chapter on New-Product Decisions, I searched for useful writings on the subject. I was aware of the high rate of new product failure, especially for consumer product launches. I felt that several mistakes were made by management, one of which was a failure to understand the consumer adoption process.

A colleague told me that the best source of information on the consumer adoption process was to be found in a book by Everett M. Rogers called *Diffusion of Innovations*. Everett wrote the book in 1962 and it was already an established classic. I read the book from cover to cover and it was a revelation. He introduced so many propositions about the stages of the consumer adoption process, the variation among people in their penchant for trying new products, the role of personal influence and opinion leaders, the categorization of five adopter stages, the influence of product characteristics on the rate of adoption, and many other concepts. Just to summarize Everett's concepts in my 1967 book took up five printed pages (from 342 to 347). I acknowledged the source with the following footnote (46):

> The consumer adoption process represents a specialized application of principles of buying stages and learning described in Chapter 4 (Buyer Behavior). I am indebted to Everett M. Rogers' *Diffusion of Innovations* (New York: Free Press of Glencoe, Inc., 1962) for the account that follows.

This same section describing Everett's ideas, with some updates, remained in every edition of my book through the present 12th edition published in 2005.

I did not meet Everett until some years later at a seminar. He approached me and said that he admired my work. I told him that it was I who admired his work and that his work shaped much of my thinking.

I saw Everett on a few other occasions and he was always the gentlemen and the enthusiast about our meetings. I also discovered his new work on the use of theatre to help market a social cause. My great regret is that I didn't meet Everett on enough occasions to become close friends.

Everett was one of two influences that helped expand my view of marketing applications. My colleague, Professor Sidney Levy, opened my eyes to the broader applications of marketing theory and the diffusion of innovation. Here I would like to give an account of the history of the movement known as the broadening of marketing.

The broadening movement in marketing emerges

The broadening movement was an effort to free the marketing paradigm from the narrow confines of commercial marketing and to show its application to a far larger number of contexts where exchange and relationship activities take place.

Until 1970, marketing language and theory focused on explaining how goods and services are priced, promoted and distributed in commercial markets by for-profit firms. Transactions and payment were considered central to the definition of markets and marketing. Other domains of exchange activity, such as the efforts of museums, performing arts groups, churches, social agencies, city governments, social action groups, and celebrities to attract and serve visitors, members, donors, clients, fans and others were outside the purview of marketing and its concepts. The problems faced by these groups at best were examined by public relations practitioners and press agents.

Some of us began to believe in the late 1960s that these non-commercial organizations faced "marketing-like" problems that could be fruitfully addressed with marketing language and concepts. So in January 1969, Professor Levy and I published "Broadening the Concept of Marketing" (Kotler and Levy, 1969).

We defended this broadening proposal on several grounds:

1. Marketing would help the practitioners in non-commercial sectors become more successful in pursuing their goals.
2. The marketing field would benefit by recognizing new issues and developing new concepts that could be brought back and offer insight into commercial marketing practice.
3. By expanding its territory, marketing would gain more attention and respect for what it can produce.

4. Marketing as a discipline for study would become more attractive to a wider audience of young people who have little interest
   in the commercial for-profit world.

As we advanced these arguments, some marketing scholars felt
distinctly uncomfortable. They felt that the broadening movement
would dilute the substance of marketing. "If marketing is so many
things, then it is nothing." Professor David Luck championed the
opposition (Luck, 1969). He warned that the broadening movement
would damage marketing. Kotler and Levy then issued a rejoinder
titled "New Form of Marketing Myopia: Rejoinder to Professor Luck"
(Kotler and Levy, 1969).

The issue finally came to a head in 1974 when Professor William
Nickels mailed a survey to randomly selected marketing professors
on whether they thought that the concept of marketing should be
expanded to include the marketing of schools, charities, politicians
and other non-business activities. Nickels reported that "More than
90 percent of the responding professors agreed that the marketing
concept should be broadened to include the efforts of nonbusiness
organisations to satisfy society's needs" (see Nickels, 1974:147).

Broadening then led marketers to investigate a number of new
areas, particularly social marketing, educational marketing, performing arts marketing, museum marketing, church marketing, and the
marketing of cities, states, and nations.

Social marketing turns the corner

Of these several areas, I would like to focus the discussion on social
marketing, the area where Everett's work and my own work over-
lapped. Everett became deeply interested in my work on social
marketing. He liked the framework that we were developing and
referred to it in his efforts to understand how to bring about behavioral
changes that are good for the individual and/or the society.

In July 1971, Gerald Zaltman and I published "Social Marketing:
An Approach to Planned Social Change" (Kotler and Zaltman, 1971).
We chose the term "social marketing" to cover efforts to market social
causes such as "Don't smoke," "Say No to Drugs," "Don't Litter,"
"Eat Healthier Foods and Exercise," and many other causes. We

Plate 6.1
Ev Rogers in Indonesia in front of a simmering volcano in 1971. Ev spent a good part of that year traveling to countries of Asia, Africa, and Latin America, studying innovative family planning programs and social marketing approaches in contraceptive promotion. In Indonesia, for instance, he studied the important role of *dukuns* (midwives) in dispensing reproductive health services. In 1973, he published a book titled *Communication Strategies for Family Planning*
Source: Ev Rogers. Provided to co-editor Singhal in 2000

wanted to show that marketing concepts and principles could be used to influence people to adopt more positive behaviors and discontinue negative behaviors.

After working on several applications of social marketing, I felt ready to write a full book on what I learned about social marketing. My graduate student, Eduardo Roberto and I co-authored *Social Marketing: Strategies for Changing Public Behavior* (1989). Further work and research led to the publication of a second edition in 2002 with Eduardo Roberto and Nancy Lee re-titled *Social Marketing: Improving the Quality of Life*.

During this period we were heartened by the attraction of several capable scholars to the field including Alan Andreasen, Christopher Lovelock, Charles Weinberg, Michael Rothschild, Paul Bloom, and others. We were pleased about the growing recognition of social marketing by the US Agency for International Development, the World Bank, the Center for Disease Control, and other domestic and international organizations. Social marketing centers had also been established at the University of South Florida in Tampa,

Plate 6.2
Ev Rogers (right) and Arvind Singhal (left) with a volunteer worker of the Kenya Network of Women with AIDS in the Kayole slums on the outskirts of Nairobi, Kenya. Ev's work on diffusion of innovations had a close affinity with social marketing practices in the areas of family planning, HIV prevention, and environmental conservation
Source: Personal file of co-editor Singhal

Carleton University in Ottawa, Canada, and the University of Strathclyde in Scotland. Over eighty empirical studies of social marketing programs have appeared in the literature since 1980.

Social marketing differs from other types of marketing in that the objective is not to benefit the marketer but to benefit the target audience and the general society. It should be further noted that social marketing can be carried out by individuals, informal groups, or formal organizations including for-profit and not-for-profit organizations. Its goal is not to market a product or service *per se* but to influence a social behavior that usually carries high public consensus. Products and services can be involved, of course, as is the case of influencing individuals to use condoms and vasectomies in contraceptive social marketing programs.

Distinctions can be made among different types of social marketing programs based on whether there is low or high involvement, one time or continuing changes, or whether they involve individual or groups. Examples are shown in the following box:

One-time behavior	Low involvement	High involvement
Individual	Donating money to a charity Registering to vote Signing up for Medicaid	Donating blood
Group	Voting for a change in a state constitution	Voting out restrictive membership rules in a club
Continuing behavior		
Individual	Not smoking in elevators	Stopping smoking or drug use Practicing family planning
Group	Not driving over 55 mph Driving on the correct side of the road	Supporting the concept of an all-volunteer army

Social marketing programs have proven extremely effective in several countries. Consider the following:

- In Honduras, after two years of broadcasting specific messages, 60 percent of rural women interviewed had used the government's new oral rehydration salts and some 35 percent of all cases of infant diarrhea had been treated with oral therapy.
- In Columbia some 800,000 children were immunized during a single three-day massive campaign.
- In Indonesia the Nutrition Communication and Behavior Change Project showed that by 24 months of age, 40 percent of the project infants were better nourished than infants in the comparison group.
- In Baltimore, techniques of social marketing developed by the Agency for International Development in Mali, Egypt, and Bangladesh were being tested for their application to

Plate 6.3
Ev Rogers (right) and his wife Corinne with Mechai Viravaidya (left), the architect of Thailand's family planning and HIV/AIDS programs. Ev greatly admired Mechai's acumen for creatively marketing social causes. This photo was taken in Bangkok in 2001
Source: Ev Rogers. Provided to co-editor Singhal in 2002

domestic problems of illiteracy, immunization, and population control.

Social marketing projects similar to these had been carried out by Everett Rogers and his associates (see Chapter 9).

In closing

Everett was especially interested in developing new techniques to further social change, including the use of theatrical performances to dramatize social problems and social solutions. Everett's work on the intricacies of the adoption processes of new products and ideas remains a major cornerstone of our work and those of social marketers around the world.

References

Harvey, P. D. 1999. *Let Every Child be Wanted: How Social Marketing is Revolutionizing Contraceptive Use Around the World*. Boston, MA: Auburn House.

Kotler, Philip. 1967. *Marketing Management: Analysis, Planning, Implementation and Control*. Englewood Cliffs, NJ: Prentice-Hall.

Kotler, Philip and Sidney J. Levy. 1969. New Form of Marketing Myopia: Rejoinder to Professor Luck. *Journal of Marketing* 33 (July): 55–57.

Kotler, Philip and Eduardo Roberto. 1989. *Social Marketing: Strategies for Changing Public Behavior*. New York: Free Press.

Kotler, Philip, Eduardo Roberto, and Nancy Lee. 2002. *Social Marketing: Improving the Quality of Life*. Thousand Oaks, CA: Sage Publications.

Kotler, Philip and Gerald Zaltman. 1971. Social Marketing: An Approach to Planned Social Change. *Journal of Marketing* 35 (3): 3–12.

Luck, David J. 1969. Broadening the Concept of Marketing—Too Far. *Journal of Marketing* 33 (July): 53–55.

Nickels, W. G. 1974. Conceptual Conflicts in Marketing. *Journal of Economics and Business* 27 (Winter): 140–43.

7

Communication and Social Change in Developing Countries

SRINIVAS MELKOTE

I first met Srinivas in 1989. His university department had a spot opening for a visiting faculty member. He had called Ev, who had called me. I had just returned from a year of dissertation field research and writing in Asia. I flew to Bowling Green and met the faculty and saw the obvious advantages of being able to work with Srinivas on communication and development issues. When a star scholar like Ev not only publishes prolifically but also teaches and trains a "generation" of students, the network created provides many opportunities to its members.

JIM DEARING

I first met Srinivas in 1984 during his job-talk at Bowling Green State University, where I was an MA student in the Radio-TV-Film Program. During his 45 minute presentation, which centered on his dissertation topic— an investigation of the diffusion of the World Bank's Training and Visit (T&V) extension program in India, Srinivas quoted Rogers some 53 times. My notes from Srinivas' presentation were brief: "Rogers said this about diffusion, Rogers said that about diffusion, Rogers should not have said this about diffusion ... Rogers blah blah blah blah." I ended my notes with the question: "Who the hell is Rogers?" Some six months later, I was filling the Stanford doctoral application with the hope to study with Rogers. Thank you, Srinivas for the introduction.

ARVIND SINGHAL

ON A CHILLY NOVEMBER MORNING IN 1986, I WAS PRESENTING A PAPER on the weaknesses of diffusion of innovations (DOI) research to a roomful of delegates at the Speech Communication Association's annual conference in Chicago. I had recently written and defended a doctoral dissertation critiquing the DOI research and practice, and in my presentation I was delivering an aggressive critique of Ev Rogers' work. Half way through my tirade, I noticed Ev Rogers sitting a few rows down listening and nodding his head (as if in agreement). Taken aback by his presence, I managed to conclude my presentation in a more diplomatic tone. After the session, Ev walked up to me and struck a very pleasant conversation. Making no mention of my presentation, he inquired about me, Bowling Green (where I was teaching), and Joe Ascroft (my graduate advisor and former student of Ev at Michigan

---

My intellectual journey with Ev

Ev Rogers played a big part in my intellectual development as a critical scholar. As an undergraduate student of communication in the early 1970s, I was introduced to the writings of Rogers (1962), Rogers and Svenning (1969), Rogers and Shoemaker (1971). These readings helped develop in me a strong interest in the field of development communication, motivating me to enroll in graduate school and hone my knowledge of communication and development theory as well as skills in empirical research methods. Both in my MA and M.Phil (Master of Philosophy) programs in India, I used Rogers' books and writings as my guide to theory, methodology, and practice. Family planning studies were very popular in India at that time and I did a KAP survey for my M.Phil thesis using Rogers' book, *Communication Strategies for Family Planning* (1973), as my guide. In 1980, I began graduate studies at the University of Iowa, and wrote a thesis that critically evaluated the contribution of diffusion of innovations research to development communication theory. All along, I have been struck by Ev's phenomenal contribution to this field.

In 1983, I met Ev for the first time at the ICA convention in Dallas. Since then the relationship turned to one of active mentoring by Ev. In the 1980s, he encouraged me to write a 'text book' in communication and development to pull together the myriad strains of work in development and communication. The book (Melkote, 1991) was published with a foreword by Ev. Our lives crisscrossed in many other interesting ways. My academic advisor at Iowa (Joe Ascroft) was Ev's former student at Michigan State University while my first graduate student at Bowling Green (Arvind Singhal) ended up as Ev's doctoral student at USC (Plate 7.1).

Plate 7.1
Ev, Arvind, and Srinivas at AEJMC's 2000 convention in Phoenix, Arizona, after a
session in honor of Ev Rogers' contributions to international communication
Source: Personal files of the author

State University). This is the quintessential image of Ev that I have
since carried in my head: A courteous, friendly, affectionate, and supportive mentor.

Writing this festschrift reinforces Ev Rogers' enormous influence
on my intellectual journey, beginning with my undergraduate days
in India. In this chapter, I reflect on this journey, reviewing the major
milestones in the field of communication and development, and especially Ev's seminal contribution in this area.

Organized development assistance and the dominant paradigm of development

The genesis of the field of communication and development one may
argue lies in the organized development assistance programs following
World War II (WWII). Political and economic leaders from Western
Europe and the United States met in Bretton Woods, New Hampshire

in 1944 to assess Europe's need for reconstruction following the devastation of WWII. Multilateral behemoths were created and vested with crucial functions. The World Bank would provide credit to encourage development activities, the International Monetary Fund would regulate global monetary and exchange rate policies, and the General Agreement on Tariffs and Trade (GATT) would liberalize international trade. For the World Bank, the immediate task at hand was to facilitate capital transfers to rebuild Europe. Thus, consistent with the global climate at that time, the attention of the multilateral agencies and the US was consumed by rehabilitation work in war-ravaged Europe. The US launched the Marshall Plan, the first and largest government-sponsored foreign assistance program.

The success of the Marshall Plan in the late 1940s and 1950s, inspired similar efforts to develop countries in the Third World, many of whom recently gained political independence from their colonial masters. Concern for the plight of the poor people in the developing countries motivated US President Truman to propose, in 1949, the Point Four program (Daniels, 1951), a Third World version of the Marshall Plan.

A dominant paradigm guided development theorizing and influenced development communication theory and practice. Rogers (1976a: 121) noted that, "this concept of development grew out of certain historical events, such as the Industrial Revolution in Europe and the United States, the colonial experience in Latin America, Africa, and Asia; the quantitative empiricism of North American social science, and capitalistic economic/political philosophy." Rogers (1976b) summarized the main elements of this dominant development thinking:

1. Economic growth through industrialization and accompanying urbanization was key to development. The assumption was that development performance could be measured quantitatively in economic terms.
2. The scientific method was dominated by Western quantitative empirical research traditions. Technology was to be capital-intensive and labor-extensive, imported predominantly from the West.
3. To guide and speed up the process of development, planning was centralized and controlled by economists and bankers.

4. Underdevelopment occurred due to problems within developing nations rather than in their external relationships with other countries.

Developing countries were encouraged to invest in a program of industrialization such as big hydroelectric projects, steel industries, and manufacturing units, imitating the developed countries of North America and Western Europe. Development performance was measured by quantitative indicators such as gross national product (GNP) and per capita income. These indicators were considered objective and straightforward to measure, especially when compared with alternative concepts such as freedom, justice, and human rights. They were also consistent with the quantitative and empirical bias of North American social sciences (Nordenstreng, 1968; Rogers 1976b).

The 1960s, named as the First Development Decade by the United Nations, was a period of great optimism. Goals for economic growth were established in the newly-independent developing countries that were consistent with the goals of UN agencies, especially of the World Bank. The emphasis was on technological transfer from the North to the South. People in the Third World needed to discard their traditional ways and willingly adopt the technological innovations that brought such extraordinary progress to the countries of the North. This provided a niche for education and communication/media activities in the development process; they were saddled with the task of upgrading human skills and knowledge (Schramm, 1964).

Modernization at the micro level

All modernization theories emphasizing social change were not necessarily at the macro level. While social and institutional evolution was considered necessary for modernization, some argued that this could not occur unless individuals changed first (Weiner, 1966). Weiner believed that attitudinal and value changes were prerequisites to creating a modern, socio-economic political system. The intellectual source for this school of thought was Weber's (1964) thesis on the *Protestant Ethic* and the general trend in American sociology on value-normative complexes. These scholars posited that modernization of the developing countries was dependent on changing the character of individuals living there to resemble more closely the attitudinal and value characteristics of people in Western Europe and North America (Hagen, 1962; Inkeles, 1966; Lerner, 1958; McCleland, 1966). Ev Rogers' 1969 book (with Lynne Svenning), *Modernization among Peasants*, studied peasants and subsistence farmers in India, Nigeria, and Colombia, as they constituted a majority of the rural population in these and other developing countries. Consistent with the prevailing theories at that time, he assumed that modernization could not occur unless peasants were individually and collectively persuaded to change their traditional ways of life.

Role of media in the modernization paradigm

The role of the mass media in development was accorded a central position in the modernization paradigm. Leading development scholars such as Wilbur Schramm (1964) reiterated that the modernization of industrial and agricultural sectors in developing nations required the mobilization of human resources. Education and mass media, then, were vested with crucial responsibility in the process of mobilization of human resources.

The prominent role of the mass media in modernization was clearly implied in Lerner's (1958) and Lakshmana Rao's (1963) research and other influential studies in the 1950s and 1960s. These studies complimented the postulates of the dominant paradigm of development that articulated an exogenous bias. Mass media served as effective vehicles for transferring new ideas and models from the West to the developing countries and from urban to rural areas. Schramm (1964) echoed this exogenous bias in his influential book *Mass Media and National Development*. He noted that in the developing countries villages were steeped in traditional habits and the spark to develop economically and socially would come from seeing positive images of the developed countries through the mass media. The mass media thus functioned as a bridge to the outside world. Rogers and Svenning (1969) posited that the mass media were entrusted with the task of preparing individuals in developing nations for a rapid social change by establishing a "climate of modernization." Thus, at the macro level, the modern mass media in developing countries were used in a top-down manner to disseminate modern innovations to the public.

The mass media were thought to have a powerful and direct influence on individuals. This powerful effects model of mass media effects seemed to hold in the developing countries in the 1950s and 1960s in spite of the fact that this model had been discarded earlier in the US. The mass media were viewed as vehicles of wide dissemination. Thus, two new biases, namely the pro-mass media bias and the pro-literacy bias were evident in development theory and practice. The mass media were considered as magic multipliers of development benefits, and as harbingers of modernizing influences.

Over time, the mass media by their very presence signaled development and progress. Lerner (1958) and Schramm (1964) showed a high correlation between the indices of modernity and availability of mass media outlets: The more developed the nation, the higher the availability of mass media outlets. The converse was also considered to be true. In an attempt to reduce the gap between nations labeled as mass media haves and have-nots, UNESCO suggested a minimum standard for mass media availability in developing countries. The establishment of a critical minimum of mass media outlets was strongly encouraged if the developing nations were to achieve overall national development. Information was thus considered as the missing link in the development chain. The quality of information available and its wide dissemination was a key factor in the speed and smoothness of development. Adequate mass media outlets and information would act as a spur to education, commerce, and a chain of other related development activities.

Diffusion of innovations

While scholars and policy-makers were supporting macro-level media initiatives, diffusion of innovations theory gradually evolved as a local-level framework to guide communications planning for modernization. Diffusion of innovations theory emphasized the ability of media messages and opinion leaders to create knowledge of new practices, and persuade the target audiences to adopt the exogenously introduced innovations.

The notion of exogenously induced social change was implicit in diffusion practice and research. The earliest definition of development was "a type of social change in which new ideas are introduced into a social system in order to produce higher per capita incomes and levels of living through more modern production methods and improved social organization" (Rogers and Svenning, 1969: 18). Modernization, or the "development" of the individual, was seen as "the process by which individuals change from a traditional way of life to a more complex, technologically advanced, and rapidly changing style of life" (ibid.: 48). The necessary route for this change from a traditional to a modern person was understood as the communication and acceptance of new ideas from sources external to the social system (Fjes, 1976). In the dominant paradigm, communication was visualized as the central link through which exogenous ideas entered the local communities. Diffusion of innovations research established the importance of communication in the modernization process at the local level.

Over time, diffusion theory proved to be inadequate as a guide for communications planning in development campaigns, and principles and methodology of social marketing have risen to the fore for the strategic, scientific determination of message strategies to promote social causes (see Kotler, this volume, and 1984; Piotrow et al., 1997). Major social marketing themes have included family planning, nutrition, maternal and child health, and HIV/AIDS prevention and control (see Singhal and Rogers, 1999).

Deconstruction of the dominant models of development

Today, there is widespread criticism and deep cynicism about the dominant paradigm of development. Critics argue that the 'development machine' is very powerful because of its vast reach and institutional backing. The 1944 Breton Woods conference put in place a powerful array of institutions to steer the world past the pitfalls of underdevelopment. These institutions have a monolithic nature, are opaque in organizational structure, have a rigid hierarchy, a technocratic culture, and a penchant for social engineering. While they have made useful contributions to development in the past, the reality of the 21st century is very different from the 1940s. Today, themes such as diversity, human welfare, community oriented participatory initiatives, and transparent modes of collective action reflect the new priorities (Honadle, 1999) and call for a new set of institutional arrangements based on the conditions and priorities that exist now. The legitimacy of the dominant paradigm is being challenged on several fronts, ranging from critiques of its scientific and economic foundations, to critiques by fundamentalist religious movements, to the postmodernist, poststructuralist, feminist, and other groups.

The concept of modernity is central to the dominant paradigm of development. Many of the negative consequences of this paradigm, and associated structures and discourse, flow directly from its inherent biases. Critics point out that the stage theory of development and the linear bias of social change have straightjacketed objects of development into frozen states wherein they share common characteristics. Uprooted from their histories and cultures, communities in the developing countries have become pliable objects to be manipulated by development experts. For people and communities far removed from the center, developmentalism has eroded their control over their lifestyles and their use of local community resources. The monoculture being spread by the development discourse has eroded viable alternatives to the industrial, growth-oriented society and crippled humankind's capacity to meet an increasingly different future with creative responses.

The development process in developing countries did not fit the assumptions implicit in the dominant paradigm of development. The paradigm worked better as a description of social change in Western Europe and North America than as a predictor of change in developing countries. The neo-classical economic model that suggested a *trickle-down* approach to development benefits started losing credibility in the 1970s (Seers, 1977). The world-wide recession of the 1980s and the neo-liberal economic reforms in the Third World countries left them further behind. Neo-Marxist scholars made serious criticisms of the dominant paradigmatic model. To them, underdevelopment was not a process distinctly different from development. In fact, they constituted two facets of the same process. The *development of underdevelopment* in Third World nations was and is related to the economic development of Western Europe and North America (Frank, 1969).

The criticisms of the sociology of development models were directed at the abstractness of the social theories (Portes, 1976), the ahistorical nature of the propositions (Abraham, 1980), and incorrect nature of development indicators (Portes, 1976) that constituted the "evolutionary universals." Additonally, the value-enactment models of Hagen (1962), Inkeles and Smith (1974), Lerner (1958), McCleland (1966), Rogers (1962), Rogers and Svenning (1969), and others were criticized for their ethnocentrism and for neglecting to account for the influence of structural constraints on individual action and enterprise.

The dominant paradigm was criticized further for its negative view of culture, especially religious culture (Singer, 1972; Srinivas 1973), for its patriarchal biases (Braidotti et al., 1994), and for its androcentrism (Sachs, 1992). In the mainstream view, local cultural traditions had to be destroyed if the developing nations and peoples wanted to modernize. This notion no longer has overt supporters, though modernization processes still function to destroy, appropriate, or absorb indigenous traditions.

Critique of communication approaches in the modernization framework

Modernization theories provided the epistemological foundation for the initial theories in communication for development. This led to inheritance of historical and institutional biases emanating from propaganda research conducted in the US between World War I and II. During this period, the mass media were viewed as powerful instruments that could be successfully used to manipulate people's opinions and attitudes, and thereby their behaviors, in a relatively short period of time (Glander, 2000; Simpson, 1994). This bias of powerful effects of the media was incorporated in development communication theories during the 1950s and 1960s. Thus, the initial biases set the norm for the field that was not necessarily appropriate for the socio-economic and cultural conditions that existed in Asia, Africa, the Caribbean, or Latin America.

By the 1970s, it became increasingly clear in Asia and in Latin America that socio-economic structural constraints greatly diminished the power of mass media in overcoming problems of development (Beltran, 1976; Rogers, 1976a). The process of development was not as straightforward and clear-cut as conceptualized earlier. And the mass media, far from being an independent variable in the change process, were themselves affected by many extraneous factors. Much of the earlier communication research with its exaggerated emphasis on the individual-blame causal hypothesis regarding underdevelopment obfuscated the social-structural, political, and institutional constraints acting against the individual's efforts to change. Scholars contended that there was a benign neglect of social-structural and political constraints on development because "alien premises, objects, and methods" (Beltran, 1976) influenced the field of communication research. The mass media, in particular, were criticized for (*a*) their trivial and irrelevant content (Shore, 1980); (*b*) giving rise to a *revolution of rising frustrations* (Lerner, 1958) in developing nations; and (*c*) increasing the knowledge gap (Tichenor, Donohue, and Olien, 1970) between the advantaged and disadvantaged sectors of a population.

"New" development objectives and roles for communication

Starting in the mid-1970s, the ferment in the field of development and the role of communication in the development process led to disenchantment with the dominant paradigm. While Ev Rogers played an important role in strengthening the postulates of the dominant paradigm through his work in modernization of developing societies and the diffusion of innovations, he was one of the first to admit the problems with the earlier models and theories in development and communication. First, he re-defined the meaning of development, moving away from the earlier technocratic, overly materialistic, and deterministic models. Rogers defined the "new" development as "a widely participatory process of social change in a society, intended to bring about both social and material advancement (including greater equality, freedom, and other valued qualities) for the majority of the people through their gaining greater control over their environment" (Rogers, 1976a). Goulet (1973) explicated his ideas of "real" development. This description of development was holistic and included a clean environment; growth with equity; provision of basic needs such as food, shelter, education and medical care; meaningful employment and relationships with others; and a harmonious relationship between culture and change. Wang and Dissanayake (1984) emphasized the improvement in the quality of life for the majority and protection of nature and local cultures.

Rogers (1976a) outlined alternative approaches to development that indicated several new goals for meaningful and real development in the Third World: (*a*) equity in distribution of information and other benefits of development, (*b*) active participation of people at the grass-roots, (*c*) independence of local communities (or nations) to tailor development projects to their own objectives, and (*d*) integration of old and new ideas, traditional and modern systems, endogenous and exogenous elements to constitute a unique blend suited to the needs of a particular community.

The idea of *self-development* gained popularity, starting in the 1970s (see Hedebro, 1982; Masani, 1975; Neurath, 1962; Schramm, 1977; Williamson, 1991). In other words, user-initiated activity at the local level was considered essential for village level development. Thus, the emphasis was not so much top-to-bottom flows of information and messages from a government official to a mass audience, but importantly, bottom-up flows from users to sources, and horizontal communication flows of communication between people. People need to have open discussions, identify their needs and problems, decide on a plan of action, and then use a specific medium of communication and an information database most appropriate to their needs. Thus, while the mass media are helpful and often necessary, they are not sufficient for the tasks at hand. The emphasis, then, is not on big media but appropriate media. Along these lines, Havelock (1971) suggested a *problem-solving* model that put the spotlight on the needs of users and their diagnosis of their problems. In this model, the needs of the users, as well as their problem-solving strategies, were studied intensively. The need for information, then, was the prerogative of the user at the village level rather than an authority at the top.

Rogers (1976a: 141) summarized the chief roles of communication in self-development efforts. He suggested that they (a) provide technical information about development problems and possibilities, and about appropriate innovations, in response to local requests, and (b) circulate information about the self-development accomplishments of local groups so that other such groups might perhaps be challenged to achieve a similar performance.

The role of mass media, then, in self-development efforts was of a catalyst in change rather than serving as the prime mover. In these approaches, the role and place of communication in social and behavioral change was radically different from the postulates of the modernization paradigm.

Participatory communication strategies

As previously indicated, many scholars and practitioners over the past three decades have favored active participation of people at the grassroots. On the surface, these signaled a positive departure from the earlier overly top-down and prescriptive approaches. However, the structure of elite domination was not disturbed. Diaz-Bordenave (1980) noted that in these new approaches, the participation that was expected was often directed by the sources and change-agents. In these so-called bottom-up approaches to development, people were induced to participate in self-help activities, but the basic solutions to local problems were selected and implemented by external development agencies. Critics argue that true participation should encourage social and political action by the people at all levels.

The term "participatory communication" has been frequently misunderstood and misused. Participation has been defined and operationalized in many ways: from pseudo participation to genuine efforts at generating participatory decision making (Ascroft and Masilela, 1989; Diaz-Bordenave, 1989; Freire, 1970; S. A. White, 1994). Attempts at operationalization of the term "participation" range from those that reflect the dominant paradigm—*the participation-as-a-means approach*, to those that genuinely represent the case for a context-based paradigm —*the participation-as-an-end approach* (Ascroft and Masilela, 1989: 12; Dervin and Huesca, 1997). The participation-as-an-end approach has received support from many scholars and administrators (Alamgir, 1988; Bamberger, 1988; Diaz-Bordenave, 1989; Kothari, 1984; Teheranian, 1985). They argue that participation must be recognized as a basic human right. It should be accepted and supported as an end in itself and not just for its results (Diaz-Bordenave, 1989).

Participatory communication models have suffered from a lack of a theory of participation. Some scholars have posited that Habermas' theory of communicative action (1984; 1989) provides an analytical approach to the problems of definition and scale of participatory activities including communication (see Jacobson, 2003). Jacobson argues that Habermas' theory of social action provides a framework for distinguishing between different types of communication in social change utilizing the theory's typology of action types.

In Habermas' conceptualization, communication constitutes an action type (see Habermas, 1984). The key objective is whether the action is undertaken to achieve understanding or manipulation. Communicative action is defined as action to achieve mutual understanding whereas any other type of action that is oriented to colonize other people's "lifeworld" is considered to be manipulative and defined as strategic action. Jacobson (2003) argues that this analysis of Habermas' work is useful to anchor definitions of participatory communication as well as specify the scale of activities. The definition of communicative action underlines the objectives of participatory communication, signifying co-equal exchange of knowledge and information, a discursive negotiation of validity claims, and a non-linear process of communication that is necessarily multi-way between the different actors. Second, in terms of scale, communicative action links analysis of participatory communication from the microsocial arena (i.e., interpersonal and small group communication activities) to the public sphere that involves the use of mass media. The theory also pulls in culture by providing categories for analysis of positive and negative cultural change at multiple levels. Scholars point out that Habermas' work may be used as an analytical framework to evaluate specific development/participation programs and their design. Program administrators can maximize the effects of communicative action types and minimize or eliminate manipulative communication practices.

Empowerment as an alternative paradigm for social change

Although the practice of participatory communication has stressed collaboration and co-equal knowledge sharing between the people and experts, a local context, and cultural proximity, the outcome in most cases has not been true empowerment of the people, but the attainment of some indicator of development as articulated in the modernization paradigm. Thus, participatory approaches have been encouraged, though the design and control of messages and development agendas usually have remained with experts. Also, issues of power and control by the authorities, structures of dependency, and power inequities have not been addressed adequately within developing country settings (Wilkins, 1999). Thus, most of the approaches, including the participatory model are viewed as old wine in new bottles.

The postmodernist deconstruction of the participatory development paradigm puts the focus squarely on the contemporary power relations in society and the structures of inequities that they create and strengthen. For "real" social change to occur for individuals and groups trapped in the margins, the search is for development communication models that address and overcome systemic barriers. Some approaches that look fruitful in this endeavor are participatory action research (PAR), empowerment strategies, organizing for social change approaches, and liberation theology practices. These approaches, while originating in different spheres of action, share much in common.

Participatory action research (PAR)

PAR encompasses an experiential methodology. In this process, the people develop on their own methods of consciousness-raising or critical awareness of their existential situation; the knowledge that is generated or resuscitated is by collective and democratic means; and, this is followed by reflection and critical self-evaluation, leading to endogenous participatory social action. This in essence forms the praxis (Rahman, 1991). PAR has emerged as a forceful methodology cum action approach, principally as a reaction to the degradation of the economic and social conditions of poor and marginalized groups. PAR is dedicated to resuscitating both the power of marginalized people and their popular knowledge. The knowledge that PAR attempts to generate is specific, local, non-Western, and non-positivist. Importantly, it is used to initiate collaborative social action to empower local knowledge and wrest social power inherent in knowledge away from the privileged (Friesen, 1999).

Domination of the poor and marginalized come about in at least three ways: (a) control over the means of material production, (b) control over the means of knowledge production, and (c) control over power that legitimizes the relative worth and utility of different episteologies (Rahman, 1991). Those who have social power will legitimize their knowledge and techniques of knowledge generation as superior. As long as there are inequalities in knowledge relations between different sections of a society, there will be inequities in the relations of material production. Nearly all of the knowledge of the oppressed and the marginalized has been disqualified as inadequate and unscientific by the dominant forces (Foucault, 1980). Therefore, in PAR an important objective to achieve the liberation of the poor and the oppressed is to recapture their knowledge and narratives. Thus, the basic ideology of PAR is that endogenous efforts and local leaders will play the leading role in social transformation using their own praxis. The PAR approach, then, by resuscitating and elevating popular knowledge, attempts to create a counter-discourse, disrupts the position of development as articulated by the dominant discourse as problematic, causes a crisis in authority (Gramsci, 1971), and creates a space for marginalized groups to influence social change (K. White, 1999).

Empowerment strategies

It is usually futile and may be even unethical for communications and human service professionals to solve minor and/or immediate problems, while ignoring the systemic barriers erected by societies that perpetuate inequalities among citizens. Certainly sustainable change is not possible unless we deal with the crucial problem of lack of economic and social power among individuals at the grassroots. Over 30 years ago, Latin American communication scholars such as Beltran (1976) and Diaz-Bordenave (1976), among others, observed the oppressive social, political and economic structures that exist in developing countries and that constitute barriers to progressive social change. Yet, the strategies that were followed have failed to directly address these constraints. Individuals are impoverished or sick or often are slow to adopt useful practices, not because they lack knowledge or reason, but because they do not have access to appropriate or sustainable opportunities to improve their lives. This is an issue of power. Unless we are willing to recognize this and act on it, our work will either be ineffective or superficial, functioning as temporary band-aids for larger problems. If development communication is to continue to play

an effective role in social change processes, researchers and practitioners must address fundamental problems of unequal power relations.

As in the case of "participatory communication" the term "empowerment" too has been misunderstood or misused. While empowerment as a construct has a set of core ideas, it may be defined at different
levels: individual, organization, and community; and operationalized
in different contexts (Rowlands, 1998). Several working definitions
of empowerment are available. However, given the nature of our work,
which can be described as directed social change, and given the power
inequities in societies that are posited as the major impediments to
achieving meaningful change, it is important that the working definitions be linked directly to the building and exercise of social power
(Speer and Hughey, 1995). Put succinctly, empowerment is the me-
chanism by which individuals, organizations, and communities gain
control and mastery over social and economic conditions (Rappaport,
1981; Rappaport, Swift, and Hess, 1984); over democratic participation in their community (Rappaport, 1987; Zimmerman and Rappaport,
1988); and over their stories.

The concept of empowerment is heuristic in understanding
the complex constraints in directed social change. It clarifies the
empowerment-oriented outcomes and provides a useful niche for
development support communication. The construct of empowerment has been mentioned quite often in the communication for development literature, but the terms, best practices, levels of analyses,
and outcomes have not been thoroughly explicated. In Table 7.1, I
attempt to articulate elements for a conceptual framework of development support communication that is informed by the goals of the
empowerment model. Table 7.1 provides a framework to compare
the theories under the modernization paradigm with approaches
under the empowerment model on several criteria. The phenomena
of interest in the two approaches are vastly different and so are the
underlying beliefs. The bias in the modernization paradigm was to
favor exogenous ideas and innovations over the local. In the absence of
active local people participation, such exogenously introduced changes
most often result in social engineering by the government or the elite.
In addition, the modernization approaches have been criticized for
their pro-innovation and victim-blame hypotheses. The differences

Table 7.1

Comparison of development communication theories and approaches in the
modernization and empowerment frameworks

	Development communication in the modernization framework (diffusion of innovations, social marketing)	Development communication in the empowerment framework (participatory action research, empowerment strategies)
Goals	National and regional development, people development, community improvement	Empowerment of people, social justice, building capacity and equity
Belief	Underdevelopment due to economic, political, cultural, geographic, and individual inadequacies; existence of a single standard (as articulated by experts)	Underdevelopment due to lack of access to economic, political and cultural resources; underdevelopment due to lack of power and control on the part of the people; diversity of standards
Bias	Cultural insensitivity, environmentally unsustainable; standardization; change directed by external sources and ideas; deterministic process toward a predetermined end dictated by an external agency; pro-innovation bias; individual as locus of change and blame; victim blame hypotheses	Cultural proximity, ecological; diversity; change directed and controlled by endogenous sources and ideas; open-ended and ongoing process of change; system blame hypotheses; community or group is paramount
Context	Macro and micro settings; very little interest in local cultures or power relationships and structural impediments in host society	Local and community settings; cognizant of formidable power inequities and systemic constraints
Level of analysis	Nation, region, individual	Individual, group or organization, community
Role of change agent	Expert, benefactor, non-participant	Collaborator, facilitator, participant, advocate for individuals and communities, risk-taker, activist

CONTINUED ON THE NEXT PAGE

TABLE 7.1—CONTINUED

	Development communication in the modernization framework (diffusion of innovations, social marketing)	Development communication in the empowerment framework (participatory action research, empowerment strategies)
Communication model	Linear, top-down, transmission of information using big mass media; media treated as independent variables with direct and powerful effects; pro-source bias; asymmetrical relationship (subject–object)	Non-linear, participatory, used to convey information as well as build organizations; increased use of small media, indigenous media, group as well as interpersonal communication; media treated as dependent variables; communication used for transaction, negotiation, understanding and not for powerful effects of a source; symmetrical relationship (subject–subject); horizontal flows of communication influence
Type of research	Usually quantitative (surveys), some use of focus groups, contextual or evaluation research	Quantitative and qualitative, longitudinal studies, labor-intensive participatory action research
Best practices	Prevention of underdevelopment; remedy through/ by experts; blame the victim; individual adjustment to a dominant norm; use of mass media to spread standardized messages and entertainment; messages that are preachy, prescriptive, and/or persuasive	Activate social support systems, social networks, mutual help and self-help activities; participation of all actors; empower community narratives; facilitate critical awareness; facilitate community and organizational power; communication used to strengthen interpersonal relationships
Outcomes desired	Modernization; economic growth; political development; infrastructural development; change in people's attitudes and behavior toward modernization objectives leadership	Increased access of all citizens to material, psychological, cultural and informational resources; honing of individual and group competence, skills, useful life and communication skills at the local level; honing of critical awareness skills; empowered local organizations and communities

are stark when it comes to the communication models used. The empowerment model focuses on a symmetrical relationship between relevant actors with communication participants treated as subject–subject rather than as subject–object (as in modernization approaches).

A discussion of the overarching frameworks brings into sharp focus the communication models used by change agencies. Communication models have traditionally looked at communication as a process of moving a message through some channel with the hope that it will reach the receiver and that there will be an effect. The process is usually linear, top-down, prescriptive, preachy and quite often technical in nature. This transmission-oriented approach to the communication process is valuable but it must be extended to include its organizational value. Empowerment requires more than just information delivery and diffusion of technical innovations. The objective of development support communication (DSC) professionals is to work with individuals and communities at the grassroots so that they participate meaningfully in the political and economic processes in their societies. This calls for grassroots organizing (Kaye, 1990) and communicative social action on the part of the poor, women, minorities and others who have been consistently and increasingly marginalized in the process of social change.

Organizing for social change approaches

The importance of organizing for social change initiatives that facilitate empowerment, especially at the grassroots, has gained ground in the last two decades and promises a bright future for the emerging area in communication for empowerment. Rogers and Singhal (2003) summarize the objectives of this theoretical approach as combining "elements of organizational communication and development communication in order to understand the process through which a group of disempowered individuals organize to gain control of their future" (ibid.: 73). One of the earliest documented examples of an effective local organization concerns the mothers in the Korean village of Oryu Li (Rogers and Kincaid, 1981). The group of women progressed to larger self-help projects buoyed by the success of their initial attempts to organize. In the long run, some of the power held by males shifted to others in the community leading to an empowerment of marginalized groups, especially women. In more recent decades, in certain parts of India, leadership training and organization-building led to an increasing sense of empowerment among marginalized women dairy farmers, more effective dairy cooperatives, and greater milk production (Papa et al., 2000). In Bangladesh, the Grameen (Rural) Bank has significantly empowered poor women and concomitantly brought positive development to the communities (Papa, Auwal, and Singhal, 1995; 1997; Papa, Singhal, and Papa, 2006).

The implication for development support communication (DSC), then, is a reconceptualization of its role. Greater importance will need to be directed to the organizational value of communication and the role of communicative efforts in empowering citizens. In essence, what I am advocating for DSC is a move away from effecting "development" (as articulated by the dominant paradigm and the helping professions) to assisting in the process of empowerment through organizing.

Liberation theology and its practice

Few of the writings on development communication in mainstream traditions have considered the positive impact of religion and spirituality in critical social change. Despite widespread negative attitudes toward religion, most who spend time in developing countries observe that religious affiliations and spiritual motivations frequently play key roles in project success (see Melkote and Steeves, 2001). The type of theology that actively supports development for personal and collective empowerment is called *liberation theology*. Perhaps the most influential scholar to apply liberation theology specifically to education and communication practice is Paolo Freire (1970; 1973). As liberation theology assumes that attaining full humanity means freedom from oppression, in both its external and internal forms, Freire begins with the premise that the purpose of development is liberation. Liberation requires a process of conscientization, i.e., the individual's increasing awareness of oppression and accompanying actions to overcome it.

The implications of Freirian ideas are clear. For development communication practice, the central focus should be on face-to-face emancipatory dialogue. The success of the awakening process via dialogue requires spiritual practice through a form of communication seldom examined by communication specialists in the past. The combination of dialogic communication, spiritual practice, and other forms of religious communication practice could be used as an effective strategy for critical social change (see Melkote and Steeves, 2001). In Latin America, liberation theology is largely manifested in the emergence of *Base Ecclesial Communities.* These communities of worship, social analysis, and activism have played important roles in development for liberation throughout the continent (Cook, 1994; Dawson, 1999). While liberation theology has been most often associated with Christianity, other religions such as Buddhism, Hinduism, Islam, and Judaism have operationalized their own versions of theology into practice for development and liberation (see Melkote and Steeves, 2001). The social activism of Gandhi using the Hindu liberation perspectives; the work of Sulak Sivaraska in creating a variety of grassroots social welfare and development organizations (see Rothberg, 1993) and the Sarvodaya Shramadana Movement (Ariyaratne, 1987) in Sri Lanka using the Buddhist liberation theologies; and Family Life Education Projects (see Amoa and Assimeng, 1993) in Ghana using Islamic liberation thought represent other well-known examples of Freirian ideas in practice.

Conclusions

Empowerment through participation, grassroots organizing, and/or dialogic action may take a long time to mature and achieve significant results. The individuals and communities at the periphery of the social, economic, political or cultural spectrum of a society should, at a minimum, have the capacity to (*a*) perceive and articulate their social, historical, economic, and political realities, (*b*) operationalize their needs, (*c*) identify resources they need, (*d*) identify, articulate and operationalize possible solution alternatives, (*e*) identify and gain access to individuals, agencies, or organizations that are crucial to meeting their needs or solving their problems, (*f*) build communication skills such as presenting issues cogently, (*g*) gain skills in conflict resolution, negotiation and arbitration, and finally (*h*) be able to organize and lead. These skills are unevenly distributed among people in a society with the individuals at the margins worse-off. This provides a useful niche to development support communication workers and scholars to assist as facilitators or enablers in the empowerment process.

Achieving empowerment is not an easy task. It not only requires dealing with enclaves of power and influence that are deeply anchored in global and national structures, but also the active participation of individuals and communities in intervention efforts affecting their welfare. However, it is the right thing to do if we are truly interested in appropriate and sustainable social change.

References

Abraham, Francis. 1980. *Perspectives on Modernization: Toward a General Theory of Third World Development*. Washington, DC: University Press of America.

Alamgir, Mohiuddin. 1988. Poverty Alleviation through Participatory Development. *Development* 2 (3): 97–102.

Amoa, B. D. and J. M. Assimeng. 1993. *Report on Family Life/Welfare Activities in Religious Organizations in Ghana*. Accra, Ghana: UNFPA.

Ariyaratne, A. T. 1987. Beyond Development Communication: Case Study on Sarvodaya, Sri Lanka. In N. Jayaweera and S. Amunugama (eds), *Rethinking Development Communication*, pp. 239–51. Singapore: Asian Mass Communication Research and Information Center.

Ascroft, Joseph and Sipho Masilela. 1989. From Top-Down to Co-Equal Communication: Popular Participation in Development Decision-making. Paper presented at the seminar on *Participation: A Key Concept in Communication and Change*. University of Poona, Pune, India.

Bamberger, Michael. 1988. *The Role of Community Participation in Development Planning and Project Management*, EDI Policy Seminar Report 13. Washington, DC: World Bank.

Beltran, Luis Ramiro, S. 1976. Alien Premises, Objects, and Methods in Latin American Communication Research. *Communication Research* 3 (2): 107–34.

Braidotti, R., E. Charkiewicz, S. Hausler, and S. Wieringa. 1994. *Women, the Environment and Sustainable Development*. London: Zed Books.

Cook, G. 1994. The Genesis and Practice of Protestant Base Communities in Latin America. In G. Cook (ed.), *The New Face of the Church in Latin America: Between Tradition and Change*, pp. 150–55. Maryknoll, NY: Orbis.

Daniels, Walter M. 1951. *The Point Four Program*. New York: H. W. Wilson.

Dawson, A. 1999. The Origins and Character of the Base Ecclesial Community: A Brazilian Perspective. In C. Rowland (ed.), *The Cambridge Companion to Liberation Theology*, pp. 109–128. Cambridge, UK: Cambridge University Press.

Dervin, B. and R. Huesca. 1997. Reaching for the Communicating in Partici-patory Communication: A Meta-theoretical Analysis. *Journal of International Communication* 46 (2): 46–74.

Diaz-Bordenave, Juan. 1976. Communication for Agricultural Innovations in Latin America. In E. M. Rogers (ed.), *Communication and Development: Critical Perspectives*, pp. 43–62. Beverly Hills, CA: Sage Publications.

———. 1980. Participation in Communication Systems for Development. Unpublished paper. Rio de Janeiro.

———. 1989. Participative Communication as a Part of the Building of a Partici-pative Society. Paper prepared for the seminar *Partici-pation: A Key Concept in Communication for Change and Development*, Poona, India, February.

Fjes, Fred. 1976. Communications and Development. Unpublished paper, College of Communications, University of Illinois, Urbana-Champaign.

Foucault, M. 1980. *Power/Knowledge*. New York: Pantheon Books.

Frank, Andre G. 1969. *Latin America: Underdevelopment or Revolution*. New York: Monthly Review Press.

Freire, P. 1970. *Pedagogy of the Oppressed*. New York, NY: The Seabury Press.

———. 1973. *Education for Critical Consciousness*. New York: The Seabury Press.

Friesen, E. 1999. Exploring the Links between Structuration Theory and Partici-patory Action Research. In T. Jacobson and J. Servaes (eds), *Theoretical Approaches to Participatory Communication*, pp. 281–308. Creskill, NJ: Hampton Press.

Glander, T. 2000. *Origins of Mass Communications Research during the American Cold War*. Mahwah, NJ: Lawrence Erlbaum.

Goulet, D. 1973. "Development"... or Liberation? In C. Wilber (ed.), *The Political Economy of Development and Underdevelopment*. New York: Random House.

Gramsci, A. 1971. *Selection from the Prison Notebooks*. New York: Internationalist.

Habermas, J. 1984. *The Theory of Communicative Action: Reason and the Rational-ization of Society*, Vol. 1. Boston, MA: Beacon Press.

———. 1989. *The Structural Transformation of the Public Sphere: An Inquiry into a Category of Bourgeois Society*. Cambridge, MA: MIT Press.

Hagen, Everett E. 1962. *On the Theory of Social Change*. Homewood, IL: Dorsey.

Havelock, R. G. 1971. *Planning for Innovation through Dissemination and Utilization of Knowledge*. Ann Arbor, MI: University of Michigan, Institute for Social Research.

Hedebro, Goran. 1982. *Communication and Social Change in Developing Nations: A Critical View*. Ames, IA: Iowa State University Press.

Honadle, G. 1999. *How Context Matters: Linking Environmental Policy to People and Place*. West Hartford, CT: Kumarian Press.

Inkeles, A. 1966. The Modernization of Man. In M. Weiner (ed.), *Modernization: The Dynamics of Growth*, pp. 138–50. New York: Basic Books.

Inkeles, A. and D. H. Smith. 1974. *Becoming Modern: Individual Change in Six Developing Countries*. Cambridge, MA: Harvard University Press.

Jacobson, T. L. 2003. Participatory Communication for Social Change: The Relevance of the Theory of Communicative Action. In P. J. Kalbfleisch (ed.), *Communication Yearbook*, Vol. 27, pp. 87–123. Mahwah, NJ: Lawrence Erlbaum.

Kaye, G. 1990. A Community Organizer's Perspective on Citizen Participation Research and the Researcher–Practitioner Partnership. *American Journal of Community Psychology* 18 (1): 151–57.

Kothari, Rajni. 1984. Communications for Alternative Development: Towards a Paradigm. *Development Dialogue* 1 (2): 13–22.

Kotler, P. 1984. Social Marketing of Health Behavior. In L. W. Frederiksen, L. J. Solomon, and K. A. Brehony (eds), *Marketing Health Behavior*, pp. 23–39. New York: Plenum Press.

Lerner, Daniel. 1958. *The Passing of Traditional Society: Modernizing the Middle East*. New York: Free Press.

Masani, M. 1975. Introduction. In M. Masani (ed.), *Communication and Rural Progress*, pp. 1–6. Bombay: Leslie Sawhny Programme in Training for Democracy.

McCleland, David C. 1966. The Impulse to Modernization. In M. Weiner (ed.), *Modernization: The Dynamics of Growth*, pp. 28–39. New York: Basic Books.

Melkote, S. 1991. *Communication for Development in the Third World: Theory and Practice*. New Delhi: Sage Publications.

Melkote, S. and H. L. Steeves. 2001. *Communication for Development in the Third World: Theory and Practice for Empowerment*. New Delhi: Sage Publications.

Neurath, Paul. 1962. Radio Farm Forum as a Tool of Change in Indian Villages. *Economic Development and Cultural Change* 10: 275–83.

Nordenstreng, Kaarle. 1968. Communication Research in the United States: A Critical Perspective. *Gazette* 14 (3): 207–16.

Papa, M. J., M. A. Auwal, and A. Singhal. 1995. Dialectic of Emancipation and Control in Organizing for Social Change: A Multitheoretic Study of the Grameen Bank in Bangladesh. *Communication Theory* 5: 189–223.

———. 1997. Organizing for Social Change within Concertive Control Systems: Member Identification, Empowerment, and the Masking of Discipline. *Communication Monographs* 64: 219–49.

Papa, M. J., A. Singhal, D. Ghanekar, and W.H. Papa. 2000. Organizing for Social Change through Cooperative Action: The [Dis]empowering Dimensions of Women's Communication. *Communication Theory* 10: 90–123.

Papa, M. J., A. Singhal, and W. H. Papa. 2006. *Organizing for Social Change: A Dialectic Journey of Theory and Praxis*. New Delhi: Sage Publications.

Piotrow, P. T., D. L. Kincaid, J. G. Rimon II, and W. Rinehart. 1997. *Health Communication: Lessons from Family Planning and Reproductive Health*. Westport, CT: Praeger.

Portes, Alejandro. 1976. On the Sociology of National Development: Theories and Issues. *American Journal of Sociology* 82 (1): 55–85.

Rahman, M. A. 1991. The Theoretical Standpoint of PAR. In O. Fals-Borda and M. A. Rahman (eds), *Action and Knowledge: Breaking the Monopoly with Participatory Action-Research*, pp. 13–23. New York: Apex Press.

Rao, Lakshmana. 1963. Communication and Development: A Study of Two Indian Villages. Ph.D. dissertation, University of Minnesota.

Rappaport, J. 1981. In Praise of Paradox: A Social Policy of Empowerment over Prevention. *American Journal of Community Psychology* 9 (1): 1–25.

———. 1987. Terms of Empowerment/Exemplars of Prevention: Toward a Theory for Community Psychology. *American Journal of Community Psychology* 15 (2): 121–44.

Rappaport, J., C. Swift, and R. Hess (eds). 1984. *Studies in Empowerment: Steps Toward Understanding and Action*. New York: Haworth.

Rogers, E. M. 1962. *Diffusion of Innovations*. New York: Free Press.

———. 1973. *Communication Strategies for Family Planning*. New York: Free Press.

———. 1976a. Communication and Development—The Passing of the Dominant Paradigm. In E. M. Rogers (ed.), *Communication and Development: Critical Perspectives*, pp. 121–48. Beverly Hills, CA: Sage Publications.

———. 1976b. The Passing of the Dominant Paradigm—Reflections on Diffusion Research. In W. Schramm and D. Lerner (eds), *Communication and Change*, pp. 49–52. Honolulu, HI: University Press of Hawaii.

Rogers, E. M. and D. Lawrence Kincaid. 1981. *Communication Networks: Toward a New Paradigm for Research*. New York: Free Press.

Rogers, E. M. and F. F. Shoemaker. 1971. *Communication of Innovations: A Cross-Cultural Approach*. New York: Free Press.

Rogers, E. M. and A. Singhal. 2003. Empowerment and Communication: Lessons Learned from Organizing for Social Change. In P. J. Kalbfleisch (ed.), *Communication Yearbook*, Vol. 27, pp. 67–85. Mahwah, NJ: Lawrence Erlbaum.

Rogers, E. M. and Lynne Svenning. 1969. *Modernization among Peasants*. New York: Holt, Rinehart and Winston.

Rothberg, D. 1993. A Thai Perspective on Socially Engaged Buddhism: A Conversation with Sulak Sivaraksa. *ReVision* 15 (3): 121–27.

Rowlands, J. 1998. *Questioning Empowerment, Working with Women in Honduras*. London: Oxfam.

Sachs, W. 1992. Environment. In W. Sachs (ed.), *The Development Dictionary: A Guide to Knowledge as Power*, pp. 26–37. London: Zed Books.

Schramm, Wilbur. 1964. *Mass Media and National Development: The Role of Information in the Developing Countries*. Stanford, CA: Stanford University Press.

———. 1977. Communication and Development—A Re-evaluation. *Communicator* April: 1–4.

Seers, Dudley. 1977. The Meaning of Development. *International Development Review* XIX (2): 2–7.

Shore, Larry. 1980. Mass Media for Development: A Re-Examination of Access, Exposure, and Impact. In Emile G. McAnany (ed.), *Communications in the Rural Third World*, pp. 19–45. New York: Praeger.

Simpson, C. 1994. *Science of Coercion: Communication Research & Psychological Warfare 1945–1960*. New York: Oxford University Press.

Singer, Milton. 1972. *When a Great Tradition Modernizes: An Anthropological Approach to Indian Civilization*. New York: Praeger.

Singhal, A. and E. M. Rogers. 1999. *Entertainment-Education: A Communication Strategy for Social Change*. Mahwah, NJ: Lawrence Erlbaum.

Speer, P. W. and J. Hughey 1995. Community Organizing: An Ecological Route to Empowerment and Power. *American Journal of Community Psychology* 23 (5): 729–48.

Srinivas, M. N. 1973. Comments on Milton Singer's Industrial Leadership, the Hindu Ethic and the Spirit of Socialism. In Milton Singer (ed.), *Entrepreneurship and Modernization of Occupational Cultures in South Asia*. Duke University: Program in Comparative Studies on South Asia, Monograph No. 12, pp. 279–86.

Teheranian, Majid. 1985. Paradigms Lost: Development as Communication and Learning. *Media Development* XXXII (4): 5–8.

Tichenor, P. J., G. A. Donohue, and C. N. Olien. 1970. Mass Media Flow and Differential Growth in Knowledge. *Public Opinion Quarterly* 34: 159–70.

Wang, Georgette and Wimal Dissanayake. 1984. Culture, Development and Change: Some Explorative Observations. In G. Wang and W. Dissanayake (eds), *Continuity and Change in Communication Systems*, pp. 3–20. New Jersey: Ablex.

Weber, Max. 1964. *The Sociology of Religion*. Boston, MA: Beacon Press.

Weiner, Myron. 1966. Introduction. In M. Weiner (ed.), *Modernization: The Dynamics of Growth*. New York: Basic Books.

White, K. 1999. The Importance of Sensitivity to Culture in Development Work. In T. Jacobson and J. Servaes (eds), *Theoretical Approaches to Participatory Communication*, pp. 17–50. Creskill, NJ: Hampton Press.

White, S. A. 1994. Introduction: The Concept of Participation. In S. A. White, K. S. Nair, and J. Ascroft (eds), *Participatory Communication: Working for Change and Development*, pp. 15–32. New Delhi: Sage Publications.

Wilkins, K. G. 1999. Development Discourse on Gender and Communication in Strategies for Social Change. *Journal of Communication* 49 (1): 46–68.

Williamson, A. H. 1991. The Fogo Process: Development Support Communication in Canada and the Developing World. In F. L. Casmir (ed.), *Communication in Development*, pp. 270–88. Norwood, NJ: Ablex.

Zimmerman, M. A. and J. A. Rappaport. 1988. Citizen Participation, Perceived Control, and Psychological Empowerment. *American Journal of Community Psychology* 16 (5): 725–50.

8

Implementing Strategic Extension Campaigns: Applying Best Practices and Lessons Learned from Ev Rogers

RONNY ADHIKARYA

For those of us who were not conducting diffusion projects in the 1960s, it is easy to underestimate the profound impact of university and government extension services on the development of the diffusion paradigm. The extension services provided ready infrastructure with local access into communities for the investigation of adoption, implementation, communication channels, time, social influence, and the all-important degree of innovativeness of adopters. Ev was foremost in working with extension colleagues to test ideas about diffusion. Trained in this emphasis, Ronny Adhikarya is an exemplar of the savvy research-infused practitioner. It is in him and research-practitioners like him that we are perhaps most likely to realize the potential of Ev's long efforts in explicating the process of diffusion.

JIM DEARING

In the summer of 1988, I was invited by the Rockefeller Foundation to the idyllic town of Bellagio, located on Lago di Como in northern Italy to present findings from our India Hum Log *project (see Singhal et al.'s chapter, this volume). "If you get to Rome, look up Ronny Adhikarya at FAO," Ev told me. I did. Some years later, Ronny involved me in several FAO (Food and Agriculture Organization of the United Nations) and World Bank learning networks that he founded—on strategic extension campaigns, environmental education, knowledge utilization through learning technologies (KULT), and HIV/AIDS. These learning networks met regularly in Malaysia, Thailand, Indonesia, the Philippines, China, and Egypt. Through these meetings, I immediately grasped the influence of Ev Rogers on Ronny, as also the seminal contributions that Ronny made in developing, up-scaling, and franchising strategic extension campaigns in countries of Asia, Africa, and Latin America.*

ARVIND SINGHAL

IN 1972, AS A RESEARCH STAFF MEMBER OF EAST–WEST COMMUNICATION Institute (EWCI) in Honolulu, I purchased a new, silver sports car—the Ford Capri. As my work involved overseas travel for five to six months a year, the Capri was available for rental to EWCI's visitors. In late 1972, when I was on one of my overseas trips, I learned that the famous Ev Rogers had rented my Capri. I returned to Honolulu excitedly, meeting Ev for the first time. Ev wrote me a personal check for the car, which I cashed in right away. In retrospect, I should have saved and framed Ev's check. At that time, I did not know how much influence Ev would have on my life and career.

For many of us development practitioners and communication scholars, Ev Rogers was one of the founding fathers of development communication. His writings on the diffusion of innovations (Rogers, 1962) were widely applied in development communication programs dealing with agriculture, family planning, nutrition, education, and environment conservation.

During my graduate work at Cornell in the early 1970s, Ev's books—*Modernization among Peasants* (Rogers and Svenning, 1969) and *Diffusion of Innovations* (Rogers, 1962)—were required textbooks. Further, we had a heavy dose of Rogers' publications and "fugitive materials" (i.e., conference papers, consultancy reports, unpublished articles) as required reading. When I was preparing my master's thesis on the use of folk media and traditional communication networks to support family planning programs in rural Java, Indonesia (Adhikarya, 1972), Ev was writing his book *Communication Strategies for Family Planning* (Rogers, 1973). During my thesis defense in 1972, my committee members asked me to operationalize several of Rogers' diffusion concepts, e.g., heterophily and homophily, social networks, and the well-known S-curve of adoption. These concepts, as explained later, influenced many development communication practices that I undertook in later years, including the design and implementation of strategic extension campaigns (SEC) in many developing countries.

In the present chapter, I trace my professional journey, highlighting the influence of Ev Rogers on my work, and, in so doing, describe the development and institutionalization of the SEC approach in various developing countries.

The Honolulu Network's influence on
development communication practice

I was fortunate to be at the East–West Communication Institute (EWCI) in Hawaii during its heyday in the 1970s. The EWCI was a leading "think-tank" and "incubator" for family planning communication programs supported by USAID and other international and multilateral agencies, providing training and advisory services to decision-makers and managers of public health and population communication programs of over 55 developing countries. Ev Rogers was one of the EWCI's key resource persons along with other luminaries of development communication such as Wilbur Schramm, Daniel Lerner, Ithiel de Sola Pool, Harold Lasswell, Fred Yu, Donald Bogue, Bill Sweeney, Gloria Feliciano, and Nora Quebral. These resource persons congregated two to three times a year in Honolulu for their "intellectual retreats" with EWCI staff.

Most of the population and health-related Information, Education, and Communication (IEC) strategies advocated by the EWCI's "network" were derived predominantly from Rogers' diffusion of innovations theory (Rogers and Shoemaker, 1971). Between 1972 and 1977, I personally witnessed the widespread applications of diffusion theory in family planning communication programs in 26 countries of Asia, Near East, and Eastern Africa. Diffusion theory had a significant impact in diminishing the "tabooness" of family planning concepts and methods, and in increasing the cost-effectiveness of peer-based group communication processes using social networks. Diffusion theory also made possible strategic applications of the different stages of adoption process and S-curve analysis for message design and audience segmentation purposes. The resulting applications included the use of (*a*) small community-based groups to stimulate contraceptive adoption, such as mothers' clubs in Korea and Indonesia, (*b*) incentive systems for change agents, (*c*) traditional midwives to reduce heterophily gaps between medical doctors and clients, (*d*) group dynamics and peer influences of social networks, (*e*) integrated mass and interpersonal channels, (*f*) piggy-backing onto Other People's Networks (OPNs) or commercial channels (the precursor to the social marketing approach), (*g*) use of folk or traditional media (the precursor to entertainment-education), and others.

The above diffusion-centered ideas were cross-fertilized with the creativity of early population communication practitioners such as Bill Sweeney, Lyle Saunders, Sam Keeney, Don Bogue, Phyllis Piotrow, Bob Gillespie, Richard Manoff, Phil Harvey, Jim Echols, Chuck Blackman, Frank Wilder, Jeff Tsai, Cesar Mercado, Larry Kincaid, and the four famous Asian "communication musketeers"— Juan Flavier, Mechai Viravaidya (a.k.a. Mr "Condom" in Thailand), Haryono Suyono, and Lukas Hendrata. As a result, many exemplary development communication programs were implemented in Korea, Taiwan, the Philippines, Singapore, Indonesia, Thailand, and Iran during the 1970s and 1980s. This heady intellectual exposure influenced my professional career in later years.

Lessons from my Stanford years

I earned my doctoral degree from the Institute for Communication Research at Stanford University during 1978–81 under the guidance of Ev Rogers. My doctoral dissertation investigated transnational knowledge transfer from US communication scholars and schools to their counterparts in the ASEAN (Association of South-East Asian Nations) countries (Adhikarya, 1983). Research in five Asian countries revealed that Asian communication scholars were heavily using Ev Rogers' books, concepts, and research reports.

At Stanford, I began to more fully grasp the reasons for Ev Rogers' widespread global influence—on both academicians and practitioners. I witnessed how he developed personal networks, partnered with his collaborators, and coached his students. Despite his "star" status as professor and a hectic work schedule, he was approachable, informal, and genuinely interested in teaching large undergraduate classes, graduate seminars, and counseling individual students, especially international ones. He was also a very engaging storyteller—hugely popular with his students, colleagues, and friends.

Ev Rogers used a coaching method instead of an instructional one. He was a pro at building student trust and confidence, making learning comfortable, and memorable. He made students feel as if it was he who was learning from them. The questions he asked were not intended to cross-examine but to solicit useful ideas, opinions, and advice. Such "discovery-based" learning processes were highly effective. Ev used similar rapport-building techniques in dealing with policy makers, donors, development practitioners, colleagues, and subordinates.

Being around Ev, I learned that in order for ideas to diffuse, personal networks needed nurturing. Only then could one create a global network of knowledge champions. These lessons at Stanford were highly important in my own professional career with United Nations agencies and the World Bank.

Couscous@Marrakech and a "belly-gram"

Ev Rogers continually revised and updated his ideas and writings. An example was his updated writings on the diffusion of innovations model vis-à-vis the knowledge (benefits) gap published in *Communication and Development: Critical Perspectives* (Rogers, 1976). To disseminate these ideas more widely in Asia, an article entitled "Communication and Inequitable Development: Narrowing the Socio-Economic Benefits Gap" (Adhikarya and Rogers, 1978) was published in *Media Asia*.

When I asked Ev what we should do with the "token" honorarium we received from the publishers, he suggested we take several of our Stanford friends for a couscous dinner at the Marrakech Restaurant. Over dessert and Moroccan coffee, a belly-dancer provided entertainment. When Ev's next birthday arrived, he was greeted with a surprise birthday gift: a belly-gram. Belly dancers arrived at Ev's home to sing "happy birthday."

Reality check: Applying concepts in the field

During my career with the United Nations' Food and Agriculture Organization (FAO) in Rome (1981–96) and later with the World Bank in Washington, DC, I met countless agricultural and development decision-makers and practitioners worldwide and observed their programs in action. Not surprisingly, most agricultural extension and development outreach activities were based on Rogers' diffusion theory, or drew from his book, *Modernization among Peasants* (Rogers and Svenning, 1969). Knowing that Ev Rogers was a pragmatic communication scholar who sought to bridge theories with practical on-the-ground problem-solving, I involved him in several strategic FAO and World Bank consultations. Ev appreciated the opportunity to conduct "reality-checks" of his concepts, ideas, and experiences with development practitioners and decision-makers.

Two of my books, *Strategic Extension Campaign* (Adhikarya, 1994) and *Motivating Farmers for Action* (Adhikarya and Posamentier, 1987), were much influenced by Ev's work on diffusion of innovations and communication networks. For instance, I applied the S-curve concept of the adoption process in developing and designing knowledge-attitude-practice (KAP) surveys of potential beneficiaries to implement strategic communication or extension campaigns. More importantly, the lessons learned from Ev were applied in developing SEC's operational modalities, practical implementation approaches, and replication strategies in many developing countries.

What is the strategic extension campaign (SEC)?[1]

The "Strategic Extension (or 'communication')" Campaign (SEC) methodology was developed during my work for the FAO of the United Nations in Rome, Italy in the early 1980s. SEC emphasizes the importance of *people's participation* (i.e., intended beneficiaries such as field extension workers and small farmers) in strategic planning, systematic management, and field implementation of agricultural extension and training programs.

A demand-driven and needs-based communication method

Strategic Extension Campaign (SEC) is a strategically planned, problem-solving, and participatory-oriented extension program, conducted in a relatively short time period, aimed at increasing awareness/knowledge level of an identified target beneficiaries, and altering

---

[1] For complete illustrations and detailed discussion on the SEC planning process, management operations, field implementation and evaluation results of the campaigns conducted in various countries, see Adhikarya (1994, 1987) and www.fao.org/docrep/u8955e/u8955e00htm and http://www.fao.org/sd/EXdirect/EXan0003.htm.

their attitudes and/or behavior towards favorable adoption of a given idea or technology, using specifically designed and pre-tested messages, and cost-effective multi-media materials to support its information, education/training, and communication intervention activities (Adhikarya, 1994). SEC is not an alternative to the conventional extension program or activity, but rather an integral part of the programs of an agricultural extension service.

SEC was labeled as an "extension" activity since the methodology was applied in agricultural "knowledge" management programs. Its extension (i.e., communication) strategies and messages are specifically developed and tailored based on the results of a *participatory* problem identification process on the causes of farmers' *non*-adoption, or inappropriate practices, of a given recommended agricultural technology. The SEC technology transfer and application approach is needs-based, demand-driven, and has a problem-solving orientation. The SEC program starts with a farmers' KAP survey whose results are used as planning campaign inputs and as a benchmark for summative evaluation purposes.

The conceptual framework and operational phases of SEC are outlined in Figure 8.1 (Adhikarya, 1994 and 1987). All 10 operational phases include participatory approach activities by soliciting relevant *feed-forward* (i.e., information on needs) and *feedback* (i.e., information on results) from target beneficiaries. The SEC method advocates the need to carry out extension activities in a *planned, systematic, sequential, and process-oriented manner* to produce a *synergic* effect.

SEC capacity development and quality assurance

The SEC approach involves training staff to master the whole extension process, rather than only some elements of the process (Figure 8.2). A series of participatory approach workshops are conducted for extension personnel, subject-matter specialists, trainers, and farmer leaders on the skills of extension program planning, strategy development, message design and positioning, multi-media materials development, pre-testing and production, as well as management planning, implementation, monitoring, and evaluation. These training workshops develop local institutional capacity in the SEC methodology.

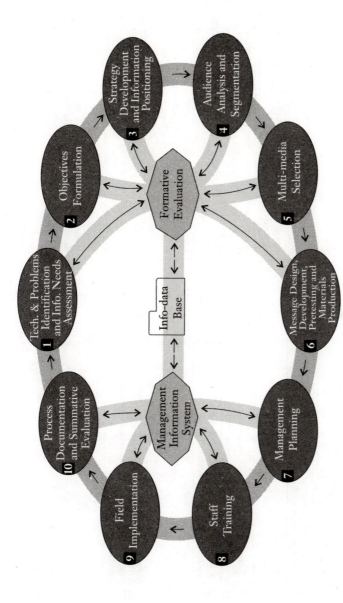

Figure 8.1

Conceptual framework for extension campaign planning: 10 operational phases

Source: Adapted from Adhikarya and Posamentier, 1987. For more detailed information on similar frameworks, see Adhikarya and Middleton, 1979

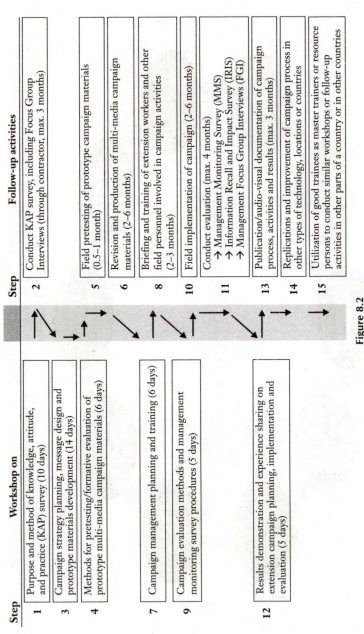

Figure 8.2

Implementation steps for strategic extension campaign and personnel training

As we show later through case studies, empirical evaluations of SEC using Information Recall and Impact Surveys (IRIS), Focus Group Interviews (FGI), and Management Monitoring Surveys (MMS) demonstrate positive changes in farmers' KAP vis-à-vis the recommended technologies as well as significant economic benefits. Such results have been reported from Bangladesh and Malaysia (on rat control), Thailand (on pest surveillance system, horticulture development), Malaysia (on integrated weed management), Zambia (on maize production), and Malawi, Jamaica, and Morocco (on population education).

Some useful features of SEC

Participatory strategic planning applications

SEC focuses on specific issues of a given agricultural technology recommendation. Its main aim is to solve or minimize problems which caused non-adoption of such a recommendation by intended beneficiaries. It selects, prioritizes, and utilizes only the most relevant information which can maximize the effectiveness of extension efforts.

SEC activities concentrate on meeting the information, education and training needs of intended beneficiaries. SEC activities are geared at *narrowing the gaps* between knowledge, attitudes, and/or appropriate practice levels of target beneficiaries vis-à-vis the agricultural technology recommendations. Ev Rogers' early work in family planning communication (Rogers, 1973), especially in using respondents' KAP data and contraceptive choice studies to address the needs and problems of non-acceptors, provides a conceptual model for using KAP survey in SEC.

Furthermore, the focus of SEC activities is to create a demand (through information and motivation approaches) and/or to satisfy the demand (through education and training) among intended target beneficiaries. Such a method applies bottom-up participatory planning procedures to give the highest priority to the needs of target beneficiaries.

In planning SEC activities, the intended *beneficiaries are consulted* regarding their priority concerns and needs. Further, SEC tries to assess farmers' local indigenous knowledge, values, and belief systems on farming practices which may be good, need to be improved, or perhaps need to be discouraged. So SEC believes in "start with what people already know," and "build on what they already have."

The SEC approach stresses the need to provide strategic, critical, and quality (as opposed to quantity of) information, which must also include non-technological information, given that the reasons for non-adoption of agricultural technologies are often related to socio-psychological, socio-cultural, and socio-economic factors. Appropriate behavioral science principles are thus applied to extension problem-solving and in information positioning, which is *responsive* rather than prescriptive in nature.

The SEC method is responsive to intended beneficiaries' agricultural development problems and information needs because its extension objectives, strategies, methods, messages, and multi-media materials are specifically developed based on survey results of their knowledge, attitude, and practices vis-à-vis the recommended agricultural technology. An example of such campaign objectives is provided in Table 8.1.

Table 8.1
Specific and measurable campaign objectives for
the rat control campaign in Penang state, Malaysia

Identified problems among farmers	*Formulated extension campaign objectives (based on KAP survey results)*
1. Inadequate knowledge of the value of physical methods and cultural practices regarding rat control	To raise the proportion of rice farmers' level of knowledge/appreciation concerning the value and benefits of cultural practices from 67% to 75%, and physical rat control practices from 31% to 45%
2. Little knowledge of the different functions and characteristics of different rodenticides	To raise the proportion of rice farmers' level of awareness and knowledge by improving their understanding regarding the different functions and characteristics of two types of rodenticides. (*a*) Chronic poison baits from 61% to 70% (*b*) Chronic poison dust from 22% to 40%

CONTINUED ON THE NEXT PAGE

TABLE 8.1—CONTINUED

Identified problems among farmers	Formulated extension campaign objectives (based on KAP survey results)
3. Misconception that rats are "intelligent" and thus unlikely to be successfully controlled	To reduce the proportion of nice farmers' misconception that rats are unlikely to be controlled successfully because they are "intelligent" from 52% to 35%
4. Lack of group and collaborative efforts in controlling rats	To encourage greater participation of rice farmers in group and/or collaborative efforts in controlling rats, by increasing the proportion of rice farmers' level of favorable attitudes towards such efforts from 60% to 70%
5. Farmers normally do not take voluntary action to control rats until crop damages are visible	To increase the proportion of rice farmers who believe that rat control is not a waste time from 55% to 65% in order to encourage them to take action before their crops are damaged
6. Inappropriate application of different rodenticides in different situation/stages	(*a*) To increase the proportion of rice farmers' knowledge on the correct application of rodenticides with regard to: • Rate of application of acute poison from 11% to 40%; chronic poison (baits) from 23% to 40%; and chronic poison (dust) from 67% to 75% • Time of application of acute poison from 47% to 60%; chronic poison (baits) from 39% to 50%; and chronic poison (dust) from 41% to 55% • Location to place acute poison from 43% to 55%; chronic poison (baits) from 43% to 55%; and chronic poison (dust) from 78% to 80% (*b*) To increase the proportion of rice farmers' level of appropriate practice in rodenticides application with regard to: • Rate of application of acute poison from 12% to 24%; chronic poison (baits) from 23% to 40%; chronic poison (dust) from 32% to 40% • Time of application of acute poison from 28% to 35%; chronic poison (baits) from 28% to 35%; chronic poison (dust) from 43% to 50%

CONTINUED ON THE NEXT PAGE

TABLE 8.1—CONTINUED

Identified problems among farmers	Formulated extension campaign objectives (based on KAP survey results)
7. Lack of motivation of most farmers who have more than one job, to spend more time and effort to control rats in order to increase their yields and income	To motivate and encourage rice farmers to spend more time and efforts to control rats in order to increase their crop yields income, by increasing their perception that controlling rats is more beneficial than doing other jobs, from 37% to 50%
8. Superstition that rats will take revenge on behalf of their "dead friends" by causing worse damages	To reduce the proportion of rice farmers' misconception regarding their superstitious belief that rats take revenge on behalf of their "dead friends" by causing worse damages from 54% to 50%
9. Non-practice of simultaneous planting which could disrupt food supply for rats during part of the year	To encourage more rice farmers to engage in simultaneous planting in order to reduce time for rats to have continuous food supply by enhancing positive attitudes towards that practice; from 79% to 85%

Source: Adapted from Adhikarya, 1994.

Human and behavioral dimensions considerations

To minimize heavy "technology-bias" of many extension activities, the SEC method gives adequate considerations to *human behavioral* aspects which facilitate or impede adoption, or the continued practice by farmers of recommended agricultural technologies. Without sufficient understanding of their positive or negative attitudes and behavior towards a given technology, the "technology transfer" process would be slow and ineffective, For instance, in the Rat Control Campaign in Penang Malaysia only 19 percent of farmers surveyed before the campaign disagreed with a superstitious belief that "rats will take revenge on behalf of their dead friends by causing worse damages." Unless this attitudinal problem is mitigated or neutralized, the technological recommendations for rat control might be of little value (Adhikarya, 1994).

The *segmentation* of extension problems, objectives, strategies and information needs according to a target audience's levels of knowledge, attitude and practice in regards to a given recommended technology is not only conceptually important, but practical and useful as well. Problems related to low knowledge level require different solutions than those related to attitudinal problems.

The implications of the different KAP levels greatly influence the development of problem-solving strategies, message design, selection of multi-media mix (including when and how to utilize group and interpersonal communication channels, such as extension workers), and materials development (Adhikarya, 1994).

Cost-effective multi-media approach

National extension services face a shortage of field personnel to reach large number of farmers in widely spread geographical areas. Moreover, these workers are usually overburdened. Such over-reliance on extension workers is neither technically sound nor operationally efficient.

Some extension functions such as awareness creation, information delivery, and motivational campaigns can be more effectively and efficiently performed by other means, channels, or non-extension groups, including the increasingly accessible and low-cost mass communication channels (i.e., local radio stations, rural press, folk and traditional media, posters, flipcharts, silk-screened printed materials, audio-cassettes, slide-tape presentations, leaflets, and comics) to disseminate standardized and packaged messages. Local resource persons (such as teachers, religious leaders, and school children) can serve as "intermediaries" in reaching farmers. In essence, the SEC method employs a multi-media approach whereby cost-effective *combination of mass, personal and group communication* channels (including extension workers and trainers) and materials are efficiently utilized to reduce extension cost and efforts, and to increase its effectiveness in dealing with larger number of beneficiaries.

Many of these communication activities are derived from Ev Rogers' research on the use of traditional authorities (e.g., traditional midwives or barefoot doctors, etc.), intermediaries (e.g., change agents and satisfied clients), small group interactions, and use of interpersonal networks, and engaging mass media approaches (such as entertainment-education).

In addition to conventional multi-media campaign materials such as pamphlets, posters, flipcharts, and radio spots, the two SEC activities for Tubectomy/Ligation and Rat Control in Bangladesh in early

1980s mobilized school children, teachers, pesticide dealers, community leaders, field health educators, and laborers as intermediary channels (Figure 8.3).

In addition, seed dealer stores, tea-stalls, mosques, bus stops, local dispensaries, factories, and schools were used as distribution (or display) points. Mini-posters were "piggy-backed" on coconut-oil bottles (most rural Bangladeshis treat their hair with coconut oil) and matchboxes. Comic sheets were distributed and essay competitions organized through secondary schools to facilitate student discussion about campaign messages with their often illiterate parents. Entertainment-education songs and soap-operas were broadcast through radio. Such approaches in using "Other People's Network or Resources" have now been mainstreamed as "social marketing" communication methods.

Narrowing the inequitable benefits gap

The SEC method also gives special attention to narrowing the inequitable benefits gap between large and small farmers which may occur as a result of a campaign. While the notion of a knowledge-gap was originally introduced by Katzman (1974), the strategy to mitigate the problem was also discussed, among others, in Rogers (1976); Shingi and Mody (1976); Adhikarya and Rogers (1978). Ev Rogers and I wrote about this issue in *Communication Yearbook III* (Rogers and Adhikarya, 1979). To narrow information gaps, strategies such as "message redundancy" and "ceiling effects" were applied in two rats control campaigns[2] in Bangladesh (Adhikarya and Posamentier, 1987).

The 1983 Bangladesh SEC was aimed at wheat farmers to increase adoption of rat control practices from 10 to 25 percent in one year. The three-month campaign covered 11 districts as its primary target area, which accounted for about 91 percent of the total wheat acreage, and about 91 percent of the total wheat production in Bangladesh. Due to some political considerations (i.e., "equity" issue, etc.), the other 10 districts in the country were considered as a secondary target area of the campaign, and very minimal campaign inputs were provided here. For evaluation purposes, these areas thus served as a "control" group.

[2] For complete illustrations and detailed discussion on these two campaigns in Bangladesh, please see Adhikarya and Posamentier (1987).

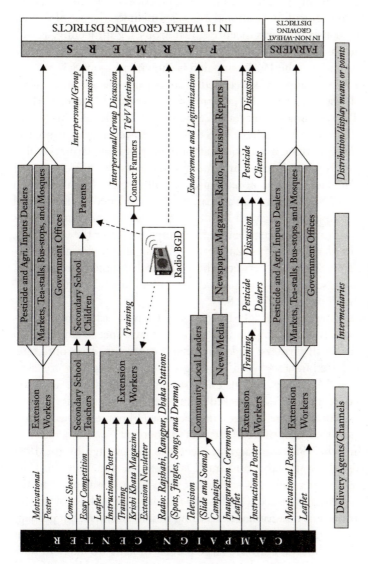

Figure 8.3

Strategic multi-media plan of the 1983 rat control campaign

The campaign's target beneficiaries were segmented according to their levels of knowledge, attitudes, and practices concerning rat control. Positioning of motivational messages included the use of various appeals such as religious incentive, fear arousal, guilt feeling, as well as a ridicule appeal that served as a discussion point. The multi-media strategy plan for the 1983 campaign is shown in Figure 8.3.

The 1983 campaign succeeded in increasing the adoption of rat control practices from 10 percent of farmers to 32 percent (Figure 8.4), exceeding the target of 25 percent. Cost-benefit analysis of the SEC showed net gains of US$ 834,295. However, evaluation data showed the increase was accounted for mainly by large farmers (cultivating more than 5 acres) and medium farmers (with 2–5 acres of land). No increase was noted among small farmers (with less than 2 acres). The 1983 campaign appeared to have widened the rat control practice gap between small farmers and large or medium farmers which was only 6 percent before the campaign. After the campaign, the gap widened to 17 percent between the small and the large farmers, and to 8 percent between the small and the medium farmers. Likewise, the gap also widened between medium and large farmers, from 0 to 9 percent (Figure 8.5).

Consequently, the 1984 SEC campaign consciously devised strategies to narrow the campaign effects gap. It gave special emphasis on reaching small farmers, and minimizing campaign drop-outs rate. Message "redundancy" and "ceiling-effects" strategies were used (Rogers and Adhikarya, 1979). These strategies worked well. Adoption of rat control practices increased from 41 to 63 percent among small farmers. Among large farmers, the increase (14 percent) was significantly less than that of small farmers (22 percent).

While the 1984 campaign reduced the gap created by the 1983 campaign between large and small farmers, the gap after the 1984 campaign (9 percent) was still wider than what it was prior to the 1983 campaign (6 percent). This gap may have been due not only to socio-economic disadvantages accruing to small farmers, but perhaps also because rat control practices depend on the degree of rat problems faced. Farmers who cultivate large parcels of land are likely to have more rat problems than do small farmers. Thus the need for rat control is felt more keenly by large farmers as compared to small farmers.

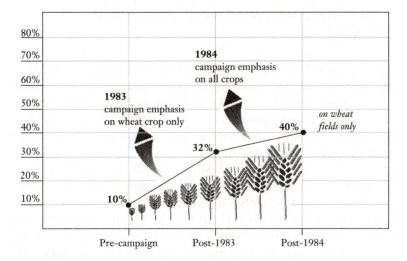

Figure 8.4
Percentage of adoption of rat control practices
by wheat farmers on wheat fields only

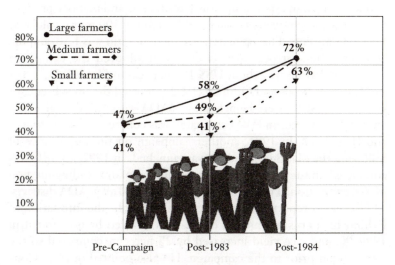

Figure 8.5
Percentage of adoption of rat control practices by large, medium,
and small farmers in all locations

The case of integrated weed management in Malaysia

The Strategic Extension Campaign (SEC) on Integrated Weed Management (IWM) was carried out in 1989 by the Muda Agricultural Development Authority (MADA) in North Malaysia with assistance from FAO. The campaign addressed a weed problem which was fast becoming serious with the wide-spread implementation of direct-seeding method or rice planting.

One of the objectives of the SEC on IWM was to train a core-group of MADA staff in the process of designing a systematic extension and training program based on SEC principles. In addition to the FAO staff, six of Malaysia's Department of Agriculture (DOA) staff members who were trained during the FAO-assisted SEC on rat control in Malaysia were the main resource persons for the SEC on IWM. The campaign was conducted from January to September in 1989.

The campaign was initially undertaken in Districts III and IV of MADA for 30,000 farm families. Mohamed and Khor (1988) reported that the campaign expenditure was US$ 46,400, and that rice production in the campaign areas increased by about 9,500 tons—valued at US$ 2.33 million. The estimated cost-benefit ratio was 1:50, and the economic benefit per farm family who adopted the campaign recommendations was about US$ 195 per season (Table 8.2).

Mohamed Noor and Othman (1992) reported that in subsequent years, other SECs were launched by MADA without external assistance. For instance, an IWM campaign was conducted for Districts I and II in 1990. In 1991, another campaign on the importance of following the planting schedule was launched. In 1992, an SEC was conducted on the correct planting techniques of dry seeding method of rice cultivation. These two campaigns covered all MADA districts.

Ho (1994) reported that as a campaign result, the infestation of Echinochloa crusgalli and E. colona was reduced by 66 percent in 1989–90, and rice yield increased by 27 percent, compared to the 1988 season prior to the campaign. Ho also pointed out: "... Continuous implementation of SEC on IWM from 1990 to 1993 over the entire Muda area has shown remarkable results. The dry-seeded first season rice yields have increased steadily, reaching 4.2 tons/hectare in 1993. Meanwhile the wet-seeded second season rice yields

Table 8.2
Cost and benefit analysis of Integrated Weed Management Campaign (in US$)

Acreage loss	1988	4,938 hectares
	1989	2,661 hectares
Production gain after campaign		2,277 hectares
Production estimates		1 hectare = 4.2 tons = $244.45
Financial gain after the campaign		2,277 × 4.2 × 224.45 = *$2,337,773*
Total savings		$2,337,773
Total campaign expenditure		$46.409
Cost/benefit ration		*1:50*
		For each $1 invested, a return of $50 was gained
Campaign target		30,000 farm families
Estimated farm families who adopted/practiced campaign recommendations		40% of target audience = 12,000
Average economic benefit per farm family who adopted campaign recommendations		2,337,773 ÷ 12,000 = *$195*

have consistently been above 5 tons/hectare. It is noteworthy that over the same period, the usage of herbicides has declined."

Lessons learned for up-scaling SEC

User-friendly guidelines

One of the lessons learned from the SEC replications, up-scaling, and franchising for various development programs in many countries is the critical need to have a theoretically-sound, explicitly-clear, user/reader-friendly, process-oriented, operationally manageable, and. practical generic conceptual framework for flexible adaptations in different contexts.

The SEC conceptual framework and the management operations steps and procedures (see Figures 8.1 and 8.2) provided generic guidelines for a Standard Operating Procedure (SOP) in planning, designing, implementing, managing and evaluating the activities. The two SEC books were developed, written and packaged in a "process documentation" format complete with empirical assessment results, and step-by-step process-oriented guidelines for generic replications or adaptation (Adhikarya, 1994; Adhikarya and Posamentier, 1987).

Similarly, Rogers' diffusion of innovation concepts, such as the process and stages of adoption, provided clear guidelines for operationalizing and applying SEC processes for several different purposes in different contexts. One of the reasons that Ev Rogers' books are widely-circulated among communication scholars, development practitioners, and decision-makers is due to his reader-friendly writing style.

In a shopping alley in Sorrento, Italy

In the summer of 1985, Ev visited with us in Rome, Italy for rest and recreation. My wife and I took him on a two-day trip to Sorrento and the isle of Capri for fine dining, wine, and Tarantella music. While engaging in a "passeggiata"—leisurely walk—through a small alley of restaurants, gift shops, and small boutiques, we saw one of Ev's books, *Silicon Valley Fever* (Rogers and Larsen, 1984), in one of the quaint shops.

Ev, a little surprised to see his second-hand book on sale at this store, remarked "…now I know why this book will be a best seller."

Ev later told me that this book (published in nine languages) sold more copies than any of his other books.

"Cloning" multiplier knowledge champions

Another critical requirement for up-scaling SEC involves capacity development for a core-group of knowledge advocates (or champions) who bond into networks of communities of practice, and cultivate a network mind-set. Opportunities to share vertically and disseminate horizontally the know-how by network members should be encouraged and promoted. Strategic alliances with other relevant networks, which can complement and add value to the accomplishment of a common objective, should be actively supported.

As explained previously, in implementing SEC activities, staff training through various SEC workshops is a requirement to ensure quality
assurance. Moreover, these workshops also provide bonding opportunities to network members and "SEC integrity" buy-ins for
potential SEC resource persons—who are "certified" to handle such
responsibilities after multiple training workshops. These resource
persons function as multiplier SEC knowledge champions by training
other practitioners and trainers. Experienced SEC network members are also provided opportunities to serve as SEC consultants or
trainers in other organizations locally, nationally, or internationally
(Adhikarya, 1994).

However, successful networking cannot be accomplished only by
forming, developing and nurturing a formal group of SEC network

---

The Toronto mini-reunion

In 1997, I organized a mini-workshop as part of the Global Knowledge
Conference in Toronto. The conference, sponsored by the World Bank
and the Canadian government, included participants such as Premier
Jean Chrétien, UN Secretary General Kofi Annan, World Bank's
president, James Wolfensohn, UNESCO's director general, Federico
Mayor, Presidents of Uganda, Mali, and Costa Rica, Nobel laureates
(Joseph Stigliz, Jose Maria Figueres, Arno Penzias), and business
leaders such as Michael Dell, CEO of Dell, Jean Monty, CEO of
Nortel, and others.

In our mini-workshop session, we tried to reunite Ev Rogers with
some of his friends and collaborators. Our plan was to have the three
outstanding Asian development communicators on the panel: Haryono
Suyono (Coord. Minister of Social Affairs and former Minister of
Population, Indonesia), Juan Flavier (Senator and former Minister of
Public Health, the Philippines), and Mechai Viravaidya (Senator and
Chairman Population and Community Development Association,
Thailand). Unfortunately, Mechai Viravaidya could not make it and
Haryono Suyono who was on his way to Toronto was recalled by the
Indonesian president for an emergency cabinet meeting.

However, eight of Ev's former students and collaborators, representing many countries and continents, posed for a photo with Ev
(Plate 8.1).

Plate 8.1
The Toronto mini-reunion. From left to right are Manfred Oepen (Germany), Arvind Singhal (India and USA), Dennis Foote (USA), Joseph Mbindyo (Kenya), Ev Rogers, Corinne Shefner-Rogers (Canada and USA), Ronny Adhikarya (Indonesia and USA), and Marco Encalada (Ecuador). The picture was taken by Senator Juan Flavier of the Philippines who considered Ev to be one of his "gurus"
Source: Personal files of the author

members. A critical task in networking lies in brokering partnerships and collaborations with other existing networks, including introducing network members to other professional contacts. Ev Rogers was a master at brokering such network contacts.

With his wide-ranging international teaching, research, and consulting experiences and excellent intercultural communication skills, Ev had an extensive network of personal contacts and intellectual followers worldwide. I witnessed many of his networking activities in Asia, but Ev Rogers footprints spread across Europe, Latin America, and Africa. After Ev passed away, when I shared the news with Professor Royal D. Colle of Cornell University, he noted: "Probably no news in the communication field has traveled to all corners of the world so quickly as this. This is a tribute to Ev's many friends and colleagues."

Franchising SEC

The SEC method has been replicated with FAO assistance in many countries in Asia, Africa, the Near East and the Caribbean, covering topics such as line sowing method of rice cultivation, maize production, cocoa cultivation, tick-borne disease control, contour tillage, HIV/AIDS prevention, population education, plowing with drought animal power, and others. In addition to various SEC replications within a country, the multiplier effects of its method are felt beyond national boundaries. Extension specialists from Ghana, Malawi, Ethiopia, France, Malaysia, Thailand, and the Philippines, who were trained by FAO on the SEC method now serve as resource persons to train their counterparts in similar SEC replications in Sri Lanka, the Philippines, Malaysia, Thailand, China, Liberia, Zambia, Malawi, Kenya, Uganda, Morocco, Tunisia, Rwanda, Burundi, Guinea, Jamaica, and Honduras.

The SEC method has now been applied in, up-scaled through, and franchised to, many agricultural development programs in at least 19 countries of Asia, the Near East and Africa, initially supported through FAO/United Nations' projects. In addition, other development agencies have also applied SEC methods, e.g., GTZ for Environment Education, Thailand's Royal Project for the Highland Horticultural Development Program, the Department of Fisheries in Western Australia (Machin, Dearded, and Lacey, 2003) for Aquaculture.

The up-scaling and franchising of SEC was also used as a model for the development and implementation of a Knowledge Utilization through Learning Technologies (KULT) Program which I later founded and managed at the World Bank.[3]

---

[3] A similar approach (as SEC) in network building through capacity development was applied when I managed and implemented the Knowledge Utilization through Learning Technologies (KULT) Program at the World Bank in Washington, DC. To leverage its limited human resources, and multiply the global training impact of the World Bank as a "Knowledge Bank," the World Bank Institute (WBI) through the KULT Program developed a "self-destructing" capacity enhancement program with a five-year exit strategy. Its objective was to improve training quality and the global competitiveness of developing countries' training institutions and their core-staff. After the five-year period,

In closing

One of the most remarkable traits of Ev Rogers was his "personable personality" which facilitated wide-ranging professional and social interactions with him. Ev Rogers had a phenomenal memory and could recall with ease the slightest details of people whom he may have met decades ago, including their professional background, hobbies, and even, sometimes, the names of their children. Through his personality and highly effective professional networking, genuine personal relationships developed among members of the large "Rogers" clan. Such a personalized international networking "system" among communication knowledge champions may be one of the main reasons for the wide diffusion and rapid adoption of Ev Rogers' concepts, principles, research findings, and consulting recommendations—many of which have been operationalized and applied globally.

While Everett Rogers is no longer with us, his legacy—the "invisible college" of networks he developed over the last five decades—is functioning well and will live on. The "multiplier knowledge champions" nurtured by this Rogers' network will continue to contribute in enriching communication scholarship and in improving development communication practice worldwide (as illustrated by the contributors to this volume).

KULT Program alumni and network members were expected to continue the efforts, through franchising arrangements, to ensure program sustainability and institutionalization. By the end the five-year period in June 2002, the KULT Program workshops had benefited 922 participants (who are trainers/educators or training managers) and resource persons from 258 training and/or development-oriented institutions in 63 countries. The fee-based KULT Program's workshops had a 63 percent "Repeat Clients Rate" (i.e., participants from the same institutions which had previously sent participants to the workshops). The KULT Program and its partner institutions had successfully built strategic alliances with at least 45 global corporations, leading national companies and reputable institutions as workshop sponsors, among others, Cisco, SONY, Microsoft, ACER Computers, Avaya, Hilton, Shangri-La Hotels, Reuters, and others. The KULT Program continues and is managed by a KULT Program Partners Consortium. Its alumni have their own virtual professional information network: The International Society for Improving Training Quality (isitQ).

References

Adhikarya, Ronny. 1972. The Intensification of the Communication Strategies in Family Planning Programs in Rural Java: With an Emphasis on the Use of Traditional Communication Networks. Master's thesis. Department of Communication Arts, College of Agriculture, Cornell University.

———. 1983. *Knowledge Transfer and Usage in Communication Studies: The US–ASEAN Case*. Singapore: Asian Mass Communication Research and Information Centre (AMIC).

———. 1994. *Strategic Extension Campaign: A Participatory-oriented Method of Agricultural Extension*. Rome: Food and Agriculture Organization (FAO)/ United Nations. Also published in French and Spanish; available on CD-ROM in English. Web version: www.fao.org/docrep/u8955e/u8955e00.htm or www.fao.org/sd/EXdirect/EXan0003.htm.

Adhikarya, Ronny and J. Middlton. 1979. *Communication Planning at the Institutional Level: A Selected Annotated Bibliography*. Honolulu, HI: The East-West Center.

Adhikarya, Ronny and Heimo Posamentier. 1987. *Motivating Farmers for Action: How Strategic Multi-Media Can Help*. Foreword by Everett M. Rogers. Eschborn, Frankfurt: Deutsche Gesellschaft für Technische Zusammenarbeit (GTZ).

Adhikarya, Ronny and Everett M. Rogers. 1978. Communication and Inequitable Development: Narrowing the Socio-Economic Benefits Gap. *Media Asia* 5 (1): 3–9.

Ho, N. K. 1994. Integrated Weed Management of Rice in Malaysia: Some Aspects of the Muda Irrigation Scheme. A paper presented at the FAO–CAB International Workshop on Appropriate Weed Control in Southest Asia, Kuala Lumpur, Malaysia, May.

Katzman, Natan. 1974. The Impact of Communication Technology: Some Theoretical Premises and Their Implications. *Ekistics* 225: 125–30.

Machin, Daniel, Mandy Dearded, and Peter Lacey. 2003. *Marrron Aquaculture Strategic Extension Campaign—An Interim Report*. Perth: Dept. of Fisheries, Western Australia. Web version: www.regional.org.au/au/apen/2003/3/ 080machind.htm.

Mohamed, R. and Y. L. Khor. 1988. *Survey Report of Farmers' Knowledge, Attitude, and Practice (KAP) on Weed Management in the Muda Agricultural Development Authority (MADA)*. Penang: Universiti Sains Malaysia.

Mohamed Noor, A.S. and A. B. Othman. 1992. *Strategic Extension Campaign (SEC) Training Programmes and Activities in Malaysia Since 1988*. Telok Chengai, Malaysia: Extension Training and Development Centre (PLPP), Department of Agriculture.

Rogers, E. M. 1962. *Diffusion of Innovations*. New York: Free Press of Glencoe.

———. 1973. *Communication Strategies for Family Planning*. New York: Free Press.

———. (ed.). 1976. *Communication and Development: Critical Perspectives*. Thousand Oaks, CA: Sage Publications.

Rogers, E. M. and Lynne Svenning. 1969. *Modernization among Peasants: The Impact of Communication*. New York: Holt, Rinehart and Winston.

Rogers, E. M. and F. F. Shoemaker. 1971. *Communication of Innovations: A Cross-Cultural Approach*. New York: Free Press.

Rogers, E. M. and Ronny Adhikarya. 1979. Diffusion of Innovations: An Up-to-Date Review and Commentary. In Dan Nimmo (ed.), *Communication Yearbook III*. New Brunswick, NJ: Transaction Books.

Rogers, E. M. and D. Lawrence Kincaid. 1981. *Communication Networks: Towards a New Paradigm for Research*. New York: Free Press.

Rogers, E. M. and Judith K. Larsen. 1984. *Silicon Valley Fever: Growth of High Technology Culture*. New York: Basic Books.

Shingi, P. and B. Mody. 1976. The Communication Effects Gap: A Field Experiment in TV and Agricultural Ignorance in India. *Communication Research* 3 (2): 46–58.

9

Entertainment-Education and Health Promotion:
A Cross-Continental Journey

ARVIND SINGHAL, KIMANI NJOGU,

MARTINE BOUMAN, *and* ELIANA ELÍAS

Sometimes when you're out of town, the future can go by. That happened to me in Los Angeles. In the spring of 1989, Ev was hosting what would become the first international conference on entertainment-education and social change. I remember looking through the conference agenda on a flight over-seas, wondering how this new entertainment emphasis fit into the scholarship of diffusion and social change. Well, many large-scale international projects later, we know. Arvind, in particular, and many of his colleagues worldwide have been instrumental in pushing this research and practice agenda forward and giving it scholarly meaning.

JIM DEARING

EV ROGERS WAS THE QUINTESSENTIAL STORYTELLER. HE HAD A STORY for every occasion, and it did not matter if you had heard it previously. Stories, vignettes, and examples were integral to his teaching, writing, and mentoring. He believed in "entertainment-education" (E-E) and was its consummate practitioner—much before the term E-E was officially coined.

Appropriately, the present chapter is co-constructed by us—the four authors—as a series of stories, interwoven, knitted, and patterned in ways to discuss the entertainment-education strategy in health promotion. One of us (Arvind) took primary responsibility for knitting and interweaving our respective narratives, and that's why sometimes you will hear our voices independently, and sometimes collectively. The "storytellers" of this chapter hail from *four* different countries

---

"First, get their attention!"[1]

There is even a story about how Ev got interested in storytelling. Once, when Ev was about 8-year-old, the Rogers family on their way to Carroll in the family car, encountered a neighbor with his team of mules. The mules, hitched to a heavy wagonload of grain, balked at crossing a bridge over a small stream. The neighbor was beating the mules on their heads with a wooden stick. When Ev's father, out the open car window, asked why he was hitting the mules, the neighbor answered: "Well, first you have to get their attention. Then you can teach them something" (Rogers, unpublished manuscript). This lesson was not lost on Ev. Without fail, Ev began a lecture with an interesting anecdote, or started a book chapter or a journal article with a vivid story.

---

on *four* different continents, each bringing a unique contextually-situated perspective on the use of entertainment-education and health promotion.

In order to make sense of these E-E stories, perhaps readers may find it useful to learn a bit about (*a*) the four storytellers, including their connection with Ev Rogers and with each other, and (*b*) the rising stock of the E-E strategy in health promotion.

About the storytellers

Arvind Singhal, born and raised in India, was Ev's doctoral advisee at the USC Annenberg School and, over a period of two decades, collaborated with Ev in studying and writing about entertainment-education health promotion initiatives in India, Peru, Mexico, China, Tanzania, South Africa, Thailand, Kenya, and Brazil (Singhal and Rogers, 1999; 2002; and Singhal et al., 2004). In 2005, a few months before this volume went to press, the USC Annenberg School's Norman Lear Center honored Arvind with the first Everett M. Rogers Award for Outstanding Achievement in Entertainment-Education.

---

[1] This story was narrated by Ev Rogers many a time and is featured in Rogers (n.d.).

Kimani Njogu, born and raised in Kenya, earned his Ph.D. from Yale University in linguistics, and collaborated with Ev on the famous *Twende na Wakati* E-E project in Tanzania, serving as chief trainer of the Tanzanian scriptwriting team. Kimani has scripted, produced, and directed numerous E-E initiatives on reproductive health, HIV/ AIDS, and environmental conservation around the globe—in Kenya, Uganda, St. Lucia, Madagascar, and several other countries. Kimani hosted the African Soap Summit held in Nairobi in June 2003, and he and Arvind have collaborated on getting E-E initiatives underway in China, India, Vietnam, and Laos.

Martine Bouman, born and raised in Netherlands, earned her Ph.D. from Wageningen Agricultural University in the Netherlands, writing about the difficult collaborative process between media professionals and health educators in E-E. Martine hosted the Third International Entertainment-Education and Social Change Conference in Arnhem, Netherlands in 2000, and presently serves as Managing Director of the Netherlands Entertainment-Education Foundation (NEEF) and founder and principal of Bouman E&E Development, an organization that works closely with Dutch media producers to incorporate health storylines in popular drama. In the late 1990s, Martine and Arvind served as advisors to the *Soul City* E-E initiative in South Africa.

Eliana Elías, born and raised in Peru, studied social communications at the University of Lima, and is co-founder and Executive Director of Minga Perú, a non-governmental organization that promotes reproductive health and gender equality in the Peruvian Amazon. Eliana is an Ashoka Foundation Fellow—a prestigious global recognition for social entrepreneurship. Eliana invited Arvind to serve on Minga's board a few years ago, and they work closely in framing Minga's communication and social change initiatives in Peru and South America.

The rising tide of entertainment-education

Over the past decade or two, E-E has become a major approach to health promotion and disease prevention (Piotrow et al., 1997; Singhal et al., 2004). *Entertainment-education* is the process of purposely designing and implementing a media message to both entertain and educate, in order to increase audience members' knowledge about an educational issue, create favorable attitudes, shift social norms, and change overt behavior (Singhal and Rogers, 1999; 2002). E-E is not a theory of communication. Rather, it is a communication strategy to bring about behavioral and social change. E-E approaches have tackled a wide variety of social issues, including HIV/AIDS prevention, small family size, maternal and child health, and gender inequality.

The general purpose of entertainment-education interventions is to contribute to the process of directed social change, which can occur at the level of an individual, community, or society. E-E contributes to social change in two ways. First, it can influence audience individuals' awareness, attitudes, and behavior toward a socially desirable end. Here the anticipated effects are located in the individual audience members. An illustration is provided by a radio soap opera, *Twende na Wakati* (Let's Go with the Times), in Tanzania that convinced several hundred thousand sexually-active adults to adopt HIV prevention behaviors (like using condoms and reducing their number of sexual partners) (Rogers et al., 1999). Second, it can influence the audience's external environment to help create the necessary conditions for social change at the system level. Here the major effects are located in the interpersonal and social-political sphere of the audiences' external environment. The entertainment-education media can serve as a social mobilizer, an advocate or agenda-setter, influencing public and policy initiatives in a socially-desirable direction (Wallack, 1990). For instance, the 1999 *Soul City* domestic violence series in South Africa mobilized community action, women's marches, and the speedy passage of domestic violence legislation in South Africa (Usdin et al., 2004).

In 2006, numerous organizations are involved in utilizing the E-E strategy for health promotion and disease prevention on a worldwide basis, including the Johns Hopkins University's Center for Communication Programs, Population Communications International in New York, The Centers for Disease Control and Prevention (CDC) in Atlanta, The BBC World Service Trust, Population Media Center in Vermont, Soul City Institute for Health and Development Communication in South Africa, Puntos de Encuentros in Nicaragua, Twaweza

Communications in Kenya, Minga Perú in Peru, the International Rice Research Institute in the Philippines, the Netherlands Entertainment-Education Foundation (NEEF) in the Netherlands, and countless others. Departments of communication and public health are now particularly oriented to studying or teaching about the E-E strategy (Singhal and Rogers, 2002).

Today, a map of the world would show E-E almost everywhere— as evident from the *four* stories that follow. Collectively, these stories highlight not only some of the main events in the research documentation of the E-E strategy in health promotion (Singhal's Story 1), but also its creative applications in East Africa (Njogu, Story 2), Netherlands (Bouman, Story 3), and the Peruvian Amazon (Elías, Story 4).

Story 1. Planting the E-E seed: A journey with Ev Rogers[2]

Primary storyteller: Arvind Singhal

In my first semester (Fall 1985) of doctoral work at the University of Southern California's Annenberg School for Communication, Ev Rogers showed a three minute videotape of the popular Indian soap opera, *Hum Log* [We People], illustrating its purposive combination of entertainment and education as a means of promoting social change. A few months previously, in India, I witnessed first-hand the effects of *Hum Log* on Indian audiences. A hush fell in our living room when Ashok Kumar, a highly respected Indian movie actor (akin to Burt Lancaster), delivered the 30-second epilog at the conclusion of each episode, summarizing the intended social message, raising rhetorical questions for the viewers to ponder, and providing viewers with guides to action. *Hum Log* viewers wrote some 400,000 letters to Ashok Kumar in response to his epilogs. Animated discussions about *Hum Log* were common in social gatherings as India was gripped by a *Hum Log* fever (Singhal and Rogers, 1989).

Ev first became aware of entertainment-education television soap operas in 1975, when a Mexican television official doing graduate work at Stanford told him about *Simplemente Maria*, a 1969–71

---

[2] This section draws upon Singhal and Rogers (1999), and Backer et al. (2005).

Plate 9.1
Ev Rogers and Arvind Singhal in the basement of Arvind's parents' home in New Delhi in 1986 sorting through a sample of 20,000 letters written by *Hum Log* viewers. Arvind's mother, Shashi, wonders what a US-based university professor would do with these letters
Source: Personal file of author Singhal

Peruvian television soap opera, which influenced its viewers to enroll in literacy and sewing classes, modeling their behaviors after María, its protagonist (Singhal, Obregon, and Rogers, 1994). Through this Mexican student, Ev also learned of Miguel Sabido, a producer-director-writer at Televisa, the Mexican commercial network, who had implemented the unique idea of combining entertainment with education in telenovelas. Only in-house evaluation research on the effects of Sabido's telenovelas had been conducted in Mexico, and these studies had not found their way into the mainstream of communication science literature. However, when the Mexican soap opera experience was transferred to India in the form of *Hum Log* in 1984–85, it presented a unique opportunity for scholarly research. Within six months of that Fall 1985 class session at USC, Ev and I had secured a grant from the Rockefeller Foundation in New York to conduct an evaluation of *Hum Log* (Singhal and Rogers, 1988).

Such were the beginnings, some two decades ago, of our collaborative journey on the path of entertainment-education. With colleagues

Plate 9.2
Ev Rogers and Arvind Singhal with the *Hum Log* survey research team in New Delhi, India in 1987. Standing behind on extreme left is Dr B. R. Patil, a close collaborator of Ev during his three-country diffusion study in the 1960s, and by his side is Bill Brown (at that time a doctoral student at USC)
Source: Personal files of author Singhal

at USC, University of New Mexico, Ohio University, Michigan State University, and other institutions, Ev and I studied entertainment-education initiatives in India, Peru, Mexico, China, Tanzania, South Africa, Thailand, Kenya, and Brazil. In 1997, seven years after I finished my doctoral dissertation on E-E (Singhal, 1990), and after two highly effective entertainment-education conferences at USC (in 1989) and at Ohio University (in 1997), we sensed that the time was ripe for a book on the topic. By this time, scores of entertainment-education initiatives were underway in dozens of countries, and the stock of entertainment-education as a health promotion strategy was on the rise.

On a bumpy bus ride in Costa Rica in 1997, while driving toward San Jose, the capital city, Ev pulled out his signature purple pen and a notepad and initiated our book's outline. A few months later, at the International Communication Association 1998 convention in Jerusalem, Israel, we met with Linda Bathgate, the communication editor for Lawrence Erlbaum Associates (LEA), and a contract was signed. In mid-1999, *Entertainment-Education: A Communication*

Plate 9.3
Ev Rogers and Arvind Singhal hold a copy of *Entertainment-Education* at the University of Miami, Coral Gables, Florida in 2002. In the center is Rasha Abdullah, an Egyptian scholar of communication studies
Source: Personal files of author Singhal

Strategy for Social Change (Singhal and Rogers, 1999) was published. A year later, it was honored with National Communication Association's Distinguished Scholarly Book Award in Applied Communication, and was widely adopted as a text in communication and public health courses at various US and overseas universities.

In 2002, with the encouragement of Professor Michael Cody, the then editor of *Communication Theory*, Ev and I edited a special issue of the journal on E-E (Singhal and Rogers, 2002). As there were several excellent submissions, and we could only accommodate six articles in the journal issue, we broached the idea of an edited volume on E-E, once again with LEA. This 22-chapter volume—representing multiple E-E projects from across the world and signifying multiple theoretic and methodological approaches to E-E—was published in 2004 (Singhal et al., 2004).

In closing

In retrospect, back at USC in the fall of 1985, Ev Rogers had clearly grasped the potential of the entertainment-education strategy in health promotion. Once the seed was planted, and nurtured, a tree would follow.

Story 2. The "Mother Hen" of radio soaps in East Africa

Primary storyteller: Kimani Njogu

In February 1993, in Dar-es-Salaam, Tanzania, I was leading a workshop organized by Radio Tanzania, the United Nations Fund for Population and Development (UNFPA), and Population Communications International (PCI) to plan for the broadcasts of *Twende na Wakati* (Let's Go with the Times), an entertainment-education radio soap opera on HIV prevention and family planning. As I was introducing the notion of the cliffhanger as an artistic device for deliberate suspension of melodramatic action, Ev Rogers and his collaborator Peter Vaughan walked into the seminar room. After taking a quick photograph of the proceedings, Ev joined our discussions and noted: "I like the cliffhanger because it not only hooks audience members but, even more interestingly, opens possibilities for other storylines!" Ev's insightful statement was to resonate throughout the course of this workshop, and I have found myself returning to it repeatedly since then in my design of E-E programs.

After the workshop at Radio Tanzania, we went for dinner to the Kilimanjaro Hotel, where I learned two important things. First, a watertight, pre-post, treatment-control research design was in place for evaluating *Twende na Wakati* (to be led by Ev Rogers and Peter Vaughan), and, second, Ev Rogers had committed to contributing in developing the capacity of entertainment-education research in Tanzania by opening an avenue for Ramadhan Swalehe and Verhan Bakari,[3] both of Population Family Life Education Program (POFLEP) in Arusha, to undertake graduate study in communication at the University of New Mexico. Both Swalehe and Bakari would study aspects of *Twende na Wakati* (TNW) in their respective sojourns in Albuquerque (where Ev Rogers was based), and return to Tanzania to continue work on E-E and HIV/AIDS prevention.

---

[3] Bakari spent a semester at the University of New Mexico while Swalehe earned an MA degree.

Plate 9.4
Ev in front of the POFLEP headquarters in Arusha, Tanzania in June, 1994. Ev was in Arusha to plan the second national survey for *Twende na Wakati*. Notice the *Twende na Wakati* insignia on the POFLEP vehicle
Source: Peter W. Vaughan

Such inclusiveness, foresight, and intuition came naturally to Ev Rogers and symbolize, for us his legacy to the field of entertainment-education and health promotion.

Theory-based message design in *Twende na Wakati*

The design of *Twende na Wakati* drew upon Bandura's social learning theory (also called social cognitive theory), which states that learning can occur through observing media role-models, and that this vicarious learning can be is more effective than direct experiential learning. Miguel Sabido, a creative Mexican writer-producer-director had adapted Bandura's theories to designing E-E soaps (see Bandura's chapter, this volume), and I was privileged to be directly trained by Miguel Sabido in the mid-1980s in this approach.

Three types of role-models were consciously incorporated in the storyline for *TNW*: (*a*) those who support the educational value (positive role-models) (*b*) those who reject this value (negative role-models), and (*c*) those who change from negative to positive behavior (transitional role-models) during the soap opera's broadcasts. Transitional characters start out as negative role-models, or at least are unsure about adopting the desired behavior. When transitional characters change their attitudes and behaviors toward the educational value, their transformation is reinforced and explained in the epilogs (which are brief statements by a prestigious individual that connects the episode to an individuals' lives). Each time a positive role-model or a transitional character performs the socially desirable behavior (such as adopting family planning, for example), they are rewarded immediately in the storyline. Each time a negative role-model performs a socially undesirable behavior, he/she is immediately punished. For example, in *TNW* Mkwaju (literally "walking stick") is a negative role model for sexual responsibility; he is a truck driver who is promiscuous, sleeps with commercial sex workers, and contracts AIDS. He is punished by losing his prestigious job, his family, and eventually his life (Rogers et al., 1999).

The effects of *TNW*

The effects of *TNW* were measured in a field experiment in which most of Tanzania was exposed to this entertainment-education radio soap opera (the treatment), while the broadcasts were blocked from a large central region of the country (Dodoma) for two years from 1993 to 1995 (the control, or comparison, area). Multiple types of evaluation data were gathered including before/during/after personal interviews with about 3,000 respondents in the control and treatment area each year for five years, point-of-referral data on family planning adoption at 79 clinics in the treatment and control areas, focus group and in-depth interviews with new family planning adopters in the control and treatment areas, and much more (Rogers et al., 1999).

TNW was an audience hit. In its first few years, some 55 percent of Tanzanians listened to the radio soap opera, and about half of those individuals listened regularly (that is, to at least one or both of the episodes that were broadcast each week). The program had strong effects on the adoption of family planning methods in Tanzania, with 23 percent of listeners reporting that they adopted because of exposure to *TNW*. Some 82 percent of listeners reported adopting a method of HIV prevention because of listening to the radio broadcasts

(Rogers et al., 1999; Vaughan et al., 2000; Vaughan and Rogers, 2000). Most of these adopters changed to monogamous sexual relationships, while others adopted condoms, or else stopped sharing razors or needles. According to Vaughan (2003: 5): "The most important behavior change that we were able to measure was a change in the number of sexual partners for both men and women .... There was a secular downward trend in this variable of about 0.3 partners for men and 0.5 partners for women ... and the decline was greater in the treatment than it was in the comparison area." The cost-benefits of *TNW* were also impressive: Less than $1.00 (US) per adopter of family planning and less than 10 cents (US) per adopter of HIV prevention. These figures are very important in a desperately poor nation like Tanzania, where the per capita income today is only $150 per year.

Fast forward to 2005. Initially slated for broadcast for two years (1993 to 1995), *TNW* is still being broadcast in Tanzania, some 12 years after its launch. In 2005, the program is broadcast on Radio Tanzania Dar-es-Salaam, Radio Tanzania-Dodoma, Sauti ya Tanzania-Zanzibar, Radio Faraja-Shinyanga, and Sauti ya Injili-Kilimanjaro. By far, it is the longest-running and most popular radio program in Tanzania of all times. Over the years, *TNW* has won numerous international recognitions, including the Global Award for Media Excellence for Best Radio Program in Population Reporting, and UNESCO's Award for meritorious and innovative programming to improve communication in rural communities.

Moreover, the *TNW* experience has opened numerous avenues for the growth of entertainment-education programs in East Africa, and in other parts of the world. In East Africa, scriptwriters and producers trained for *TNW* were key in initiating *Zinduka*, a radio soap on reproductive health and child survival; *Mnazi Mmoja*, a radio serial designed to encourage voter-education; *Vijana Wetu*, a radio serial on adolescent reproductive health; *Bibi Msafiri* on civic education; and *Baragumu la Haki* and *Mambo Bomba* on youth and sexuality.[4]

---

[4] *Mambo Bomba* (Cool Stuff), a radio youth magazine with a soap opera component, was another program inspired by *Twende na Wakati*. It was produced by Radio Tanzania under the Africa Youth Alliance (AYA) Project. The skills gained by youth in developing *Twende na Wakati* contributed to the development of *Mambo Bomba*.

Outside of East Africa, the trainers, scriptwriters, and researchers of *TNW* applied the lessons they learned in Tanzania to launch reproductive health and environmental conservation E-E programs such as *Apwe Plezi* [After the Pleasure] in St. Lucia and *The Coconut Bay* in the Eastern Caribbean Islands (Vaughan, Regis, and St. Catherine, 2000). Other E-E and health promotion projects that directly benefited from the *TNW* experience were *Sarivolana*, an E-E soap opera in Madagascar, *Banadda Twegande* in Uganda, and *Usigo Unake*, an E-E soap in Namibia.

In closing

So, *TNW* represents a mother hen for the increased proliferation of E-E in East Africa and outside.[5] Further, the research design and publications from the *TNW* project in Tanzania have contributed significantly to our understanding of how and why entertainment-education works as a health promotion strategy.

The invisible hand of Ev Rogers continues to guide the diffusion of E-E practice and research worldwide.

Story 3. Turtles and peacocks: Lessons in E-E collaboration from the Netherlands[6]
Primary storyteller: Martine Bouman

One morning in June 1991, as I waited in the lobby of a small hotel in the interior of Finland to undertake a tour of the famous North Karelia community health project, I noticed a friendly, distinguished-looking man, sitting in a comfortable chair. I extended my hand and said: "Hello, I am Martine Bouman from the Netherlands. Are you

---

[5] *TNW* has also inspired (and been inspired by) other work in East Africa, notably the Kenyan radio soap opera *Ushikwapo Shikamana*. Both serial dramas are in Kiswahili the national language of Kenya and Tanzania, and shared common design elements, including formative research; development of a values grid; positive, negative and transitional role models; and culturally sensitive storylines.

[6] This section draws upon some previous writings of author Bouman (1999; 2002; 2004).

the bus driver?" The man smiled, took my hand, and said: "Very nice to meet you, Ms. Bouman. Yes, we will be travelling together, although I will not be driving." Unsure about what his role would be on our tour, I told him about my interests in health promotion (at that time I worked with the Netherlands Heart Foundation), and especially in entertainment-education. When I casually mentioned the Indian television series *Hum Log* [We People] as one of the E-E television examples known to me, the man's eyes gleamed and he noted: "Hello, I am Ev Rogers. I know this project very well."

I was very familiar with Ev Rogers' writings on *Hum Log* (Singhal and Rogers, 1988), and not recognizing Ev Rogers in person in that Finnish hotel lobby was embarrassing, to say the least. Over the next few days, we talked about E-E, and I shared with Ev my plans to write a thesis on the subject. When I asked him if he would consider serving as one of my (long-distance) Ph.D. supervisors, Ev grinned about his rapid promotion from bus driver to doctoral committee member.

The metaphor of the bus driver is especially apt for Ev Rogers. In the driver's seat, Ev guided many E-E journeys, including mine in Netherlands. He was friendly and radiant, welcoming, and inclusive. He introduced me to many E-E fellow travelers, including his collaborator on the India *Hum Log* research project, Arvind Singhal (whom I first met in New Delhi, India in 1992).

As I began my doctoral thesis at Wageningen Agricultural University (WAU), I discovered that Ev's ties with the Netherlands went back several decades. One of Netherlands' most respected scholars in agricultural extension at WAU, professor Anne van de Ban, first met Ev Rogers in 1958 at Ohio State University (and later at Michigan State University), when he was studying at the University of Wisconsin. They became good friends and Ev visited van de Ban in Wageningen, prior to the publication of the first 1962 edition of *Diffusion of Innovations* to learn more about innovation diffusion experiences in the Netherlands (and, more generally, in Europe). Another Dutch scholar from WAU, Niels Röling, earned his Ph.D. from Michigan State University in the late 1960s when Ev was teaching there, and participated in the famous three country (India, Nigeria, and Brazil) diffusion study of agricultural innovations that Ev spearheaded.

Plate 9.5
Ev and Martine Bouman after Martine's doctoral defense at the University of Wageningen, the Netherlands, in 1999. Soon after they first met in Finland, Ev graduated from being a "bus driver" to Martine's doctoral committee member
Source: Martine Bouman

When, three decades later, Ev participated on my doctoral thesis committee at WAU, many of these bonds were reinforced and strengthened.

Turtles and peacocks

In my doctoral dissertation, published as a book, *The Turtle and the Peacock: The Entertainment-Education Strategy on Television*, I examined how health communication specialists and television professionals collaborate in producing E-E programs. My analysis included an identification of the hindering and facilitating collaboration factors, as also how these influencing factors could be managed (Bouman, 1999). I referred to the media-professionals (writers, producers, and directors) as "peacocks": they are creative, flamboyant, ego-centric, focused on aesthetics of presentation, and interested in gaining attention. Displaying their beauty and artistry, they eschew scholarly oversight of their work, which they believe as being an unnecessary hindrance. In contrast, I labeled the content-driven health educators as "turtles": they are slow, dull, steeped in both scientific and bureaucratic procedures, questioning, and nitpicking. Interestingly, while most E-E investigations around the globe included audience effects research and/or "reception" studies, our work in the Netherlands looked at the front-end, collaborative production processes characterizing E-E (Bouman, 2002; 2004). That is, in order to create entertainment-education, how can the entertainers and the educators come together, and could the problems associated with such a union be addressed.

In the past 15 years, I have been intimately involved in several E-E projects in the Netherlands to foster collaboration between the "peacocks" and "turtles." The first attempt was *Villa Borghese*, a 1992 co-production purposively designed and implemented to promote a healthy lifestyle, initiated by the Netherlands Heart Foundation (where I was then based).[7] *Villa Borghese* was broadcast on Thursday evenings, in primetime (8:25 P.M. to 9:15 P.M.). The setting is the lavishly decorated interior of Villa Borghese, a health farm in the Dutch countryside. In one scene, for instance, we see Maarten (played by Hugo Haenen), with his new lover, *Villa Borghese*'s dietician Laura (played by Linda de Wolf), dressed in a sexy oversized silk shirt. As they kiss, she pushes him away: "I can smell you picked up smoking again! Why?" Maarten replies: "I'm so sorry. I think it's the stress. I'm really trying to quit." He convinces her of his good intentions, and together they fall in bed, where she begins to undress him (Bouman, 2004).

The lessons from *Villa Borghese* provided understandings of the collaborative processes involved in an E-E co-production (Bouman, 1999; 2002; Bouman and Van Woerkum, 1998; Bouman and Wieberdink, 1993; Wieberdink, 1992; Zandvliet, 1998), including the difficulties when "peacocks" and "turtles" try to come together. Building on the *Villa Borghese* experience, other collaborative television projects followed in the Netherlands, including the hospital drama series *Medisch Centrum West* in 1992–94 (Bouman, Maas, and Kok, 1998), and the television series *Costa!* in 2001 (Van Empelen and Kok, 2002).

Costa!, broadcast in the fall of 2001, was the result of in-script-participation initiated by Stichting Soa Bestrijding, the Dutch

---

[7] Other examples of Dutch E-E television interventions in the late 1980s and early 1990s are the comedy series *Familie Oudenrijn*, the *Way of Life Show*, docu-drama *Twaalf Steden, Dertien Ongelukken*, the comedy series *Oppassen*, the hospital drama series *Medisch Centrum West*, and the game and talk show *Op leven en Dood*.

Foundation Against Sexually Transmitted Diseases. *Costa!* was broad-cast on Monday evenings during primetime (9:30 P.M. to 10:15 P.M.). Its setting is a beach club in Salau, on the Spanish Costa del Sol. In one of the scenes, for instance, we see Frida (played by the hottest Dutch actress Katja Schuurman) walking to her apartment after an early morning stroll. Inside, her promiscuous roommate Agnetha (played by Froukje de Both), kisses her previous night's lover good-bye. As Frida comes in, Agnetha, barely dressed in a white bathrobe, falls back in the bed. "This is the way I like 'em best," she sighs, "No strings attached, no address, no other details, I don't even recall his name!" Frida says: "I don't want to interfere in your love-life ... but there's something to say about the dangers associated with your behav-iors." "Dangers?" Agnetha snaps back, "You needn't bother, I always make love double Dutch!" At Frida's appalled "Double Dutch?" she responds: "Yes, of course: I always use a condom, and I take the pill as well. Double protection, so nothing can happen to me!"

Twenty years ago, E-E programs like *Villa Borghese* and *Costa!* would not have been possible in the Netherlands. At that time, collab-orating with scriptwriters of popular television programs was prob-lematic, because national health organizations had strong reservations about using a popular medium like a tabloid, a soap opera, or other drama series to communicate serious health messages (Bouman, 2004). Apart from their unfamiliarity with popular culture, health organizations feared losing their respectable image.

Our work in the Netherlands suggests that in an E-E collaboration there is always tension between following systematic plans, as health communication professionals are trained to do, and following creative impulses, as comes naturally to television professionals (Runco and Albert, 1990; Van Woerkum, 1981; 1987). A health communication professional stated, "Brainstorming for television professionals [involves] ... acting out every wild fantasy, although there is a limited budget ... and some of the ideas are not at all feasible" (Bouman, 1999: 188). Health communication professionals often become annoyed (although some are also thrilled) with how television professionals indulge in fantasies and how they let their imagination run wild.

While both health communication and television professionals want a television program with high entertainment value and high viewer ratings, they focus on different goals (Pruitt and Carnevale, 1993). Health communication professionals want to influence the audience's knowledge, attitude, and behavior, while television professionals want to entertain the audience and satisfy commercial sponsor-revenue ambitions as well as their professional standards (Bouman, 2004). Health communication professionals usually have scientific training in which matters of objective information, truth, balancing of values, and standardized protocols and procedures are important. Television professionals are trained to value creativity, originality, spontaneity, and authorship. When engaging in E-E collaboration, both parties enter the process with their own professional standards and frames of reference. These two frames of reference (and perceptions of reality) often conflict in the daily practice of producing an E-E program. Health communication professionals specify their aims and goals by means of a thorough and often detailed briefing, based on their frame of reference. After briefing and discussion with the television professionals, the latter also start to work on the project from their own frame of reference. During the actual production stage, the conflict becomes more evident. While both professionals think they are doing a good job, each is questioned and criticized by the other (Bouman, 2004).

A reference frame for conflict is fought out at the production level, on the work floor. Recognizing this potential conflict, both professionals invest time in socializing with each other in order to influence the decisions that are made. But the production of the television program takes place in the domain of the television professionals, so ultimately their frame of reference proves to be the more decisive. Health communication professionals, more often than television professionals, reframe their issues. During the collaboration process, and especially at the production stage, they are confronted with controversies that are based on different perceptions of reality. Because of the deadline structure of television, which requires quick and decisive answers when problems arise, there is not much time for reflection. This results most of the time in accepting the television professionals' frame of reference. Health communication professionals only in rare cases succeed in having television professionals accept their frame of reference (Bouman, 2002; 2004).

Toward a mutual frame of reference

However, our work in the Netherlands with E-E interventions suggests that effective collaboration between "peacocks" and "turtles" can occur. The interests of both the collaborating partners can be met, when a mutual frame of reference is employed to search for common ground. In the Netherlands, we have discovered that a *coordinating mediator*, who knows both fields and can speak both languages, is key to this collaborative process. As Ev noted: "If collaborating with the turtle can get the peacock what he wants, then ultimately they will, at least to some degree, collaborate" (personal interview in the Netherlands, September 2000).

For both the "peacocks" and the "turtles," a coordinating mediator is one possible way to diminish the perceived risks involved in E-E. For health communication professionals, educational messages in entertainment television formats are complicated by the multidimensional character of the medium (a combination of text, image and sound); further, these messages are open-aired, mass-mediated and, hence not restricted to a captive audience. The outputs are thus diffused: that is, the specific educational messages can disappear behind the veneer of entertainment. To media-professionals, health education messages loom as a direct threat to their creative processes and products.

To reduce the perceived risks in E-E collaboration for both the "peacocks" and the "turtles," I helped found the Netherlands Entertainment-Education Foundation (NEEF) and Bouman E&E Development. The purpose was to establish independent organizations that could bring the different E-E stakeholders together. In 2000, NEEF organized the third international conference on Entertainment-Education and Social Change, where researchers, field workers, politicians, media professionals, and funders met on equal terms and mutually designed an EE Declaration for the future (NEEF and JHU/CCP, 2001).

To foster better coordination between different stakeholders, Bouman E&E Development recently completed a research study called *Health on Screen* in which we—the health communicators—analysed how sexual behavior and intimate relationships were portrayed in four different Dutch popular soaps and drama series—

Onderweg Naar Morgen; *Goede Tijden, Slechte Tijden*; *Costa!*; and *Najib en Julia*. After carefully watching over a hundred episodes of these four dramatic series, we identified fourteen different dramatic plots dealing with sexual issues and intimate relationships (including homosexuality, the first intercourse, [in]fidelity in relationships, and others). We also interviewed in-depth the scriptwriters of these storylines and held focus group discussions with Dutch youth (ages 13–19 years old), the primary audience of these series. This research yielded three interesting perspectives of different stakeholders—health communicators, scriptwriters, and audiences. By using actual examples of storylines we were able to start a dialogue between health communicators, scriptwriters, and Dutch youth and create an open forum for discussing the potential impact of drama portrayals and audiences' sexual behavior. One outcome of this project is the design of a mutual, overlapping frame of reference for the three stakeholders (Bouman E&E Development, 2005).

Another more recent, more exciting participatory and collaborative Dutch example of entertainment-education is based on the user-as-designer (UAD) concept. In late 2004, plans were put in place for a television-centered E-E intervention for Dutch youth titled *Find Out*. This 24-episode television series, created by Dutch youth for Dutch youth, is supported by the Dutch Health Research and Development Council, and aims to empower young people to reflect on their own beliefs, values, and practices on the use of drugs, sex, and alcohol. Supported by extensive formative and summative research, *Find Out* is a collaborative venture between various stakeholders: The National Institute for STI and AIDS Control in the Netherlands (SoaAids Nederland), Netherlands Institute of Mental Health and Addiction (Trimbos Instituut), Netherlands Institute for Health Promotion and Disease Prevention (NIGZ), Maastricht University, Bosch Film Amsterdam, and MTV–Box Television. Bouman E&E Development coordinates this project and provides formal and informal guidance to this collaborative venture.

Further, Bouman E&E Development, with financial support of the Dutch Health Research and Development Council, has initiated a large multi-university curriculum development project on entertainment-education, perhaps the first of its kind at a national level. The E-E teaching modules, being implemented in six communication and media studies programs, are designed to make health communication and television professionals become more skilled partners in designing and implementing E-E interventions.

In closing

Ev Rogers, our metaphorical bus-driver, will perhaps be pleased with the journeys that E-E has made in Netherlands.

Story 4: Entertainment-education in the Peruvian Amazon
Primary storyteller: Eliana Elías

In 1991, a cholera epidemic claimed hundreds of lives on the Peruvian coast and in the Andean highlands, threatening to become a great disaster as it advanced on the Peruvian Amazon. As a social communicator working with a development NGO, and a student preparing her thesis, I, on my own initiative, decided to validate the efficacy of the media materials for the national prevention campaign against cholera. Loaded with posters, stickers, and other campaign materials, and after a long trip by plane and boat, I arrived in Papaplaya, a riverine community of four hundred families on the Huallaga River in San Martin province.

Over the next several days, focus group interviews with community members demonstrated that most of the national campaign materials were poorly designed and many lacked cultural sensitivity. Messages like "wash your hands with soap after going to the toilet" had no relevance in the rural Amazonian riverine communities where people could barely afford soap, and where there exist no toilets. "Boil water for 20 minutes" means little in communities where one can hardly find clocks, and where "cook" is the commonly-used term, not "boil." Not surprisingly, most of the campaign materials were developed in Lima—the capital city of Peru—by "expert" health educators. Even some of the graphic designers, it was clear, only knew the Amazon region by its pictures.

As part of my job, I also interviewed local youth groups in the Peruvian Amazon who were creating other messages to control cholera.[8] They showed me a poster in which ghosts were emerging from a metal pot in which water was being "cooked" on a bonfire. They explained that "with the bubbles the 'bad' things go out from water, illness is gone, and water is ready for drinking." These youth groups, also broadcast a radio spot in which two commonly-available fruits, Cocona and Guineo (in local parlance alluding to female and male genitals, respectively) talked among themselves about the importance of washing the fruit prior to eating them. The spot became so popular that people in the market place joked about these two fruits, including the importance of cleaning them, prior to pleasurable consumption!

The creative ghost and bubbles poster and the daring radio spot were big hits in certain parts of the Peruvian Amazon region. Unlike the materials developed in Lima by "experts," these locally-produced messages were understood, remembered, and enjoyed by the Amazonian people. People told me that they "felt these messages as their own." Once local creativity was empowered and liberated, a communication circuit was established that appealed to local culture, was respectful of local idioms and metaphors, and built on peoples' previous knowledge. During those few days in the Amazonian jungle, I began to see the potential of locally-sensitive entertainment-education.

During the next four years, as I traveled extensively in Peru's Loreto region (mainly in the Amazonian riverine communities) working as consultant to health and environmental projects, I tried to engage with local sensitivities and understand local communicative practices in the context of peoples' well-being.[9] "In the Amazonian jungle everything [everybody] talks to us, you just have to know how to listen," an old village woman told me. I began to believe her. Not surprisingly, "vegetalist physicians"—or shamans—are most respected in the Amazonas—primarily on account of their unique capacity to converse with sacred plants (e.g., Ayahuasca). Norma Panduro, a

[8] They organized themselves around *Radio Oriente* (Orient Radio) and *La Voz de la Selva* (Voice of the Jungle) radio stations.
[9] These villages are located in a region that represents one fourth of the country territory. There live more than sixty indigenous peoples, which are culturally and linguistically diverse. However, due to decades of discriminatory and exclusionary policies, they lack even basic services.

vegetalist physician explained: "The sacred plant talks to us, she tells us about the 'damage' [illness] that affects the ill person, and guides us to be able to choose the plants that will cure him/her."

Naturally, I was struck by the richness of communication in the Peruvian Amazon. As heirs of an ancient oral tradition that has allowed the creation and recreation of world views and knowledge systems, where the joyous life world resists the disenchantment that comes with modern colonialism, the Amazonian peoples maintain conversation and oral narration as the locus for encounter, recall, and intergenerational transmission of old wisdom, creating new meanings and comprehension. In the Amazon region, it is common to experience lengthy talks, plenty of details, rhetoric resources, and magnificent histrionic talents—all devices that prompt and promote interpersonal closeness. One can listen to countless narratives in which human beings and nature are united, where the life-giving river and forest "mothers" constantly communicate providing, taking care, or punishing when natural resources are inappropriately used. I began to realize that in the Amazonian region, where conversation is the core of life— both for an individual and the community, health is also maintained through the exchange of messages. "Good communication" is considered part of well-being (Aquituari 2004; Panduro 2004).

A quest for culturally-sensitive communication circuits

In 1998, along with my husband, Luis Gonzales, I co-founded Minga Perú, a non-profit organization committed to fostering social justice and human rights through the promotion of better health, increased equity, and the sustainable management of natural resources for peoples of the Amazon region, especially its rural women. Minga's activities are focused in the region of Loreto, a territory comprising one-fourth of Peru's geographic area, including 146,000 square miles of the Amazon rainforest (Sypher et al., 2002). About 1 million people live in Loreto: half in Iquitos City, the main city, and the other half in some 500 riverine communities[10] along the Amazon River and its serpentine tributaries. Some 60 ethno-linguistic groups make up the

---

[10] These numbers pertain to officially-recognized riverine communities. The actual number is higher.

Peruvian Amazon, representing a non-homogenous population. The river is the main transportation channel and most people travel by manually-powered shallow canoes made of balsa wood (Farrington, 2003). Steamers, ferries, and motor boats connect major riverine routes along the Amazon. There are no roads in these remote communities, nor a dedicated power supply. There are insufficient health services: Only a few health clinics exist, mostly located in bigger riverine communities or towns.

From day one, communication was the main axis to fulfill our mission. One of our first projects was the production of *Bienvenida Salud!*, a 30 minutes radio show broadcast three times a week throughout the Loreto region of the Peruvian Amazonas. The radio program revolves around a soap opera whose main character is Pasionaria, a peasant woman that fights bravely for a better life for her, her family, and her community. *Bienvenida Salud!*, the brainchild of a group of communicators, nurses, and local actors, is in its seventh year of broadcast. By 2005, over 900 episodes of *Bienvenida Salud!* had been broadcast (Singhal and Rattine-Flaherty, 2006).

Bienvenida Salud! recreates and adapts the entertainment-education strategy to suit the local conditions of the Peruvian Amazonas. We sought to create "communicative circuits" where listeners are not just message receptors; rather, they become active co-producers of messages (Elías 2004; Neira, 2001). To foster co-production, audience members are strongly encouraged to write letters to the program, which serve as the basic input for *Bienvenida Salud!*'s radio scripts. Letters come in the form of cards, hand-sewn notes, and some are even painted on bark. Vegetable and natural colors are used as ink. To encourage audience feedback and formative inputs to designing *Bienvenida Salud!*, Minga has made arrangements with boat companies to ferry listeners' letters from the interior of the Amazon jungle to Iquitos City, where the headquarters of Minga is located. Letter-writers do not pay for this "postal" service; Minga Perú pays a small fee for each letter that is delivered (Singhal and Rattine-Flaherty, 2006).

To date, over 4,500 letters have been received where Amazonian women and men share their personal stories, ask questions about reproductive health, denounce human right violations, and provide advice about the content of the program. For instance, in

December, 2002, Romel Castro wrote in about his abusive father: "I suffered psychological abuse from my father .... He often came home drunk and would insult my mother and hit her .... Sometimes I would see blood on her face. It's a big problem for me" (quoted in Farrington, 2003: 2). Minga distills stories like the ones provided by Romel into its social dramas on *Bienvenida Salud!*, each illustrating a carefully chosen topic for the episode, such as why eradicating violence in the community is important, or how to recognize the side effects of contraceptive injections.

Bienvenida Salud! is highly popular among its audiences. Almost one out of two radio listeners in Loreto's rural areas listens to *Bienvenida Salud!*, and almost one out of three listeners of *Bienvenida Salud!* talks about the program with another person (Ventsam, 1998). Listeners also point out that what they value most about Pasionaria, the main character, is the way she faces adversity and joins with other women for collective empowerment. In the program's episodes, Pasionaria discovers her own strength, the capabilities and knowledge she has and that she ignored, resulting in a better self-image. Beyond the explicit content, the acknowledgement of women's lives in *Bienvenida Salud!* constitutes the "subtext," and is acknowledged as the main value of the program.

Some viewer stories and testimonies reinforce the value of *Bienvenida Salud!* in the Peruvian Amazon. Evarina Yumbato, a 58-year-old indigenous Cocama woman living in the riverine community of San Antonio, who assists women during delivery, admits that she did not know the danger of swelling (or water retention) during pregnancy:

> I heard that Pasionaria brings her friends to the hospital when they have swelling during pregnancy, because she says it is dangerous....
> When I observed that my oldest daughter who was in her fourth month of pregnancy had swelling on her face and feet, I brought her as soon as I could to the medical center. She had high blood pressure ... but they assisted her and she recovered.

Asunción Lozano Flores, a 28-year-old woman and mother of a 3-year-old daughter lives with her husband in Nueva Vida, a riverine community on the Itaya river, seven hours by boat from Iquitos. A regular listener for the past seven years, Asunción was inspired by *Bienvenida Salud!* to practice family planning: "I use natural methods which I combine with artificial ones," she noted. Asunción is a human rights and health activist in her community. She travels to Iquitos to hand-deliver letters of *Bienvenida Salud!* to Minga head-quarters, and pick up audio cassettes of the program which she plays during community assemblies:

> In this way it is easier for me to talk in front of all the people of my village. When they meet in an assembly I put on a cassette with *Bienvenida Salud!* and the people get excited…. They take more interest in what I'm going to explain afterwards about human rights.

Complementing Minga's on-air broadcasts of *Bienvenida Salud!* are a host of ongoing on-the-ground interventions, led by a trained cadre of community *promotoras*. Minga trains young women, using culturally appropriate materials, to work as health promoters and change agents in the communities where they live. They are carefully chosen on the strength of their personality, drive, and motivation, and trained at Minga's Tambo Training Center, located two hours away by motorboat from Iquitos City. "Tambo" means a place of rest (or home) in Peruvian Spanish. *Promotoras* come here for training from various riverine communities to learn the basics of male and female anatomy, detection of breast and cervical cancers, and simulation of the birth process (Farrington, 2003). They also implement sewing, weaving, and crocheting projects; learn carpentry; how to establish and run a fish farm; how to grow medicinal herbs; and create environmentally sustainable eco-systems through agro-forestry and small animal husbandry projects. The *promotoras* represent Minga's partners and field-based change agents, modeling healthy reproductive lifestyles, initiating community discussions and projects, and serving as local resource persons for Minga's outreach (Singhal and Rattine-Flaherty, in press). By 2005, 52 community health *promotoras* had been trained by Minga, who work closely with a network of 500 women in 35 riverine communities (of the Marañon and El Tigre river basins) in the Peruvian Amazon.

In sum, Minga Perú's work in the Peruvian Amazonas is geared toward empowering members of riverine communities, especially its women, to experience a higher quality of life; to make better informed choices with respect to their reproductive health; and to gain in self-esteem to value their sexual and human rights.

Plate 9.6
Eliana Elías (front and fourth from right in dark clothes) with *promotoras* at Minga's Tambo Training Center in the Peruvian Amazon
Source: Personal files of author Singhal

In closing

In a culturally diverse environment such as Peru, where most messages (*a*) are created in, and emitted from, a material and symbolic "center of power" (located in the capital city of Lima), and (*b*) carry a top-down homogenizing agenda, the entertainment-education approach (such as the one followed by Minga) forces the communicator to respect differences among audience members, and to be sensitive to their language, idioms, metaphors, emotions, humor, and wisdom. Also, our experience at Minga suggests that E-E proposes an educational pedagogy that values pleasure, engagement, and joy—where the learning-teaching experience is founded in an ethic of well-being rather than in one that privileges duty, fear, and guilt. E-E supports a laughing over a crying education. E-E liberates the creative capacities of people, encouraging democratic encounters through listening, discussions, and actions rather than fostering hierarchical relations.

Further, our E-E experiences at Minga Perú suggest that behind every text there is a subtext. In the Peruvian context, Amazonian women value horizontal communication, where the "different other" is not ignored. They prize the affective link and the closeness that is achieved within a community of communicators (not just listeners). E–E shows that humor, joy, and pleasure can establish a public space for meeting. It liberates the self, not severing it from the rest of life. Through E-E the self can realize that it belongs to a community, close to, together with, like in a riverine village.

Professor Rogers' writings on communication for social change, and particularly about entertainment-education, greatly inspired our work at Minga. *Bienvenida Salud!* had been on air for only a short time when Professor Rogers' and Singhal's collaborative writings on E-E (Singhal and Rogers, 1999; 2002) helped us to reassess our practice and gave us more elements to think strategically in designing and understanding the construction of the characters and in dealing with emotions and stories of our program.

Muchas gracias, Professor Rogers!

References

Aquituari, P. 2004. Siani, mi hija kukama: El nuevo brote de mi pueblo. In E. Elías and E. Neira (eds), *Salud reproductiva en la Amazonía. Perspectivas desde la cultura, el género y la comunicación*, pp. 223–28. Iquitos-Lima: Minga Perú.

Backer, T. E., J. W. Dearing, A. Singhal, and T. W. Valente. 2005. Writing with Ev: Words to Transform Science into Action. *Journal of Health Communication* 10 (4): 289–301.

Bouman, M. P. A. 1999. *The Turtle and the Peacock: The Entertainment-Education Strategy on Television*. Gouda, the Netherlands: Bouman E&E Development.

———. 2002. Turtles and Peacocks: Collaboration in Entertainment-Education Television. *Communication Theory* 12 (2): 225–44.

———. 2004. Entertainment-Education Television Drama in the Netherlands. In A. Singhal, M. Cody, E. M. Rogers, and M. Sabido (eds), *Entertainment-Education and Social Change: History, Research, and Practice*, pp. 225–42. Mahwah, NJ: Lawrence Erlbaum.

Bouman, M. P. A. and E. A. M. Wieberdink. 1993. *Villa Borghese*: A Soap Series on Heart Health. *Canadian Journal of Cardiology* 9 (Suppl. D): 145D–46D.

Bouman, M. P. A. and C. Van Woerkum. 1998. *Television Entertainment for Health: Collaboration Aspects of the Design Process*. Paper presented to the International Communication Association, Jerusalem, July.

Bouman, M. P. A., L. Maas, and G. J. Kok. 1998. Health Education in Television Entertainment: A Dutch Drama Serial. *Health Education Research* 13 (4): 503–18.

Bouman E&E Development. 2005. *Gezondheid in Beeld*. Research report. Gouda, the Netherlands: Bouman E&E Development.

Elías, E. 2004. Comunicar para icarar: El modelo Minga de comunicación para la salud desde la cultura. In E. Elías and E. Neira (eds), *Salud reproductiva en la Amazonía. Perspectivas desde la cultura, el género y la comunicación*, pp. 179–90. Iquitos-Lima: Minga Perú.

Farrington, A. 2003. 'Family matters' in the Amazon. *Ford Foundation Report* 34 (4): 16–19.

NEEF and JHU/CCP. 2001. *Proceedings of the Third International Entertainment-Education Conference on Social Change*. Gouda, the Netherlands: Netherlands Entertainment Education Foundation.

Neira, R. E. 2001. *Del silencio a la acción. Minga Perú y el proyecto—Promotoras Comunitarias. Informe de evaluación*. Lima: Minga Perú.

Panduro, N. 2004. Viviendo bien: mucha salud y cuidado del alma y la comunidad. In E. Elías and E. Neira (eds), *Salud reproductiva en la Amazonía. Perspectivas desde la cultura, el género y la comunicación*, pp. 261–68. Iquitos-Lima: Minga Perú.

Piotrow, P. T., D. L. Kincaid, J. Rimon II, and W. Rinehart. 1997. *Health Communication: Lessons from Family Planning and Reproductive Health*. Westport, CT: Praeger.

Pruitt, D. G. and P. J. Carnevale. 1993. *Negotiation in Social Conflict*. Buckingham: Open University Press.

Rogers, E. M. n.d. *The Fourteenth Paw: Growing Up on an Iowa Farm in the 1930s*. Unpublished manuscript.

Rogers, E. M., P. W. Vaughan, R. M. A. Swalehe, N. Rao, P. J. Svenkerud, and S. Sood. 1999. Effects of an Entertainment-Education Radio Soap Opera on Family Planning Behavior in Tanzania. *Studies in Family Planning* 30: 193–211.

Runco, M. A. and R. S. Albert (eds). 1990. *Theories of Creativity*. Thousand Oaks, CA: Sage Publications.

Singhal, A. 1990. *Entertainment-Educational Communication Strategies for Development*. Ph.D. dissertation, University of Southern California.

Singhal, A., R. Obregon, and E. M. Rogers. 1994. Reconstructing the Story of '*Simplemente María*,' the Most Popular Telenovela in Latin America of All Time. *Gazette* 54 (1): 1–15.

Singhal, A. and E. Rattine-Flaherty. 2006. Pencils and Photos as Tools of Communicative Research and Praxis: Analyzing Minga Perú's Quest for Social Justice in the Amazon. *International Communication Gazette* 68 (4): 313–30.

Singhal, A. and E. M. Rogers. 1988. Television Soap Operas for Development in India. *Gazette* 41: 109–26.

———. 1989. Pro-social Television for Development in India. In R. E. Rice and C. Atkin (eds), *Public Communication Campaigns* (2nd ed.), pp. 331–50. Newbury Park, CA: Sage Publications.

———. 1999. *Entertainment-Education: A Communication Strategy for Social Change.* Mahwah, NJ: Lawrence Erlbaum.

———. 2002. A Theoretical Agenda for Entertainment-Education. *Communication Theory* 12 (2): 117–35.

Singhal, A., M. J. Cody, E. M. Rogers, and M. Sabido (eds). 2004. *Entertainment-Education and Social Change: History, Research, and Practice.* Mahwah, NJ: Lawrence Erlbaum.

Sypher, B. D., M. McKinley, S. Ventsam, and E. Elías. 2002. Fostering Reproductive Health through Entertainment-Education in the Peruvian Amazon: The Social Construction of *Bienvenida Salud! Communication Theory* 12 (2): 192–205.

Usdin, S., A. Singhal, T. Shongwe, S. Goldstein, and A. Shabalala. 2004. No Short Cuts in Entertainment-Education. Designing *Soul City* Step-by-Step. In A. Singhal, M. Cody, E. M. Rogers, and M. Sabido (eds), *Entertainment-Education and Social Change: History, Research, and Practice*, pp. 153–76. Mahwah, NJ: Lawrence Erlbaum.

Van Empelen, P. and G. Kok. 2002. *Costa! Een soap als. medium om jongeren voor te lichten over SOA.* Research report, Capaciteitsgroep Experimentele Psychologie, Universiteit Maastricht. Maastricht: Universiteit Maastricht.

Vaughan, P. W. 2003. Using Effects Research to Sustain Entertainment-Education Programs: A Case Study from Tanzania. Paper Presented at the Africa Soap Summit: Making Entertainment Useful Conference, Nairobi, June 3–7.

Vaughan, P. W., A. Regis, and E. St. Catherine. 2000. Effects of an Entertainment-Education Radio Soap Opera on Family Planning and HIV Prevention in St. Lucia. *International Family Planning Perspectives* 26: 148–57.

Vaughan, P. W. and E. M. Rogers. 2000. A Staged Model of Communication Effects: Evidence from an Entertainment-Education Radio Soap Opera in Tanzania. *Journal of Health Communication* 5: 203–27.

Vaughan, P. W., E. M. Rogers, A. Singhal, and R. M. Swalehe. 2000. Entertainment-Education and HIV/AIDS Prevention: A Field Experiment in Tanzania. *The Journal of Health Communication* 5: 81–100.

Ventsam, S. 1998. The Role of Entertainment-Education in Fostering Reproductive Health in the Peruvian Amazon: Lessons Learned from Bienvenida Salud! Master's thesis, University of Kansas.

Wallack, L. 1990. Two Approaches to Health Promotion in the Mass Media. *World Health Forum* 11: 143–55.

Wieberdink, E. A. M. 1992. *"Villa Borghese": Een verslag van de ervaringen en resultaten van het project "GVO en Drama."* Utrecht, the Netherlands: Landelijk Centrum GVO.

Van Woerkum, C. M. J. 1981. Planmatigheid versus creativiteit. *Massacommunicatie* 9 (1–2): 48–59.

———. 1987. *Massamediale voorlichting: Een werkplan* (2nd ed.). Meppel/ Amsterdam: Boom.

Zandvliet, A. 1998. De popularisering van een gezonde leefstijl. Een casestudie van de produktie van een 'soap' in de gezondheidsvoorlichting. In P. Schedler and F. Glastra (eds), *Voorlichting in veldtheoretisch perspectief*, pp. 69–85. Deventer, the Netherlands: Lemma BV.

10

Everett Rogers' Personal Journey: Iowa to Iowa

CORINNE L. SHEFNER-ROGERS

"The Lovely Corinne," as I've long referred to her as, has always been much more than that. She is the prototype of the hybrid that all of us in health communication look for: technical expertise from public health study; relational sensitivity from communication study; and a lot of first-hand knowledge about what works and doesn't in entering, studying, and making a difference in field settings. Ev saw and admired all of that. He was a large influence on her, too. Once I sat at an awards table of the World Association of Public Opinion Research. Next to me was Dr. Ruth Guttman, widow of Louis Guttman, the great innovator in survey measurement, multidimensional scaling, and factor analysis. Ruth accepted a posthumous award for her husband and vividly described, to the delight and laughter of the audience, her annoyance at how her husband couldn't stop being an intellectual. Every morning at the breakfast table, he was questioning her about her dissertation progress. That same dynamic was a part of Ev and Corinne's relationship.

JIM DEARING

For about five years (1991 to 1996), Ev and I served as UN consultants to the National Dairy Development Board in India on an initiative to empower women dairy farmers. Corinne would often accompany us on these India sojourns—to remote, rural villages in Rajasthan, Gujarat, Maharashtra, and Goa. Everywhere we went, women dairy farmers flocked around her. The two male consultants soon realized that Corinne was not only an interested co-traveler, but also a key collaborator, informant, observer, and sense-maker. Some years later, when Ev, Corinne, and I traveled through Brazil, Kenya, South Africa, and Thailand to study HIV/AIDS prevention programs, "the Corinne factor" greatly aided our learning. Over the years, the three of us, I estimate, clocked some half a million miles—across six continents. During these travels, I was privileged to see first-hand Ev and Corinne's close relationship.

ARVIND SINGHAL

EVERETT M. ROGERS WAS A SELF-DESCRIBED "SON-OF-THE-SOIL." HE grew up on an Iowa farm in the 1930s, milking cows, raising pigs and chickens, picking corn, and driving a tractor. He attended a one-room country school where the handful of students were related to one another. It was a youth he described as less-than-idyllic. Yet he attributed his later successes in life to the values and work ethic that he learned as a young farmhand from his father. Ev's life journey and career path were seamlessly intertwined. The present chapter follows Ev's life journey from his farm boy beginnings, through his career in diffusion research, to his final return to the farmland.

I first met Ev in the lobby of the Annenberg School for Communication at the University of Southern California (USC) in December 1989. I was visiting USC to determine whether I would accept their offer of admission to work on my Master's degree. During my meetings with various faculty members, all mentioned the name Everett Rogers. My background was in anthropology and I knew little about Everett Rogers' work. As I was leaving the building, I was introduced to Ev on the mosaic presidential seal that adorns the floor of the school's lobby. Ev was courteous; he encouraged me to come to USC.

During my year-and-a half at the Annenberg School (1990–91), I took two of Ev's graduate classes and worked as one of Ev's four teaching assistants for a large undergraduate communication class. After graduating from USC in May 1991, I moved to Baltimore, Maryland to take a position with the Johns Hopkins University Center for Communication Programs. Within a month, Ev showed up on my Baltimore doorstep and we began a long-distance relationship. Eventually we married (Plate 10.1) and I moved to New Mexico where Ev had taken a position as Chair of the Department of Communication and Journalism at the University of New Mexico. Throughout our marriage, I had the honor of learning more about Ev's life, and learning from Ev about life. The stories he shared reflected a man of great intelligence, solid values, and someone who loved life. I remain his number one fan.

Beginnings on an Iowa farm

Everett M. Rogers (known to all as "Ev") was born in the spring of 1931 in Carroll County, Iowa. He was the descendent of Cornish lead miners on his father's side and Alsatians on his mother's side. The

Plate 10.1
Ev and Corinne's wedding toast in 1994
Source: Personal files of the author

Iowa prairie land that became Ev's first home was purchased in 1879 by his grandfather, who migrated to the United States from Cornwall, England in the 1840s. That land was named Pinehurst Farm.

It was on Pinehurst Farm that Ev began his life-long study of human behavior. First, he learned about animal behavior: alpha male dogs, plow horses working in teams, gophers burrowing underground, opportunistic bugs in his mother's vegetable garden, and birds that pretended to be injured to divert the attention of predators from their nests, or called out to one another before a looming storm. From his father, Ev learned about soil types, crops, planting rotations, weeding, and crop yields. It was his father's behavior in particular that led to Ev's doctoral dissertation study of the adoption of agricultural technologies among farmers in Collins, Iowa. Ev's father was slow to adopt new farm practices in comparison to neighboring farmers.

Ev also learned the value of money by watching his parents stretch their earnings from the farm to feed the family, maintain the farm machinery, and re-invest in farm operations. A bank loan for farm equipment kept Ev's father up at night, and the worry was not lost on Ev. Money was never a priority for Ev, although he had a strong commitment to living within his means. He believed that if you worked hard at what you loved to do, the rewards, including money, would follow.

The Pretty Betty project[1]

At the age of 10, Ev joined the 4-H Club[2] in Carroll, Iowa. As a 4-H member, he was required to select a project that would demonstrate his skills as a young farmer. Ev wanted to raise a pig. The purpose of the 4-H project was to teach young boys and girls about the responsibilities associated with caring for livestock. 4-H members were required to maintain careful records on the costs of raising a farm animal.

Ev had $100 in his bank account when he joined the 4-H Club. A decent brood sow would cost some $400. Undaunted, and with his money in hand, Ev traveled with his father to a purebred Spotted Poland China sow auction in a neighboring town. It was mid-February, and heavy snow kept many other potential bidders from attending the auction. The early bidding yielded over $400 for each sow. Ev had doubts about his prospective sow-raising project. His father told him to be patient. The last sow to be auctioned was small with unusually fat jowls. The bidding began at $50. Ev jumped into the bidding and after a few back-and-forth bids with another farmer, Ev took the sow and her pedigree papers home for $120. Her name was Pretty Betty.

In March, Pretty Betty gave birth to six piglets. Ev rigged a light bulb in the corner of the hog house in order to warm the piglets and to keep Pretty Betty from lying down on top of them by accident. He maintained detailed records about the weight of the pigs, the cost of their feed, bedding, and protein supplements, as well as the labor costs of caring for Pretty Betty and her litter. Finally, in August, his 4-H project was ready to be brought to the Carroll County Fair to be judged. Ev earned a red ribbon (2nd place) for his project.

The Pretty Betty project gave Ev first-hand experience with the risks and benefits of farming enterprises, and taught him important management skills. He almost broke even on the cost of raising the sow's six piglets after he sold them to a livestock buyer in his hometown. He would have earned more had there not been an overproduction of pork that year. His records showed that it cost him as much to raise his six pigs as it would have cost him to raise 200 pigs (as his father did). He learned an important lesson of returns to scale. Ev was relieved that he had raised only six pigs.

[1] This vignette is adapted from Rogers (n.d.).
[2] 4-H is the youth education branch of the Cooperative Extension Service, a program of the United States Department of Agriculture. 4-H members pledge

Ev worked along side his father, a quiet man who was subtle about telling Ev what tasks needed to be completed on a given day, or how to manage a specific task. For example, Ev once told me that he was helping his father fix the roof of the dairy barn. Instead of telling Ev to be careful while working on the roof, his father said, "The first step is the big one!" Ev was adept at using similar subtlety with his students.

Ev attended a one-room country school between 1936 and 1944. He was a motivated student. He walked two miles to and from school everyday. The heavy schedule of daily farm chores forced Ev to be disciplined about his schoolwork and farm work (Plate 10.2). He had little time for leisure activities. The free time that he did have was spent reading library books that his mother brought him from her weekly trips to sell farm eggs in Carroll. He was a voracious reader, and could identify words that he would only learn to pronounce correctly in later years. He spent countless hours reading maps, and following the military events of World War II via radio broadcasts from the one radio in the living room of the farmhouse. He was fascinated by the world beyond Pinehurst Farm.

Attending Carroll High School from 1944 to 1948 marked the beginning of Ev's exposure to individuals who were different than he (later he used the term *heterophilous*). His high school classmates were of a different religion, urban, and most were from relatively well-to-do families. He was quick to observe that those students whose parents had money did not have to rush home after school to do daily chores. They could attend football games and dances. The one club that Ev belonged to as a senior in high school was the Future Farmers of America (FFA), which taught young men how to be good farmers. Through the FFA, Ev made his first trip outside of Iowa to Kansas City, Missouri for a convention. That experience made a favorable impression on Ev; it was a taste of travels to come.

As a high school student, going to college was not high on Ev's list of priorities. He anticipated becoming a farmer and spending the rest of his days on Pinehurst Farm. His high school vocational agriculture teacher, however, saw a different future for Ev. He took Ev on a field

---

to honor the four "Hs": (*a*) Head to clearer thinking, (*b*) Heart to greater loyalty, (*c*) Hands to larger service, and (*d*) Health to better living, for their club, their community, their country, and their world.

Plate 10.2
Ev with a bunny at Pinehurst Farm, Carroll, Iowa
Source: Personal files of the author

trip to Iowa State University (ISU) in Ames, some 60 miles from Carroll County. Ev liked what he saw at ISU. With the help of a scholarship and part-time job, Ev began his college career as an undergraduate in ISU's College of Agriculture in 1948.

In the summer of Ev's sophomore year, North Korea invaded South Korea and the Korean War was underway. During his junior and senior years in college, Ev signed up for Advanced United States Air Force ROTC, and was commissioned as a second lieutenant at graduation. Ev was called to active duty in 1952. He was stationed at Wright-Patterson Air Force Base near Dayton, Ohio.

General Donald Flickinger, Director of Human Factors in the Air Force Research and Development Command, also stationed at Wright-Patterson, selected Ev to become his personal aide. General Flickinger, as Ev described him, was a colorful character. He threw many parties for upper-echelon Air Force members where Ev learned to make mix drinks and tend bar. Those parties were opportunities for Ev to observe a lifestyle previously unknown to him. He was particularly struck by the drunken behavior of many of the wives of these airmen.

Flickinger was a medical doctor who gained renown during World War II by parachuting into the Burmese jungle to save the lives of downed airmen. "Flick" was interested in studying such events as ejection seat operations on fighter planes, especially why these seats were breaking the arms of the pilots who used them, and how pressurized suits could help pilots withstand G-forces during high-performance flights. Ev's position as Flickinger's aide marked the beginning of Ev's career in the human factors field, a new world for the 21-year-old farm boy with a BS degree in agriculture from Iowa. He was mingling with university scholars in the fields of human engineering, psychology, and medicine, and he began to think about graduate studies related to the human side of technology. He observed the resistances to human factors design, and, recalling his father's resistance to adopting new farm technologies, Ev again asked the question "Why did people not adopt new ideas that were obviously advantageous?" In his dissertation study, Ev argued that the diffusion of innovations was a general process, whether the innovation was in farming, medicine, or education.

The diffusion calling card

Ev completed his doctoral dissertation at Iowa State University in 1957. While I was completing my Ph.D. degree at Johns Hopkins University in the early 2000s, Ev would regale me with stories from his doctoral student days. Although I had heard some of the stories many times before, Ev never failed to make me laugh with his vivid descriptions and impersonations. When I was "crunching numbers," Ev would tell me about the young computer "geek" that he hired to conduct the statistical analyses for his dissertation study, and about how lucky I was that I didn't have to use punch-cards to run my statistical analyses. As I wrote the final chapter of my dissertation, Ev reminded me of the statistics professor on his dissertation committee whose words may very well have launched Ev's professional career. Just hours after his doctoral defense, Ev ran into the professor walking across the ISU campus. They chatted for a minute or two. As the professor turned to part company, he looked over his shoulder and told

Ev that although his Beta-weights were "sickly," his literature review would perhaps someday make a great book.

Later that day, Ev left Ames to begin his career as an Assistant Professor of Rural Sociology at Ohio State University in Columbus, Ohio. He loaded up his car and drove all night to reach Columbus in time to start teaching the next day.

Counting chickens in Colombia[3]

Ev was a particularly skilled field researcher and enjoyed teaching students the art of interviewing survey respondents. In 1964, while he was a Fulbright lecturer at the National University of Colombia in Bogotá, Ev conducted a study of the diffusion of agricultural innovations among Colombian peasants in the Andes Mountains. The questionnaire that he and his students designed asked about each farmer's adoption of a dozen agricultural innovations, for example, the use of nitrogen fertilizer and the adoption of a new variety of high-altitude bean. On a cold, rainy day, Ev and one student trudged through the rocky Andean soil to interview a rather poor farmer who lived in a one-room mud-brick and stone house with an open fire in the center to heat the house. Here Ev and his student administered the questionnaire.

The final set of questions on the questionnaire were developed to measure the socioeconomic status (SES) of the respondent, since SES is a variable that is highly related to the adoption of innovations. The farmer was asked whether he owned cows, pigs, farm implements, etc. The only livestock of value that the farmer owned were two chickens.

At the end of the personal interview, the farmer invited Ev and his colleague to stay for lunch. Colombians are known for their hospitality. Ev tried to decline the invitation since he understood the sacrifice involved for the farmer's family to feed two additional mouths. The farmer insisted. Ev and his student heartily ate the chicken and potato stew prepared by the farmer's wife.

After leaving the farmer's house, Ev went back to the completed questionnaire and located the questions about livestock. He crossed out "*dos*" (two) chickens and wrote in "*uno*" (one). Although the stew was delicious, the knowledge that he and his colleague had eaten half of the farmer's livestock left a bitter taste in Ev's mouth.

---

[3] This vignette is adapted from Rogers (n.d.).

After conducting 11 major research projects on the diffusion of innovations between 1957 and 1961, and a year of touring European research centers discussing diffusion with numerous scholars in 1961, the first edition of *Diffusion of Innovations* (Rogers, 1962a) made its debut. This book launched Ev's career. *Diffusion of Innovations* became his calling card, and helped him move to Michigan State University in 1964, then a major training center for new Ph.Ds in communication. His book opened the door to research abroad.

In 1963, Ev was a Fulbright lecturer at the Facultad de Sociologica, Universidad Nacional de Colombia, Bogotá. In 1961, a young Latin American scholar, Dr Fals Borda, heard Ev make a presentation on the diffusion of agricultural innovations at the American Sociological Society annual conference at Ohio State University. Following Ev's presentation, Fals Borda invited Ev to Bogotá for a one-year lectureship position. Ev did not speak a word of Spanish at the time of the invitation. He had one year to prepare for his overseas challenge. He enrolled in a Spanish course at Ohio State University. Within a year he was fluent enough to conduct classes in Spanish in Bogotá.

Ev told me that the experience of learning another language and teaching in another language taught him self-efficacy, and showed him that he could learn to get along in any culture. The year in Bogotá launched his scholarly adventures around the world. He lived and worked in Brazil, India, and Indonesia, and conducted research in Afghanistan, Bangladesh, Cambodia, China, Japan, Korea, Malaysia, Nigeria, Singapore, and Tanzania. He never tired of overseas travel. Many-a-time he would travel by plane for a day to reach some overseas destination like Tokyo or Jakarta, where he would give an hour-long presentation, meet with local scholars, and then fly home the following day. Ev enjoyed overseas trips as they provided ample time, free of interruptions, to engage in such scholarly endeavors as writing journal articles, grading student papers, developing research projects, and drafting book manuscripts. His carry-on travel bag was always filled with papers.

Ev's natural curiosity, whetted on the family farm, translated into a 47 year career in diffusion of innovations research. Diffusion research and teaching was the backbone of his career, and moving from one academic institution to another provided avenues for studying diffusion in a variety of fields. At Ohio State University, Ev was in a department of rural sociology where he mainly studied the diffusion of agricultural innovations. His move to Michigan State University in 1964 allowed him to broaden his study of diffusion to public health, family planning, and educational innovations in secondary schools in Thailand (Rogers et al., 1968; Rogers, 1970).

Ev found moving from one university to another intellectually stimulating. In 1973, Ev moved from Michigan State University to Ann Arbor, Michigan to become a faculty member at the University of Michigan where he helped build a new doctoral program in communication. He held a joint appointment in the School of Public Health where he pursued his interest in the diffusion of family planning innovations. In 1975, he moved to Stanford University as the Janet M. Peck Professor of International Communication and became a part of the highest-rated Ph.D. program at that time. His move to the Annenberg School for Communication at the University of Southern California in 1985 was motivated by his growing interest in new communication technologies (Rogers, n.d.).

In 1993, Ev moved to Albuquerque, New Mexico to become Chair of the Department of Communication and Journalism at the University of New Mexico (UNM). Part of the draw to UNM was being able to launch a Ph.D. program in intercultural communication. Ev loved a challenge. Upon his arrival at UNM, he drafted a proposal for this new doctoral program. Then came the lesson in navigating New Mexico politics. He walked his proposal through 14 administrative steps (including an appearance at the State Legislature), and gifted one Kashmiri rug to an individual from whom Ev needed a letter of support (this individual made it clear that a rug from Ev's collection of Kashmiri rugs would help him write that letter). In its first year, the doctoral program in intercultural communication at UNM was ranked as number one by the National Communication Association.

Ev often joked that the variable that best explained his career moves was average daily temperature; he continually moved to warmer climates. In fact, changing academic affiliations approximately every eight to 10 years fuelled Ev's intellectual vigor.

Sharing knowledge and experiences

Ev believed that knowledge gained through research was knowledge that should be shared. He conducted research on various aspects of the diffusion of innovations, such as the role of research universities in creating and transferring technological innovations, the diffusion of health interventions, cultural factors in the diffusion of health innovations, the role of the Internet in health promotion, and the effects of entertainment-education soap operas on family planning adoption and HIV/AIDS prevention. He published books on a broad range of topics, including communication networks (Rogers and Kincaid, 1981), communication technology (Rogers, 1986), the history of communication study (Rogers, 1994), media agenda-setting (Dearing and Rogers, 1996), intercultural communication (Rogers and Steinfatt, 1999), entertainment-education (Singhal and Rogers, 1999; Singhal et al., 2004), the communication revolutions in India (Singhal and Rogers, 1989; 2001); and combating AIDS (Singhal and Rogers, 2003). He was prolific and enjoyed being a "wordsmith."

Ev published hundreds of journal articles. His earliest publications focused on the elements of diffusion theory, for example, adopter categories, opinion leadership, and innovativeness (Rogers, 1959; 1961; 1962b; 1963; Rogers and Havens, 1962). In the early 1970s, Ev increasingly studied the communication of innovations across cultures, including the role of communication in social change (Rogers, 1971; Rogers and Burge, 1972; Rogers and Shoemaker, 1971). This interest continued throughout his career. Ev was energized when interviewing key figures or respondents, visiting organizations, clinics, and villages, sifting through archival materials, or talking with colleagues around the world. He was animated when sharing his knowledge and experiences through storytelling, as a teacher, a project team-leader, a colleague, and as a friend to his students. He was entertainment-education personified.

Role modeling

In the 1980s, Ev began to conduct research about applied social learning theory (now called social cognitive theory) in Latin America and

India (Rogers and Antola, 1985; Singhal and Rogers, 1988). He believed that the role of social modeling (Bandura, 1977) in motivating human behavior was key to the diffusion of pro-social behaviors.

Ev and others conducted research on the telenovela *Simplmente María*, and the television soap opera *Oshin*. *Simplemente María* was a highly popular Peruvian soap opera first broadcast in 1969, which inadvertently led to the development of the entertainment-education strategy (Singhal, Obregon, and Rogers, 1994). *Simplemente María* portrayed the classic rags-to-riches story of a rural girl, María, who migrated to the capital city in order to find work as a maid. María took literacy classes and learned to read. She also learned to sew. When the telenovela ended, María was a successful fashion designer with a boutique in Paris. María was a self-made woman whose success was the result of hard work. She was also a role model for thousands of young maids in Peru who enrolled in literacy classes and sewing classes.

Oshin was a Japanese soap opera broadcast by NHK in 1983–84. The story of *Oshin* followed the central character, Oshin, through her life, beginning in the early 1900s (Shefner-Rogers, Rogers, and Singhal, 1998). Born to a poor tenant farmer, Oshin, at seven years old, was sold by her father to a timber merchant in exchange for a bale of rice. She endured many hardships, but her spirit eventually captured the attention of an educated woman who taught Oshin basic skills, including reading, writing, arithmetic, and Japanese etiquette. Following a series of ups and downs in her life, Oshin emerges victorious with a happy family, and a highly successful business enterprise.

In many ways Ev's life mirrored the lives of the role models in the entertainment-education soap operas he studied. *Simplmente María* and *Oshin* taught audience members that problems could be solved with endurance and effort. Like María and Oshin, Ev possessed great strength of character. He worked hard to overcome economically disadvantaged beginnings in life. He was a role model for perseverance.

The constant gardener

Wherever Ev lived, and wherever he traveled, he exercised his farming roots. As soon as the ground was ripe for planting, Ev could be found with a spade in hand, tending a vegetable garden. At Stanford, Ev

Plate 10.3
Ev in the greenhouse of his Stanford home
Source: Personal files of the author

secured a plot of university land and developed a vegetable garden. In this garden he held informal meetings with his students; they discussed diffusion theory as they hoed and weeded rows of corn, tomatoes, peas, and lettuce. At his home in Stanford, he built a greenhouse where he spent many hours cultivating vegetables and fruits (Plate 10.3). In Los Angeles, his backyard was a vertical slope, but Ev turned it into terraced, fertile farmland.

In the summer of 1996, Ev and I spent a couple of months in Bayreuth, Germany where Ev was the Ludwig Erhard Professor at the University of Bayreuth. We lived in a small apartment in an architecturally striking building within walking distance of the university. On our first morning in Bayreuth, Ev found a traditional grocer (next door to our apartment) who grew seedlings. We noticed that almost every house had a garden. Many garden plots had cold-frames (slanted glass encasements that captured the heat of the sun providing warmth and moisture to the growing plants) so that households could grow vegetables during cold months. Ev was itching to buy some of the grocer's seedlings and start a garden. But where? At the back of our building, Ev found a beautiful wooden deck opening out to a perfectly manicured landscape. With a glint in his eye he said: "Here is our garden!" The following day, Ev planted lettuce and onions in the carefully tended flowerbed. I worried that the grounds-keeper would think the seedlings were weeds and pluck them. Every day, Ev and I took a garden tour to check on the little plants. We did not stay in Bayreuth long enough to enjoy the fruits of Ev's small vegetable garden, but that really was not the point. What mattered was that Ev could feel the soil on his hands. We told our friends at the University of Bayreuth about the garden so that they could reap what Ev sowed.

When we returned to New Mexico from Bayreuth, Ev adopted the idea of using cold-frames and built such frames for the garden plots in our backyard. We grew vegetables year-round. One of Ev's greatest pleasures was to share our vegetable bounty with our colleagues and friends. Throughout the summer growing season, Ev would make jam from tomatoes, kumquats, and oranges. When he was a boy, he learned how to can fruits and vegetables from his mother. When he was chair of the Communication and Journalism Department at the University of New Mexico, he used these homemade jams to expand his network contacts at the university. He learned that making a gift of these jams sometimes greased the wheels of bureaucracy.

A transformative experience

In late 2002, Ev was diagnosed with cancer. His first reaction was shock. I could count on one hand the number of times Ev had been sick (usually with a mild cold) during the 15 years we were together. I always marveled at how robust he was, and he always responded by saying that his vigor was the result of his "good peasant stock." The cancer diagnosis was a trigger event that permanently altered his/ our life.

Ev never missed an opportunity to learn something new (in this case about cancer), but this time the cost of learning was high. Together we conducted research on kidney cancer: diagnostic criteria, treatment options, risks, and outcomes. Ev required an operation to remove his left kidney. He wanted to know how this operation would affect our lifestyle and his work. There was a possibility that he would be tethered to a dialysis machine for the rest of his life. Initially, we told only our immediate family about Ev's illness.

The outcome of Ev's operation, despite its complexity, in January 2003 was positive. The recovery process required physical and psychological determination, both of which Ev had in abundance. This process also encouraged extensive self-examination. Ev spent many hours in the living room of our home in Albuquerque, looking at the snow-covered Sandia Mountains lost in thought. He had spent a lifetime analyzing data, and now he needed time to make sense of his health condition. He never once uttered a word of self-pity. Instead, he became interested in conducting communication research about cancer survivorship as a transformative experience. During his follow-up radiation treatments, Ev and I would wait in the radiation lounge at the New Mexico Cancer Research and Treatment Center (CRTC) until it was his turn for treatment. He required 40 treatments that meant we spent many hours at the CRTC. Each waiting hour was spent talking to other cancer patients, gathering information about how cancer had changed their lives. Ev re-focused his self-identity; he began to identify as a cancer survivor.

Another outcropping of Ev's cancer diagnosis was that he intensified the writing of his memoirs (Rogers, n.d.), a project that he worked on from time to time in recent years. The cancer diagnosis, and the writing of his memoirs, motivated him to strengthen his bonds with his family in Iowa. Increased correspondence with his family allowed him to revisit and corroborate stories from his childhood on Pinehurst Farm.

A few days prior to Ev's passing in October 2004, he dictated the epilog to his memoirs. He had put off finalizing the book until he was ready to let go of life.

Life's lessons

By 1980, the buildings on Pinehurst farm were taken down and the total acreage was turned to cropping. Today, the stand of pine trees on the farm continues to provide shelter to deer, birds, and other small animals. Per Ev's wishes, the Pinehurst soil is his final resting place. Although Ev's life and career propelled him perpetually forward and away from Carroll, Iowa, he never forgot where he came from, that he was a "son of the soil."

Ev had several doctrines that guided his life's work. First, "Do what you love to do and the reward will follow." In the weeks prior to his passing, Ev said that he was surprised that he had devoted some 47 years of his life to the study of the diffusion of innovations, and had never tired of his work. He always found something new to think about, write about, and test. He found his reward in the useful application of diffusion theory in a variety of academic fields and social endeavors.

The second doctrine was "Work hard at whatever you do." People would often ask Ev how he was able to be such a productive scholar. Did he sleep? He believed in working hard; his Iowa work ethic was deeply ingrained.

Third, "Treat every individual with respect." Ev was socially skilled, charming, and genuinely interested in learning about others. Countless times, when we traveled abroad, we met people whom Ev had not seen in years, sometimes decades. When he would turn to introduce me to them, he could recount their complete academic careers, beginning with the topic of their dissertation, their marital status, and the number, gender, and even ages of their children. He was the ultimate networker, always making and fostering connections.

In closing

Since Ev's passing in October 2004, I received hundreds of letters, cards, and e-mails from Ev's friends, colleagues, and former students dating back to his days at Michigan State University, Stanford, and the University of Southern California. Some notes came from individuals who had met Ev only once, at a meeting or conference, and who claimed that that single meeting had made a lasting impression or changed their lives.

What emerged from these letters, cards, and e-mails, was a picture of a truly extraordinary man. The words that were commonly used to describe Ev included generous, supportive, visionary, gentlemanly, humane, and inclusive. His students remembered such things as the purple-penned edits in very small script on multiple drafts of their papers, the way he would say "hi, hi" as he strolled down a hallway to his office, or the way he would end a sentence by asking, "No?" Almost everyone recalled his rare ability to write so eloquently and clearly about complex topics, and his keen sense for merging theory and practice in ways that contributed to the betterment of individuals in developing countries. That was the public image of Ev, the diffusion scholar.

The private side of Ev was equally magnanimous. He was loving, kind, and funny. He was always positive, and in the last two years of his life, profoundly introspective. The onset of his illness allowed him to reflect on his life and appreciate all that he had achieved.

When Ev was growing up on the family farm in the 1930s, his mother told him that the purpose of life was to leave this world a better place than when he arrived. Perhaps this book is a testimony that Ev followed his mother's advice.

References

Bandura, A. 1977. *Social Learning Theory*. Englewood Cliffs, NJ: Prentice-Hall.

Dearing, J. W. and E. M. Rogers. 1996. *Agenda-setting*. Thousand Oaks, CA: Sage Publications.

Rogers, E. M. 1959. A Note on Innovators. *Journal of Farm Economics* 41 (1): 132–34.

———. 1961. The Adoption Period. *Rural Sociology* 26 (1): 77–82.

———. 1962a. *Diffusion of Innovations*. New York: Free Press.

———. 1962b. Characteristics of Agricultural Innovators and Other Adopter Categories. In Wilbur Schramm (ed.), *Studies of Innovation and of Communication to the Public*. Stanford, CA: Stanford University, Institute for Communication Research.

———. 1963. What are Innovators Like? *Theory into Practice* 2: 252–56.

———. 1970. Group Influences on Student Drinking Behavior. In George L. Maddox (ed.), *The Domesticated Drug: Drinking among Collegians*, pp. 307–20. New Haven, CT: College and University Press.

———. 1971. Social Structure and Social Change. *American Behavioral Scientist* 14: 767–82.

———. 1986. *Communication Technology: The New Media in Society*. New York: Free Press.

———. 1994. *A History of Communication Study: A Biographical Approach*. New York: Free Press.

———. n.d. *The Fourteenth Paw: Growing Up on an Iowa Farm in the 1930s*. Unpublished manuscript.

CORINNE L. SHEFNER-ROGERS

Rogers, E. M. and L. Antola. 1985. Telenovelas: A Latin American Success Story. *Communication Research* 35: 24–35.

Rogers, E. M. and R. J. Burge. 1972. *Social Change in Rural Societies*. New York: Appleton-Century-Crofts.

Rogers, E. M. and A. W. Havens. 1962. Predicting Innovativeness. *Sociological Inquiry* 32 (1): 34–42.

Rogers, E. M., R. E. Joyce, D. J. Leu, and F. J. Mortimore. 1968. *The Diffusion of Educational Innovations in the Government Secondary Schools of Thailand*. Institute for International Studies in Education, Michigan State University, Report 5. East Lansing, MI: Michigan State University.

Rogers, E. M. and D. L. Kincaid. 1981. *Communication Networks*. New York: Free Press.

Rogers, E. M. and F. F. Shoemaker. 1971. *Communication of Innovations: A Cross-Cultural Perspective* (2nd ed.). New York: Free Press.

Rogers, E. M. and T. M. Steinfatt. 1999. *Intercultural Communication*. Prospect Heights, IL: Waveland.

Shefner-Rogers, C. L., E. M. Rogers, and A. Singhal. 1998. Parasocial Interaction with the Television Soap Operas *Simplemente Mariá* and *Oshin*. *Keio Communication Review* 20: 3–18.

Singhal, A., M. J. Cody, E. M. Rogers, and M. Sabido (eds). 2004. *Entertainment-Education and Social Change: History, Research, and Practice*. Mahwah, NJ: Lawrence Erlbaum.

Singhal, A., R. Obregon, and E. M. Rogers. 1994. Reconstructing the Story of *Simplemente Mariá*, the Most Popular Telenovela in Latin America of All Time. *Gazette* 54: 1–15.

Singhal, A. and E. M. Rogers. 1988. Television Soap Operas for Development in India. *Gazette* 41: 109–26.

———. 1989. *India's Information Revolution*. New Delhi: Sage Publications.

———. 1999. *Entertainment-Education: A Communication Strategy for Social Change*. Mahwah, NJ: Lawrence Erlbaum.

———. 2001. *India's Communication Revolution: From Bullock Carts to Cyber Marts*. New Delhi: Sage Publications.

———. 2003. *Combating AIDS: Communication Strategies in Action*. New Delhi: Sage Publications.

About the Editors and Contributors

The Editors

ARVIND SINGHAL is Professor and Presidential Research Scholar, School of Communication Studies, Ohio University. He earned his Ph.D. at the University of Southern California (USC) under Ev Rogers' guidance, and has co-authored/edited five books with him, including three award-winning volumes: *Combating AIDS: Communication Strategies in Action* (2003), *Entertainment-Education: A Communication Strategy for Social Change* (1999), and *India's Communication Revolution: From Bullock Carts to Cyber Marts* (2001). He has been principal investigator for research projects sponsored by the Ford Foundation, David and Lucile Packard Foundation, National Science Foundation, Centers for Disease Control and Prevention, and Population Communications International. His research centers on the entertainment-education communication strategy, health promotion and disease prevention, organizing for social change, and complexity science approaches to understanding organizational change. He has served as a consultant to the World Bank, UNICEF, UNDP, UN-FAO, UNAIDS, PATH, FHI, BBC-WST, IRRI, and numerous other international organizations. Singhal was the recipient of the first Everett M. Rogers Award for Outstanding Achievement in Entertainment-Education (in 2005) given by the Norman Lear Center at USC's Annenberg School for Communication. Email: singhal@ohio.edu.

JAMES W. DEARING is Professor and Director of Graduate Studies, School of Communication Studies, Ohio University. He completed his Ph.D. at the University of Southern California under Ev Rogers' guidance, and co-authored *Agenda-Setting* (1996) with Ev. He has been principal investigator for research projects sponsored by the Agency for Health Care Research and Policy, the National Science Foundation, and the Environmental Protection Agency, along with the John D. and Catherine T. MacArthur Foundation, the

W. K. Kellogg Foundation, and the Robert Wood Johnson Foundation. He studies how evidence-based practices, programs, and policies can be diffused more rapidly among practitioners in education, health, the environment, and youth development. Email: dearingj@ohio.edu.

The Contributors

RONNY ADHIKARYA retired after a 33-year career at the World Bank, the United Nations, and other international organizations. He served the World Bank until 2003 as Manager/Founder of the World Bank Institute's (WBI) Knowledge Utilization through Learning Technologies (KULT) Program in Washington, DC. He was then appointed as the Food and Agriculture Organization (FAO)/United Nations Representative for Pakistan, where he served until 2005. He has written eight books (two are also in electronic/CD-ROM version) on such topics as communication, extension, and non-formal education, as well as numerous book chapters, journal articles, and technical reports. He completed his Ph.D. under the guidance of Ev Rogers at Stanford University, and frequently collaborated with him over three decades. Email: ronny@radhikarya.com.

ALBERT BANDURA is David Starr Jordan Professor of Social Sciences in Psychology at Stanford University. He and Ev Rogers were colleagues at Stanford University for over 10 years. Dr Bandura is hailed as a giant in social psychology, having authored numerous books and hundreds of articles. His social cognitive theory is at the heart of many mass-mediated intervention programs, including the entertainment-education strategy.

MARTINE BOUMAN is Managing Director of the Netherlands Entertainment-Education (E-E) Foundation and founding principal of Bouman E&E Development. An independent consultant and researcher, she is involved with several national and international E-E television projects. She previously served as an associate researcher at the Department of Communication and Innovation Studies at Wageningen Agricultural University in the Netherlands.

Bouman's investigation of the collaboration process in E-E television resulted in the publication of her doctoral thesis, *The Turtle and the Peacock: The Entertainment-Education Strategy on Television* (1999). She served as CEO of the Third International E-E Conference in the Netherlands, in 2000.

ELIANA ELÍAS is a social communicator, Ashoka Fellow, and AVINA leader. Founder and Executive Director of Minga Perú, a Peruvian non-profit organization that promotes social justice and human dignity through the use of entertainment-education communication strategies in the Peruvian Amazon. Minga, led by Elías, has developed an Intercultural Methodology for Social Change and is using it to train social organizations in Peru and Latin America.

PHILIP KOTLER is the S. C. Johnson and Son Distinguished Professor of International Marketing at the Northwestern University Kellogg School of Management in Chicago. Author of many—if not most—of the leading books in the field of marketing management, Dr Kotler is hailed by Management Centre Europe as "the world's foremost expert on the strategic practice of marketing." Professor Kotler and Ev Rogers knew each other well, and influenced each other's writings. Email: pkotler@aol.com.

DOROTHY A. LEONARD is the William J. Abernathy Professor Emerita of Business Administration at Harvard Business School, Harvard University. She earned her Ph.D. at Stanford University where Ev Rogers chaired her dissertation committee. She has written several books and numerous other publications on innovation and organizational change, focusing on aspects such as creativity, new product and service development, and on the transfer of knowledge within and across organizations. Email: dleonard@hbs.edu.

SRINIVAS MELKOTE is Professor in the School of Communication Studies, Bowling Green State University. His research interests include the role of communication in organizing social change, media effects, and health communication. Dr Melkote did his Ph.D. under the guidance of Dr Joe Ascroft, who was a Ph.D. advisee of Ev Rogers. Email: melkote@verizon.net.

GARY MEYER is Associate Dean in the J. William and Mary Diederich College of Communication and Associate Professor in the Department of Communication Studies, Marquette University. His research interests are in applied persuasion, especially in diffusion of innovations as it relates to health promotion and disease prevention. Dr Meyer worked with Ev Rogers on an AIDS project in San Francisco and was a Ph.D. advisee of Jim Dearing at Michigan State University (hence is a second-generation advisee of Professor Rogers). Email: gary.meyer@marquette.edu.

KIMANI NJOGU is Director of Twaweza Communications and Representative of Africa Health and Development International (AHADI) in Nairobi, Kenya. He worked closely with Ev Rogers in initiating an entertainment-education radio soap opera project in Tanzania in the early 1990s. An Associate Professor of Kiswahili and African Languages, Kimani has worked extensively in the use of the arts and media for social change around the world. His current research interests are in language, popular culture, and transformative leadership in Africa. Email: knjogu@africaonline.co.ke.

CORINNE L. SHEFNER-ROGERS was married to Everett M. Rogers. They traveled, worked, and played together from 1991 to 2004. Shefner-Rogers is an Adjunct Professor in the Department of Family and Community Medicine, and in the Communication and Journalism Department, at the University of New Mexico. She also works as an international health communication consultant based in Albuquerque, New Mexico. Email: clshefner@hotmail.com.

THOMAS W. VALENTE is Associate Professor and Director of the Master of Public Health Program at the Department of Preventive Medicine, Keck School of Medicine, University of Southern California. He received his Ph.D. in Communication from the Annenberg School for Communication at USC in 1991 and then spent nine years at the Johns Hopkins University Bloomberg School of Public Health. He is author of *Evaluating Health Promotion Programs* (2002), *Network Models of the Diffusion of Innovations* (1995), and over 70 articles and chapters on social networks, behavior change, and program evaluation. Valente uses social network analysis, health communication, and mathematical models to implement and evaluate health promotion programs, primarily aimed at preventing substance abuse, tobacco use, unintended fertility, and STD/HIV infections. Email: tvalente@usc.edu.

Name Index

Subject Index